Bren

Octo~~ber 2~~0, ~~1985 - July~~

ISBN: 1468026194
ISBN-13: 978-1468026191

DEDICATION

To Kelly, the love of my life.

ACKNOWLEDGEMENTS

Many thanks to Mimi Martinez for editing, and to Kim Cypert for creating the book cover.

1 IN THE BEGINNING

There I was again, trapped in another day of lying around on the couch trying to deal with all of the crazy side effects of my latest treatment. I was so exhausted from the chemotherapy, but unable to sleep because of the steroids that I was given to help control the nausea. Even with the steroids and the other two or three anti-nausea meds I was taking I still felt sick to my stomach. I knew I needed to eat but could hardly even stand the idea of forcing food down. I could feel sores starting to form in my mouth and throat. My teeth and gums were throbbing with pain. My leg was swollen and achy from all of the fluids that had been pumped into me. My lungs hurt and it was difficult to breathe. On top of all of the pain and discomfort, my mind was really foggy and it was extremely hard to focus on anything because of the chemo-brain. Overall, I was pretty miserable.

But it wasn't a big deal. Coping with all of these discomforts was routine for me by now. After all, I had been sick like this for a few hundred days over the past couple of years. I was a pro at suffering through the physical torment that chemo gave me. I even got to be pretty good at dealing with all of the mental and emotional distress that comes along with having cancer. But there was one thing that I still hadn't fully grasped, and that was trying to wrap my mind around why all of this had happened to me. I just didn't get it. Probably like any cancer patient I had so many deep questions, like why did I have to get cancer? Why was my perfect life completely thrown out of the window? Why hadn't my prayers and faith created some kind of miracle cure? Why hadn't God done something to prevent this from happening? Did God cause this to happen to me or did he just allow nature to take its course? Why did I have to go through so much suffering? And why had this whole nightmare progressed to the point that I probably wouldn't be cured?

I had spent so much time over the past couple of years trying to find answers to these questions. I knew that I would probably never find complete answers to all of them but I felt like I had made some serious progress. I have learned and grown so much through my many miserable experiences and received blessings that I never would have received had I not been diagnosed with cancer. My understanding has come from the endless days spent studying the scriptures, praying sincerely, and analyzing everything I had ever learned and experienced in my life. It was my life experiences, mainly the hardships that I went through, that ended up being the key to my strengthening of character, recognizing the blessings I had been given, and helping me find answers to so many of these deep questions that plagued my mind for so long.

The story of my life was put into motion back in 1980. A young active, energetic, and care free girl from Houston, Texas finally said yes to the young, sound minded, charitable, and hard-working guy from St. Anthony, Idaho who had been asking her to marry him for the past year or so. They were married for time and all eternity in December of 1980. I came into the picture in October of 1981, just ten short months later, as a fat, but cute, happy baby boy. It's safe to say that my arrival came as a surprise to my parents, who were still two poor college students at Brigham Young University. I lived the first year of my life in Provo, Utah until my dad finished his degree and moved down to Sugar Land, Texas to start his career. Sugar Land is a suburb of Houston that was experiencing rapid growth around the time my parents moved there.

2 MY FAMILY

My younger sister, Laura, joined the family in 1983, just a year and a half after I was born. Then in 1985, my brother Nick came along. The house that my parents originally bought had quickly become too small for a family of five so they moved into a larger one just a few blocks away. My other sister, Mandy, was born in 1987 and my youngest sister, Whitney completed the Weaver family in 1990. We were one big happy family of seven!

Well, we were happy most of the time. Like any family, we had our fair share of scuffles. When the family has five kids it seems like there is fighting all of the time. While we were young, somebody was always crying or whining about something the other one did. It drove my parents crazy sometimes. But they were always so loving and patient with all of us. Apart from the short scraps we routinely engaged in, we all seemed to get along very well. Even though they annoyed me quite a bit, I considered my brothers and sisters to be my best friends.

Laura and I were especially close. Laura always loved to tag along with me and my friends when we were growing up. She did all kinds of things with us, even some of the boy stuff like playing in the nearby bayou and shooting birds with bb guns. When we were young I really liked having her tag along with me and my friends. She was just another fun kid to have around. However as we grew older she became interested in boys, and it bothered me how she liked to follow my friends around and flirt with them. Even still, we hung out quite a bit and had a lot of good times together.

Nick, being a few years younger than me, was the typical annoying little brother that I had to share a room with, but his goofy and spontaneous personality made him very entertaining to be around. Once we got a little older I really had a lot of fun with him doing all of the exciting boy stuff that Laura wouldn't do. He was a good friend to have around, but once he got into high school I really enjoyed hanging out with him. He was always so weird and funny that I couldn't help but laugh when we hung out together. I really missed having him around when I had to move away to go to college and grow up.

I still remember when my parents brought Mandy home from the hospital. She was such a precious baby sister to me. Plus we got along really well because we were both the sweet peacemakers of the family (most of the time). I think that's why I was so close to her when we were really young. I always tried to take care of her and make her happy. I moved away before I really got to know how much fun she was all through high school. Every time I returned from college it seemed like she had grown up a little more and become more interesting to be around. I enjoyed watching her personality and confidence develop over the course of my college years and I'm so proud of the amazing person that she has turned into.

I feel kind of bad about how my relationship with Whitney was when I was growing up. But there wasn't that much I could do about it. Whitney and I were too far apart in age for me to ever develop any kind of relationship with while I was still living at home. I was nine when she was born and by then I didn't really pay much attention to her except when she was whining, like most babies do. We really picked on her a lot because she was so much younger than us. When I moved away to college she was only nine years old – still a little kid. I always thought she was so cute, even though she was a little spoiled and used to getting what she wanted. By the time I graduated from college and got married she was starting her junior year of high school and was in that stage where it isn't cool to be around your family. It was just recently after Whitney left to go to college that I really began to get to know her better. I've seen how sweet

4

of a girl she really is inside and I'm really proud of the progress that she is making in her life.

Looking back, our family was awesome! I think we all owe it to my amazing parents. They were always so loving to each of us and taught us how to live Christ-like lives, love each other, and get along well. My parents have always been very religious. We all attended church and Sunday school every week. Plus, they tried to read us stories from the scriptures and pray together as a family every night. They set aside time almost every Monday night for us to spend time together as a family. But most of all, they practiced what they preached and always set a good example of how we should live our lives.

Apart from the love and spiritual upbringing that my parents gave us, they also taught us to be hard workers. They made us work hard in school and practice diligently at the different sports that we were all involved in. They taught us the importance of having a job while we went through high school. But one of the greatest things that they infused into our brains was the idea that we could accomplish anything that we wanted as long as we were willing to put in the work needed to achieve it.

My parents did so much to help each of us as we jumped through life's hoops. But there was another strong influence to help us along the way… and that was the amazing friends that we were all so blessed to have. When my parents moved down to Sugar Land they ended up making friends with a handful of couples that they attended church with. They all became close friends and hung out all of the time. It worked out perfectly because each of the other couples also ended up having large families with kids about the same ages as all of my brothers and sisters. The group of families did everything together, from trips to my grandparents' lake house to weekends at the beach. Sometimes it got a little crazy, like when there were only three or four moms to take care of about twenty kids, but it provided amazing childhood experiences for each of us.

Over the years, all of us kids grew up close to each other. We were together for each other's earliest birthdays up until we all moved to college. I still have a handful of friends today that I have known since before I can remember and all of their parents are like another set of parents to me. I felt like I could go to them for anything I ever needed. Over the years, after comparing my life with so many other people, I realize how unique of a childhood I actually had and I feel so blessed to have had it.

3 MY EARLY EDUCATION

When I was growing up there were four things that I focused on in my life: church, scouting, sports and school. Actually, sports were the only thing that I was really interested in. The others were things that I knew were important but mainly did them because my parents strongly encouraged me to. And by "strongly encouraged" I mean, they pretty much made me do it. Nevertheless, I worked hard and learned a lot of really important things in church, scouting, and school.

My formal education all started with a few short years at Settler's Way Elementary school. Unfortunately, I don't remember too much about my time there. I know I played football during recess, traded snacks at lunchtime, and ran from girls with cooties. I was amazed when we got the first computers put into our classrooms when I was in fifth grade. I grew up in the age where parents still felt safe to let their kids ride their bikes to school. So we rode bikes a lot and would race home every day so that we could get home and play. Other than that, my time at elementary school was a big blur.

I remember a lot more about church stuff from those years than the things I learned in school. I have always been really involved in my church. When I was little I attended church and Sunday school every week. I was taught good stories from the scriptures. I learned that God is our father and that he loves us like an earthly father loves his children. I learned the importance of prayer and tried to remember to say my prayers every morning and night. And I learned that Jesus Christ is our savior and that I should follow his example in my life. By the time I was done with elementary school I knew all of the basic stuff really well.

It was around that time, too, that my parents got me involved in Cub Scouts. At that age, scouting was cool. We got to go out on campouts, learn how to build fires, use pocket knives, and other stuff like that. But the thing I liked the most was that all of my closest friends from church were in the same program with me. Every week I got to hang out with them and learn cool things about the outdoors.

Apart from school, church, and scouting, my parents got me involved in lots of different sports. My dad is really athletic and always loved to play sports with us. As soon as we were old enough he enrolled my brother and sisters and I in almost any sport we wanted to try. I started my first swim team when I was five years old and continued swimming competitively all the way through high school. When I was seven or eight I joined community soccer, baseball, and basketball leagues and continued playing those until about the time I started middle school.

By the time I got into middle school the sports weren't quite as fun to play anymore. It seemed like all of the other kids my age had far outgrown me and I was really too small to compete much. At the end of middle school I think I was only 5'-1" and 90 pounds. Ironically, the only sport I could play was football. They let anybody on the team who was willing to play, so I signed up. But it turned out that a guy of my size isn't of any use on a football team. Even so, I was a proud member of the C-team bench warmers and made sure to look extra tough in my seventh and eighth grade team pictures.

Starting up middle school was such a change of life from elementary school. I felt so overwhelmed when it was time to make that move. I had to take care of my books and my locker, and I had to get to all of my classes on time. Plus, all of a sudden girls no longer had cooties. It was cool to be interested in girls, which created a whole new social aspect of going to school that I wasn't used to. Also, everybody was either classified as a cool person or a dork. The "developed" girls and taller boys were cool and almost everybody else was kind of a dork. My miniature size automatically removed me from the cool group, which I was okay with. At that age there weren't really any social activities going on for me to not get invited to. Plus, I was perfectly content with hanging out with my church friends and brother and sisters. Even so, I was eager to hit puberty so that I could grow up and finally fit in with everybody else a little more. Sadly though, that didn't really happen until I got to high school.

As far as my physical appearance went, not much had changed when I started high school. I was still about the same size. It wasn't unusual for older girls to point at me in the halls and say "look at how cute that little guy is." It was suddenly clear that my freshman year wouldn't be much better than middle school.

Trying to find some kind of extracurricular activity to be involved in, I followed some of my C-team football friends and tried out for the football team. But considering I was still a whole head shorter than most of the guys on the field, I decided to quit after just a few days. Plus, I found out that the school had a swim team and I felt like I would be a lot more successful at swimming than playing football. The swim team ended up being a great fit for me. The 5:45 am workouts in a cold pool were often painful and miserable, but we all goofed off together and had a good time. Plus, there was never any kind of cool group or dorky group on the swim team because when everybody runs around in a Speedo all of the time nobody really cares whether you're cool or not. You're just a part of the team. I had so much fun on that team and was able to make a lot of good friends that stuck with me throughout my high school years.

Everything got pretty hectic once life in high school kicked in. There was more pressure to do well in school so that I could get into a good college. I had never really cared too much about my grades before, but now I was starting to realize that I needed to put a little more work into it. I had to juggle my school assignments with all of the other activities that I had going on in my life. And it wasn't just swim meets and practices that took up my time either. I was still really involved in church and scouting.

I participated in weekday youth activities apart from the Sunday church services I attended. Once a week all of the youth in the congregation, a lot of which were my good friends, would get together for different types of activities which taught a little about the gospel of Jesus Christ and then provided wholesome uplifting activities. The youth leaders tried to come up with activities that involved things like service or Boy Scouts (just for the boys, of course), but a lot of times we just ended up playing basketball in the gym. I always loved playing basketball, and enjoyed most of the other activities that we had, but usually having to do the "boy scout" stuff really annoyed me.

By the time I got into high school, scouting definitely wasn't cool anymore. I was always so embarrassed by the dorky uniforms and strange rituals that go on in scouting. Even today I still think they are pretty ridiculous, but my parents always made me go no matter what. I really hated it sometimes. The only way for me to fully escape it was to finish the program by earning the Eagle Scout award. So I pushed through the hard work and dorkiness of it all and got my Eagle when I was seventeen.

At the time I really didn't enjoy scouting very much at all, but now looking back, I can see how great of a program it was for me to be involved in. I don't remember how to tie any special knots or even what merit badges I earned. But I gained a good work ethic, learned important morals, and built great relationships with people who were good examples of the type of person I needed to be. The things that I gained through the scouting program, in a way, helped to mold me into the person that I am today. And for that, I am extremely grateful for my parents' persistence in making me go all of those years.

Another important experience that helped me through high school was my church's early morning seminary class. Every school morning at 6:00 AM a scripture study class was held for anybody who wanted to attend or for anybody whose parents wanted them to attend. I'm embarrassed to say, but I was usually one of the kids who went because their parents wanted them to. It was another thing in my life that I didn't see the value of until years later. Waking up so early was often a struggle, but I managed to make it about once a week during swim season and almost every day during the swimming off season. By attending this class I was able to learn so much more about the scriptures and how the teachings in them could help me in my life. I also learned more about the basics, like faith, prayer, and repentance. But most importantly, I learned how to live a Christ-like life from the example of so many amazing teachers.

I wasn't always the best person during high school, but studying the scriptures in the morning helped remind me to try to improve each day. I went through high school always trying to stay out of trouble and to be nice to everybody that I was around. It was easy my freshman year because I was still just a little runt that didn't have too many friends and, therefore, not much of a social life. But things changed once I finally started to grow.

During the end of my freshman year and over the summer I grew about ten inches. By the time I started my sophomore year I was the size of most of the kids at school. In fact, I was even bigger than lots of them. Plus, all of the swim team workouts gave me something that I had never really had before... muscles. All of a sudden the social playing field was leveled and I was a normal kid at school. I even heard rumors here and there that girls were maybe interested in me. But that was way too unbelievable for me to comprehend. I still pictured myself as the dorky little guy that girls thought was cute because he was so small. I was always just the nice guy that girls wanted to be friends with. I was too shy to ever put any moves on anybody I was actually interested in, but throughout the course of my sophomore and junior years I gained a lot more confidence in myself. I was slowly working my way onto the cooler side

11

of the spectrum, even though that wasn't what I truthfully wanted. I didn't really care about being one of the cool people and even despised that idea a little because of the way some of them had treated me in the past. I had always told myself that I wouldn't be like that and that I would try to be nice to everybody. For the most part I was, which worked out great for me. I had lots of friends because I was a nice guy.

By the time my senior year rolled around it seemed like everybody had realized that they wanted to be around nice people more than the cool people. Suddenly my group of friends and I became more of the popular group. Life started to be a lot of fun. I had an older car that my parents had bought as the kids' car and enjoyed all of the freedoms that came along with it. I started to get involved in other activities like student council and the local club lacrosse team. I had a job as a server at a restaurant and was able to save up some pretty good money. I was applying to colleges and loving life. Everything was going great.

About half way through my senior year things began to change. I think the popularity was going to my head and I was always stressed from the time demands of school, work, church, and sports. My priorities were all mixed up with my family and church on the very bottom of the list. I started to behave differently and do things that I normally wouldn't do. I was stressed out for so long that I caved in and decided to try out alcohol as a way to have fun and escape my exhausting life. I went out and partied with my friends a couple of times. I know that drinking in high school isn't a big deal to many people, but it was something that my parents were very strict about. I knew that it would upset them if they found out, so I lied to them to cover it up, another thing that my parents were very strict about. Lying was my mom's biggest pet peeve. Before I knew it, my new behavior was causing all kinds of drama in my family. My parents were always upset with me and I had lost the respect of my brother and sisters.

The choices I had made negatively impacted everybody in the family. There was a strong feeling of peace and love in the house that was often destroyed and replaced with contention and sadness because of my actions. During my few months of acting up I learned an important lesson about how much my personal choices can affect others around me, especially those that love and care for me.

Looking back now I can see how I sometimes justified my bad decisions by telling myself things like "It's my life, I can do what I want with it." I thought that any negative consequence from my actions would just affect me and that it was okay as long as I was willing to accept the consequences of my actions. Through my experiences I learned that this concept was far from the truth. I quickly realized that our lives are so closely tied together that the decisions that we make and the things that we choose to do will always affect others around us. It's an inconvenient truth, but when we knowingly make bad choices it is all too often the people that get hurt are the ones who love and care for us the most.

I have learned that there is something about loving another person that ties our emotions to their actions or general welfare. When we love somebody and something good happens to them or they do something good it fills us with joy and happiness. On the contrary, when something bad happens to someone we love or they do bad things it tears us apart and fills us with sadness and anxiety. The amount of love we have for another seems to be related to how greatly our emotions are affected. The more we love somebody, the happier we are when they are doing well and the sadder we are when they aren't doing well. There is so much heartbreak and sadness in so many people's lives that could be prevented if people would take the time to consider how their choices might affect others. Sadly though, there seems to be a general lack of love and respect for others in the world. It is all too often that when somebody doesn't care about whether their choice is right or wrong, they don't care about hurting other people either, especially people they don't even know. This just goes to show how important it is to "love thy neighbor as thyself." If we had a general love for everybody out there it would be a lot more difficult to make a bad decision, knowing that we would probably be hurting somebody else that loved us.

Drinking with my friends was a lot of fun at the time, but it was selfish for me to take enjoyment in something that hurt others. It didn't take long for me to realize that the fun times I had weren't worth the negative impact that my lifestyle was making on my family. By the middle of the summer after my graduation I had decided to give up drinking and try to be an overall better person. I felt that moving away to college was the perfect opportunity to start over and get my life back on track spiritually.

During high school there was really only one school that I was interested in getting into... Brigham Young University (BYU). Both of my parents went to BYU and I had a lot of friends who were already attending there. It is a beautiful campus right at the foot of the mountains in Provo, Utah. Unfortunately, my application was rejected. My grades and ACT scores weren't quite high enough to get in. So I had to settle for my second choice... Rick's College. It was a junior college in a tiny town in Idaho that was a sister school to BYU. My goal was to attend there and work my butt off until my grades were high enough to transfer to BYU. I started classes during the second summer term about two months after my high school graduation.

It was a great plan to make up for my failure to get into the school of my choice. I was excited but extremely nervous to move out of my parent's house and experience life on my own. I couldn't believe that my life had progressed to the point that I was actually going to college. I was also really sad to leave my family. My brother and sisters were such good friends to me and it was hard to have to leave them behind. Nevertheless, I knew that this was just the next step in my life, and that I needed to make it no matter how hard it would be.

4 WELCOME TO COLLEGE

As my flight descended during landing I looked out the window and couldn't help but notice how small the city was. I could see the entire city out of the window of the plane. I wondered how I would survive in such a small place. Then I realized that the city I was flying into was actually Idaho Falls. Rick's College was in Rexburg, a much smaller town about thirty minutes up the road. As we drove past the potato fields, entered Rexburg, and approached campus I started to realize how different life was going to be. Rexburg didn't even have a McDonald's yet, much less anything that would provide any kind of entertainment. What was I getting myself into?

Luckily I was rooming with a good friend that I have known for as long as I can remember. Having him with me that day helped calm my nerves a lot. As we moved our stuff into our new apartment-style dorm I couldn't stop thinking about how weird the whole change was. I was going from a big house full of my brother and sisters in a community where I knew lots of people to a small apartment in a tiny town where I only knew one person. I was so scared to make that step in my life.

About an hour after hugging my mom goodbye a group of guys came and knocked on our door and introduced themselves. They all seemed like really cool guys and they lived right above us. We quickly made friends with them and invited them to come hang out whenever they wanted. After they left I felt exhausted and decided to take a short nap on the couch in the living room, but my nap was quickly interrupted by the sound of laughter. I opened my eyes and there were three cute girls standing in our dorm laughing at the goofy posters that we had put up on the walls. It was amazing! I had never woken up to cute girls in my house before. It was pretty nice. They introduced themselves, hung out for a while, and then invited my roommates and me over for dinner before they left. After meeting those girls and the apartment of guys above us my fears were completely washed away. I ended up becoming really good friends with all the people I met that day and hung out with them throughout the summer and fall semesters.

The summer semester flew by. Classes were easy and only took up a couple hours each day, which left plenty of time to play. Since there wasn't much to do in Rexburg; we had to come up with our own entertainment. We did all kinds of fun stuff, like bridge-jumping, cave exploring, and playing on the sand dunes. But mostly we just hung out with the new friends that we had made. I loved my new life, especially since I had changed my attitude and given up drinking. I just seemed to be so much happier with everything that was going on. Time flew by and before I knew it the fall semester was about to start.

The fall semester was a lot different than the summer semester. The whole environment changed because there were so many more students on campus all of the time. I wasn't able to play as much because I spent more time in class and studying. Plus, it started snowing at the beginning of October, which cut out a lot of the things that I normally did. But despite all of the changes I still had a blast! I spent most of my free time playing soccer pick-up games, hanging out at girls' apartments, and goofing off with my guy friends in the dorms. There were also all kinds of cool church and campus sponsored activities that I tried to go to as much as possible.

I loved the new life that I was living and a lot of it was because of the personal changes that I had decided to make. I tried to pray more often, read the scriptures on my own a little every day, and be more Christ-like in everything that I did. I found that it made a big difference in how happy I was. I had learned that the more I tried to follow the scriptures' teachings, the happier I became in my life. I know that this might be common knowledge to a lot of people, but at the time it felt almost revolutionary to me. I was excited about my new found knowledge and wanted to share it to help improve the lives of others. I decided that I was going to put my education on hold and go on a two year mission for my church at the end of the fall semester.

In my church young men and women between the ages of 19 and 25 have the opportunity to go on a mission trip if they choose. In reality, it's a lot bigger of an ordeal than just a simple trip. Anybody who is interested has to send in an application. The application is then reviewed by church leaders who, after praying about the individual and the needs of the different missions, decide on where the applicant will go to serve. They then mail out an envelope full of information about the mission location along with instructions on what to do.

I was so excited when I received my envelope full of information. Inside of it was information about where I would be spending the next two years of my life. I had friends who had gone on missions before. They each went to a different place around the world: South Korea, Russia, The Philippines, and Spain. I could be going anywhere. I opened it while I was still up at school. I had my family listening on the phone and all of my good friends around me. I was so excited and nervous about what it might say that I was nearly shaking. I'll never forget when I opened that envelope and read the words "You have been called to serve in the Guadalajara, Mexico mission." I couldn't believe it! I was going to Mexico! I had no idea where Guadalajara was or even how to pronounce it, but I was thrilled about Mexico. After that night I spent the next few months studying, shopping, and making all of the other preparations that I needed to make in order to live in Mexico for two years.

Time flew by and before I knew it, it was time to leave home again. But leaving home this time would be different. I wouldn't be able to just call up my family whenever I felt like it. I would only be able to call home twice a year, on Mother's Day and on Christmas. The mission leaders wanted the missionaries to be 100% focused on helping others. There would be strict rules to help prevent anybody from becoming distracted. Some of the rules would include not watching TV, calling home, shopping, dates, or swimming. Pretty much anything that took time away from the work would be against some kind of rule. On top of what I wouldn't be able to do, there would be a huge list of things that I had to do daily. Wake up at 6:00 AM, study scriptures for an hour and a half, study Spanish for an hour, miscellaneous study for an hour, do 30 minutes of exercise, leave the house at 10:30 AM, return at 9:00 PM, and go to bed by 10:00 PM. Needless to say, my life would be changing drastically!

All of the changes I would face made me scared to death to leave. I couldn't believe I was actually going through with it. It sounded so noble and adventurous at first, but now I questioned if I would even be able to survive. I wasn't going to back out though because I knew it was the right thing for me to do. I had made a commitment and I needed to follow through with it.

I'll never forget the day I left. My mom came to wake me up early that morning and the instant she turned the doorknob to come into my room a wave of anxiety washed over me. All I could do was lay there in disbelief that the day had finally come for me to leave everything in my life behind. It was a major struggle to climb out of bed that morning, but it was even harder to say goodbye to my family at the airport. I wouldn't see them for two whole years, which, at the time, was longer than anything I could comprehend. It felt like I was saying goodbye to them forever. We all tried to be strong, but each of us ended up crying before my flight had departed. I couldn't believe it. The day that I had been looking forward to and anxiously dreading for so long had finally arrived. I had left my family, friends, and everything else behind to go out and try to serve the people of Mexico.

5 THE MISSION

After leaving my family I became eager to get down to Guadalajara to get to work. But as eager as I was to get started, I couldn't just fly down to Mexico right away. I couldn't speak any Spanish, which is why I spent the first two months of my mission in a missionary training center in Utah. All missionaries spend the first month or two in a training center where they are taught the language, scriptures, communication skills, and everything else that that they might need to know to work in whatever area of the world they are going to.

Nobody ever told me how intense my time in the training center would actually be. Nearly every second of my day was planned out for me. On a typical day there I would wake up at 6:00 AM, study scriptures for an hour, get ready for the day, eat breakfast, go to Spanish classes until lunch, study scriptures for a few more hours, then study Spanish for a few more hours, eat dinner, go to some group meetings, then enjoy about thirty minutes of free time before going to bed at 10:00 PM. This was my life for almost two months. It was intense! Thankfully I was put in a group that would all be going to Guadalajara the same day as I. I became good friends with a lot of the other guys in my group. Having friends there made the experience much more bearable. Without them I don't know how long I would have lasted before calling it quits.

By the end of my time at the training center I had learned so much. I felt like I really understood the gospel of Jesus Christ and that I was fully prepared to teach it to others in a way that would help them improve their lives. I was also pretty confident at speaking Spanish. During the first two or three weeks we had covered almost everything I had learned in my three years of high school Spanish classes. By the end of the two months I could understand almost everything my gringo teacher spoke and felt like I could speak fairly well. I didn't think I would have any problems communicating when I got there. My whole group was so excited and we could hardly wait to get to Mexico to start working.

I'll never forget the day we flew down to Guadalajara. What an eye-opener! I went from the good old USA, where everything was "normal" to this bizarre, chaotic, foreign city where it seemed like nothing made sense. The houses were small and crammed together; there were no yards, the roofs were flat and had dogs on top of them. There appeared to be no traffic rules, people drove lots of small motorcycles and old Volkswagen beetles. Everything had graffiti spray painted on it, there were cobblestone roads, kids playing soccer in fields of dirt, and everybody spoke this foreign language that I was supposed to be able to understand. It was actually really exciting to see how different everything was. But the excitement quickly faded on the second day when our group was split up and we were all sent out to different parts of the city to start working.

The mission was extremely well organized. Each mission in the world has a mission president who is in charge of the whole mission. The Guadalajara mission covered about three and a half states in Mexico, with Guadalajara being the location of the mission headquarters. The entire area of the mission was divided up into about 18 zones, each being led by a zone leader. Each zone was divided into several districts with a district leader in charge. Each district was divided into areas with a pair of missionaries in each area.

I was told by the mission president that I would be working with a young man from Mexico in an area of the city called La Estancia. He picked me up in a cab and we drove off to the house that we would be living in for the next few months. Leaving my training center friends behind and going off into real Mexico with some guy I barely knew was one of the strangest and scariest experiences of my life. It was like my perfect life was replaced with some kind of weird dream that I knew I was going to be stuck in for the next two years. When we arrived, I was shocked to find out that our "house" was actually just a room in the back of somebody else's house. It had two beds, a closet, and a desk for us to study at… and that was about it. After I unpacked my stuff we rushed out for a couple of appointments to teach some families that my missionary companion had met the week before.

While I was out I realized how little Spanish I actually knew. I could barely understand my companion. He had to speak really slow and pronounce everything perfectly for me to get what he was saying. And then pretty much the only things I could say to him were things like "How do you say?" and "What does that mean?" It was so frustrating! When we returned to the house that night, I laid down in bed and thought to myself "What in the world am I doing here?" Everything was different, I couldn't communicate, and I lived in this tiny room in the back of a weird cement house full of people I didn't know. Yet I was determined to stick with it. I wasn't going to be one of those guys who quits and goes home early. I was committed to stay the full two years even though I wondered how I would ever make it without going crazy.

The next few weeks were really difficult. Every morning we woke up early, studied, and then left to go try to teach and serve people. My ability to communicate improved each day but it was still extremely frustrating. My mouth would get so tired and sore from constantly speaking Spanish. My feet and legs were always aching because we walked 15 to 20 miles a day. I was sick a lot and had the runs more often than I like to admit. I was so exhausted every night by the time we got home that I practically fell asleep the moment I laid down.

On top of all of the difficulties I was enduring, nobody really wanted to listen to us. I was in a wealthier part of the city and a lot of people just weren't interested in anything we had to offer. We had a lot of doors slammed in our faces and were made fun of quite a bit. People would turn us down even if we only wanted to do their chores or help them with anything else they might be able to think of. Sometimes it really crushed my spirits to work so hard to try to help people and not be able to find anybody that wanted it.

Life was really hard. Going through that time in my life was the hardest thing I had ever done. I prayed for strength and guidance daily and was humbled more than ever before. It was such a mental challenge just to hang in there. I thought about home frequently and sometimes wished I was still there. I wondered how I would ever make it two whole years. But with time, all of the hardships became bearable. My legs grew stronger, I got over my illnesses, and I wasn't quite as tired all of the time. After about two months the Spanish suddenly just started to click and I was able to understand almost anything. A month later my ability to speak kicked in and I could say about anything I wanted. The transition happened so quickly that it seemed like I became fluent overnight.

We also finally found a family that we were able to help that was made up of a single mother, named Cynthia, and her two boys which were under the age of 12. Cynthia and the boys' father had split up years before because of his drug and alcohol abuse. Now the mother and kids lived in a one room cement house with one wall missing. The house was in an abandoned lot that was surrounded by a cement wall with a crack that you had to squeeze through to get in. The mother was struggling to take care of her family and worried about her boys not having good friends and getting involved in drugs. They hardly knew anything about the bible because they were from a small town that had a large native population. I felt bad for them because they just didn't seem to be happy.

My companion and I ended up spending lots of time with them. We visited them nearly every day. Typically in our visits we would teach them about the gospel and share scriptures that we felt might help them. We always encouraged them to pray and read from the scriptures every day. Then, after teaching, we usually played soccer and goofed off with the kids. We invited them to go to church and get involved with good people who would be positive influences on them, particularly for the boys. Over time they began to pray, read the scriptures, and attend church regularly.

I saw amazing changes in them as they grew closer to Christ. They became closer to each other as a family. Cynthia's confidence and self-esteem improved dramatically. The language and attitude of the boys improved and they were able to make good friends at church who weren't into drugs. They were kinder and more patient with others. But most importantly, they all just seemed to be happier. I fell in love with that family and wanted the absolute best for them.

Cynthia and her family was the first of many that I was able to help throughout the two years of my mission. Each person I taught had their own unique trials and difficulties that we tried to resolve. But the outcome of our labors was always the same when they put in the work to make changes in their lives. The changes they made were always followed by newfound peace and happiness in their lives. Teaching and helping the people that I met on my mission was the most fulfilling experience of my life. At times I wished I could always be with them to continue to help them along, but I knew that wouldn't be possible.

Each missionary works in their assigned area for only four to six months, after which they are transferred to work in a different area of the mission. After seeing the amazing changes in Cynthia's family, my time in La Estancia was up and it was time for me to go. I was so sad to leave all of my newly made friends behind. I had become attached to them as I taught them the gospel and helped them with their struggles. Leaving friends behind was always difficult, not just because it was sad that I wouldn't see them again, but because I worried that they might fall away from the path that we helped them to reach. I wanted them all to remain happy and continue improving their character and their lives. Knowing that I wouldn't be able to be there to assist them was always the hardest part about moving. Nevertheless, I had to go and trust in the Lord that he would continue to help them along.

I packed up my stuff and moved across the city to an area that was completely different than my first. Here everybody was poor. The roads were either made of cobblestone or dirt. Packs of stray dogs roamed the neighborhoods and there were always people drinking and doing drugs in the streets at night. Unfortunately, I was only in that area long enough to be rejected and robbed. After only three weeks I was transferred again.

From there, I was sent to a much smaller city called Zamora in the state of Michoacán. I loved it there. It was beautiful and the people were always so nice. The whole lifestyle in that city was so much more laid back than in Guadalajara.

Sometimes people ask what I was doing on 9/11… well, I was in Zamora teaching a lady in the street. At the end of our conversation she said "You're American right? Did you hear your country is under attack?" I didn't know what she was talking about, but decided it needed to be looked into. We headed over to a friend's house and were greeted by somber faces. Our friends turned on the TV and showed us what was going on back at home. Like everybody else, I'm sure, I couldn't believe what I was seeing. We watched for a few minutes but then decided we better put our sadness behind us and get back to work. Working the rest of the day turned out to be a little difficult. Everybody we talked to said the same thing, "Hey, you're American right? Did you see what's happening?" We ended up just walking around aimlessly the rest of the day thinking about how crazy life must be back in the USA.

I ended up staying in Zamora for almost six months. I worked really hard and made lots of good friends there.

When I got the phone call that I was going to be transferred again I was sad to leave, but also ready to move on and make new friends.

This time I was sent back to Guadalajara to an area called Miravalle. It was a difficult area for me. People just weren't as interested in religion in the big busy city, which made it hard to stay motivated every day. Plus, my companion was super lazy and never seemed to care about working. Sometimes it seemed like I had to drag him along everywhere I went. I even pulled him out of bed a few mornings so we could get going. The area had lots of gang activity and sometimes it felt pretty unsafe. One time we walked out of our apartment and there was a dead guy lying in the street for everybody to see. He had been shot while trying to rob a bus.

Not all of my experiences there were bad. We made friends with some gang members, taught a young man that ended up going on a mission himself, and most amazingly, witnessed a girl who was miraculously cured of cancer. She had been diagnosed with cancer by three separate doctors to make sure that the diagnosis was correct. We met her the night before she was going in for surgery to have the cancer removed. The entire family was there and was extremely anxious about the upcoming operation. They asked us to give her a special blessing in hopes that God would heal her of her disease. After finishing the prayer we all felt the spirit of the Lord. There was a strong feeling of peace that comforted the family and the girl who was to have the operation. We left the house hoping and praying that God would strengthen them in whatever the outcome was. Upon returning a couple of days later we found out that the surgeons opened up the girl but didn't find any cancer to remove. It had magically disappeared. We had witnessed a miracle! I was excited to continue to teach her and build a relationship with that family, but unfortunately, they moved the next week and I never heard from them again.

I have thought back on that experience several times to try to figure out exactly how faith and miracles all really work. My "faith" grew that day but I sometimes wonder if it was the right kind of faith. I have learned a lot about faith and miracles but to this day they remain to be topics that I have not fully figured out. Maybe someday God will shed enough light on me about the subjects so that I can make sense of it all.

After about five long months of living in Miravalle I finally got a phone call to let me know that I was being transferred. This time I went back to the state of Michoacán, but to a smaller city named La Piedad. Again, I loved the friendly and laid back environment of the small towns. It was a perfect area. The only bad thing that happened to me was that I was stung by a scorpion while I was sleeping. Scorpions were everywhere. We would get home and find them on the walls just about every night. I was also made a district leader, which I really loved. It was so fulfilling to be able to help the other missionaries in my district and teach them the things that I had learned. Life in the mission was nearly perfect again, but after only two months a need for a zone leader arose back in Guadalajara and I was sent to fill the position.

The zone I was asked to lead was called Independencia and had 18 missionaries in it. At first I was overwhelmed by the new responsibility but I quickly came to love it. I was in charge of all of the finances, supplies, training, reports, and weekly meetings in the zone. I loved being able to help the other missionaries with whatever they needed. Apart from my leadership role, the work was pretty slow again. But I always worked hard and stayed busy taking care of the other areas in the zone. My time in that area flew by and before I knew it my two years were up. It was time to fly home to get back to my own life.

The thought of going home was absolutely overwhelming. For the past two years I had completely put others before myself. Now I had to go home and focus on

ME and what I needed to do with the rest of my life. It was weird and almost scary to have to think about stuff like what I would study, where I would live, and how I would afford to go to school. I even worried about being able to communicate. I had hardly spoken English for two years and had forgotten a lot of my vocabulary. My Spanish was way better than my English, which by then was coated with a Spanish accent.

It was also exciting to think about returning. Every day of my two years I was physically and mentally exhausted from working so hard. I couldn't wait to be able to rest and just relax. I also felt like there was so much catching up to do. I hadn't talked to my friends in two years, and I had only talked to my family four times. I had no idea about what was going on in the news, other than the fact that 9/11 happened. I also had lots of movies and TV shows to catch up on, and lots of shopping to do because all of my clothes were completely out of style. But the most exciting thing was probably the fact that soon I would be able to hang out with girls again and maybe even get a girlfriend, if any of them would actually be interested in me.

My last night in Mexico was so bitter-sweet. I couldn't wait to get back to the life I had left behind, but at the same time I couldn't stand to think about leaving my life in Mexico. All of my friends in that area threw a party for me that night. We all got together and ate carnes asadas with chorizo, charro beans, fresh salsas, and hot-off-the-press corn tortillas, and then finished the meal off with an amazing tres leches cake. It was my last taste of the authentic Mexican food that I had grown to love so much.

That night, as I lay in bed trying to go to sleep, I thought about everything I had experienced on my mission. I had been respected, loved, adored, laughed at, picked on, hated, and even chased by somebody who was threatening to kill me. I had seen everything from families finding happiness and amazing miracles, to starving children and husbands beating their wives.

The things I had gone through and witnessed made me grow in ways I never knew were possible. Observing the consequences that resulted from others' poor decisions taught me a lot about how important it is to make good decisions in my own life. I saw that the choices we make can either lead us down a path of pain and sadness or towards a life filled with peace and joy. I learned of the love that God has for each of us and how he uses commandments and rules to help protect us and maintain our happiness. I learned how the Holy Spirit can guide us in our lives, and how to follow his promptings to fulfill God's will. Most importantly, I learned how repentance and commitment to follow Christ's teachings can bring about miraculous changes in people's lives.

I had seen it happen in so many of the people that I was able to help. Through changing their lives and following Christ their trials and hardships were minimized and often completely replaced with joy and happiness. Of course it was always difficult for them to make the needed changes. Sometimes the changes were part of a long process and involved overcoming addictions, being made fun of, or even being persecuted by friends or family. But the happiness they experienced always made it worth it in the end. Seeing these miracles in other people's lives taught me that making constant improvements on my own life could bring about additional blessings and happiness for me.

On top of all of the spiritual learning I obtained, I also gained temporal skills that have helped me throughout my life after the mission. Among them were learning about people and how to communicate better, learning leadership skills and how to teach and motivate others, and probably most importantly, gaining an incredible work ethic and learning that I can accomplish great things through hard work and persistence.

Thinking that night of all of the amazing things I had experienced made me so sad to have to leave the next day. I had grown to love the Mexican people and their culture.

After two years I felt like I belonged in Mexico more than I did in the United States. It broke my heart to think that I had to leave it all behind. Despite my efforts to be tough, the sadness overtook me and the tears flowed until I was able to finally fall asleep.

6 BACK TO LIFE IN THE USA

During my flight home the weirdest thing happened. My plane had to land in Austin because of bad weather over the airport in Houston. While we were all stuck there on the runway the captain said we could pull out our phones to make calls if we needed to. Right then, almost everybody on the plane pulled out a cell phone. It was the weirdest thing. When I left on my mission nobody had a cell phone, except maybe a few adults that I knew. But almost everybody on the plane had one, even some of the teenagers. I couldn't believe it.

My flight finally made it to Houston and I was greeted by my family who was anxiously awaiting my arrival. I hugged each of them one by one and when I made it to Whitney I was completely shocked. She was about a foot taller, her face looked more grown up and even her voice had changed. It was like my sister was taken and replaced by an entirely different person.

It was really weird to be around my family again. They all had changed a little and it was hard for me to make conversation with them. Plus, I had been so far removed from normal life that they kind of thought I was weird. I wish I had more time to re-kindle my relationships with them, but unfortunately I had to leave to Rexburg, Idaho right away for the spring semester. I only got to hang out with them for about a week. It was a great week though. They introduced me to all of the good movies, TV shows, and music that I had missed. They also took me shopping to buy new clothes so that I didn't look like a dork when I got back to college. It was so fun and exciting to be able to experience everything again.

It was also really hard to adjust to all of the luxuries that we enjoy in the US. After living in Mexico for two years, everybody in the US seemed so wealthy. The houses here are huge, people drive nice cars, and everybody eats well. It made me sick that we have so much here while people have so little there. It didn't seem fair. But after thinking about it I realized that the people there were just as happy as, if not happier than the people here. Having nice things doesn't have anything to do with happiness. I knew it because some of the happiest people that I knew lived in tiny cardboard houses with dirt floors. It took me a while to get used to the difference in wealth between the two countries.

After a short week of hanging out with my family and getting used to living back in the United States I had to return to Idaho to start working on my life and finish my education.

7 WINTER SEMESTER: JAN 2003

Going back to college was so much fun. It was exciting to wear normal clothes all of the time, to be able to hang out with friends, and especially, to be able to hang out with girls. Right away I was able to make friends with a few apartments of girls that I ended up hanging out with the whole semester. I was put with random roommates that turned out to be really awesome. I loved life and had a great time.

My experiences with dating, though, weren't that great. There were lots of girls that I was interested in, but I had been out of the dating scene so long that I had completely forgotten what I was supposed to do. I didn't know how to act around girls, I had forgotten how to flirt, and I had somehow become really shy. I only went on one date that semester and it didn't turn out well at all. I didn't have a car, so we walked to the movie theater, which ended up being closed. I had no clue what to do then, so we walked all the way back to her apartment and watched a movie there. I was really awkward the whole time and she definitely noticed. There was no second date.

Apart from my problem with girls I also had a major problem with my bowels. I was always getting an upset stomach and had the runs quite a bit. At first I thought I was just adjusting to the different food, but when it didn't go away after a few months I started to think I had some kind of parasite or something. I got checked out by a doctor but he had no idea what was wrong with me. My problem was really annoying and always had me running for the bathroom. It ended up taking about two years for it to completely go away.

While I was on my mission I decided to study mechanical engineering. The only problem was that the school I went to didn't have a mechanical engineering program. I had to transfer to BYU and try to get accepted into their program. I needed to get good grades in order be accepted to BYU. Luckily, I was so used to studying and working hard on my mission, that doing school work was no big deal. I worked really hard that semester and made almost straight A's. I was also able to test out of 12 credits worth of Spanish classes since I was fluent in Spanish. All of my good grades that semester were just enough for me to get accepted to BYU for the fall.

8 BYU: SEP 2003 – SEP 2004

Going to school at BYU was an entirely different experience for me. It was an actual university and was enormous compared to the junior college I went to before. There seemed to be students everywhere I went and there were more apartment complexes than I could count. The whole experience was so exciting to me.

I decided to live with a good friend of mine in this apartment complex that was known for being extremely social. We were randomly set up with four other roommates that turned out to be really awesome. There were cute and fun girls everywhere. My roommates and I always had a lot of fun hanging out at some girls' apartments that lived down the hall from us. We were always pulling pranks and goofing off. Every night was like a weekend night and we always had a great time together.

That semester I did a little better on the dating scene too. Well, kind of. I had been home from my mission long enough that I was comfortable around girls and I remembered how to flirt again. But I still wasn't too good at getting them to like me. I only asked out girls that I was interested in and was a lot better at planning out the date. Plus, I had bought a cheap little green car with some money that I had saved up from working over the summer. Having a car made things much easier. I usually was only able to take out girls once or twice before they started playing games or screening my phone calls. Once the games started I usually lost them. I was horrible at playing the dating games. And unfortunately, BYU girls were notorious for playing them.

Everybody was always in this search for somebody who was better than what they had. I was always pretty straight forward with the girls and made it obvious that I was interested in them. Once they felt like they could have me if they wanted to, they were off to find somebody better. I quickly realized that dating at BYU was a huge mess. Luckily, I wasn't too concerned about having a serious girlfriend at the time, so it didn't bother me too much.

Another huge difference at BYU was that everybody was always so busy. Everybody was serious about their studying and lots of people worked part time as well. It seemed like nobody had time to do anything. I didn't really understand this until my classes started to pick up.

I was taking all of the engineering classes that were required to get into the program. And they were hard. That first year at BYU I took a chemistry class, two calculus classes, two physics classes, a couple of engineering classes, and a bunch of GE's. I was studying all of the time. It wasn't uncommon for me to stay in the library until 10:00 pm several nights a week. I put so much work into my classes because I wanted to be successful in school. I didn't care too much about making straight A's; I just wanted to be able to finish the engineering program with a decent GPA, something that wasn't easy to do.

I was doing pretty well, until I realized that I was running out of money and needed to get a job. Getting a job in a small town with 35,000 college students wasn't easy. I just had to take what I could get. And that, unfortunately, was a job washing dishes in a cafeteria. It was disgusting and humiliating, but it paid the bills. I loved having some money come in, but it made life much more difficult. I now had to balance school, work, and a social life. And unfortunately, the social life was the one that always got cut.

Luckily the school year was almost over and I would get a break from my crazy life. Some of my roommates and I moved into a different apartment for the summer because rent was cheaper. It was super social and had a big pool area and hot tub. We had an awesome time that summer and I made some great friends. I also got a new job waiting tables at a Brazilian restaurant called Tucanos. I made a lot more money than in the cafeteria and the work was a lot more fun. I had a really good time that summer and was able to save up enough money to pay for tuition and living expenses for the next school year.

9 BYU: SEP 2004 – SEP 2005

My second year at BYU was awesome! I moved into an apartment with a really good friend from Sugar Land that I had known for longer than I could remember along with four other great friends that I made over the summer. Since most of us paid our own way through college and had hardly any money our apartment was kind of on the lower end of the luxury scale. It was a cheap, kind of run-down place about three quarters of a mile from campus, which made for some really miserable walks to school early in the morning during the winter. But we made the best of it. We all had so much fun together. We all pitched in and rented a big TV for the school year and got some extra couches and set up stadium seating. We always had girls hanging out at our place and we were always goofing off together.

Everything in the apartment was going great until one of our roommates moved out to get married and was replaced by some really weird random guy. He did all kinds of strange things like talk to himself while taking baths, wear sunglasses inside with all of the lights turned out, and sit on his bed and stare at the wall for hours. We all kind of felt bad for him because he didn't have any friends, so we tried to invite him to hang out whenever we went anywhere. Then one time when he snapped on a friend from church that was visiting and called him a pervert and a stalker, we started to think something was wrong with him. After doing some minor investigating we found out he had schizophrenia and had recently stopped taking his medicine. We were all scared of him after we found that out. We didn't know if he was going to snap on us like he did on others. The longer he was living with us the crazier he got too, until one day we all put together a special operation to sneak into his room and get his dad's cell phone number out of his phone. We called him and let him know how he was doing which eventually led him to being admitted back to a psychiatric center for more treatment. Life with him was always interesting. I could write a whole book about all of the funny and scary experiences that we went through with him. Unfortunately, though, I don't have time for that.

That school year was insanely busy for me. I worked about 20 hours a week at Tucanos, played intramural sports, studied like crazy, and tried to meet girls with any extra time I had. Like always, school was the most time consuming. That year I spent a lot of time in the math lab, thanks to classes like multivariable calculus, linear algebra, differential equations, and the calculus 2 classes that I had to retake to get into the engineering program. It was an extremely intense school year, but somehow I survived.

I had a really rough time in the dating world that year. I didn't have a problem meeting girls that I was interested in but I was still having a hard time getting past the second or third date. It started to feel like there was some kind of force working against me. These girls I took out seemed really interested at first, but then all of a sudden it was like something would come up and they were out of there. Things like: the girl had to move away for study abroad, or they decided at the last minute to go home for the summer. It drove me crazy! At the end of the year I was really wanting something to work out and it was starting to upset me. To add to my agony, all of my best friends had serious girlfriends, four of which got engaged by the end of the year. Even my sister Laura got engaged. It felt like everybody close to me was moving on with their lives and getting married and I was still stuck behind, getting rejected left and right. It got to be pretty depressing by the end of the school year.

Once summer arrived things started to change. Jordan, my best friend at the time and former roommate, moved back to the same apartment complex as the previous summer with me and a few other really good friends. It ended up being the best summer yet. We all became really close friends and did everything together, from longboarding down Provo Canyon to taking road trips to visit cute girls.

That summer I also picked up another job waiting tables at Olive Garden to make a little extra money. I quickly learned that I couldn't take two server jobs at the same time. I got too sick of dealing with customers, so I quit. I still had my job at Tucanos, which I loved. I had been working there for about a year and a half and was good friends with everybody there. From my experience, for whatever reason, waiters and waitresses aren't really the best moral people to be around. They can be crude, bitter, and greedy, and after working there for so long it started to rub off on me. That, along with the constant sarcasm and jokes by my roommates, made my spiritual side start to slip a little. The content of my conversations and the state of my character just weren't where they should have been and it made a difference in my life. I wasn't as happy and often found myself having a bad attitude.

I learned that if I read the scriptures for 30 minutes a day and made sure to pray every morning and night, that it would help me feel happier, lower my stress level, and change my attitude. But it took a lot of work and persistence to accomplish that, especially with my busy life. I wasn't always good about it, but I knew that it was a sure way to make my life feel a little better.

10 BYU: SEP 2006 – APR 2006

My third year at BYU was probably my all around most difficult school year. It was a tough contrast from the amazing summer that I had just lived. Everything that year was really hard for me and it all started with my apartment of good friends being split up. Jordan and I moved into this really old house that was built in the 1940's because we couldn't afford the higher rent for the place that my other roommates were moving into.

We ended up in this house with three other random guys. One of them was all right, another acted tough all of the time and wouldn't ever really talk to us, and the other barely spoke English. Living there was so different for us. Mainly because we were used to bringing the social scene to our place, but now we had to leave to go have fun. We spent a lot of time hanging out at our friends place until they got serious girlfriends and got engaged. So a lot of the time it was just Jordan and I. Luckily he was an awesome friend and always fun to be around.

School that year was especially difficult. I had been accepted into the mechanical engineering program and was being hammered by classes like fluid dynamics, material science, thermodynamics 1 and 2, materials science and electrical engineering. It felt like I never had any time for a social life because I spent all of my time studying. This was super frustrating for me. I wanted to find a girlfriend so badly but didn't have any time for it.

I was always trying to meet new girls because I wanted to move on with my life and get married. Looking back now, I don't know why I was in such a rush, but at the time it was really depressing to be single when all of my good friends had somebody. I prayed a lot to find somebody but still had the same old stuff happen to me. Whenever I found someone that I really liked, after two or three dates they would either just stop answering their phones, or something would happen so that they couldn't date me anymore. It was driving me crazy. I started to wonder if I would ever find anybody.

On top of my dating problems, my spiritual side was starting to slip again. I still went to church every week, but it wasn't enough to keep me at the level that I wanted to be. I needed to be reading scriptures for 30 minutes a day but since I was so busy with school it often got put at the bottom of my priority list…and I was feeling the consequences.

I was also stressing a lot about what I was going to do about a summer internship. I had already gone to the career fairs and applied with lots of companies, but none of them called me back. It was annoying because lots of guys in my program were already hired on for the summer. I felt so rejected because nobody was interested in hiring me. That, on top of my stress from school, my failures in the dating world, and my declining spirituality, made me feel really crummy about myself.

I went home for Christmas break feeling pretty depressed. I just wanted things to work out for me. When I got home from my mission I had this vision in my head of how I wanted my life to go. My plan was to be successful in school, date around for a little while, find a girlfriend that I really liked, date her for about a year or so, get married to her, and maybe start a family about a year after that. So far it seemed like nothing was going according to plan.

During the Christmas break I met one of my dad's friends who was a mechanical engineer for a good engineering company called Fluor. When he asked me about my plans I told him that I should probably find an internship somewhere. Well, the next day he called me up and said "I have an interview set up for you. Can you be there at 1:00?" I was so shocked! I didn't really know what to say. I had absolutely no interest in living in Sugar Land that summer, but I wanted to be polite and figured I could use some interviewing experience, so I went.

After the interview I had no interest in working there, until a few weeks later they called me up and made me an offer. It was an offer that I couldn't really turn down. They were going to pay me more than I had ever dreamed of making while still in school and their office was only five minutes away from my parent's house. I could live there and save every penny I made. It was going to be great, except for one thing. I didn't have any friends there and I especially didn't think I would find anybody to date. I was excited and worried about what the summer might have in store for me. Regardless, I accepted the offer just about a month or two before the school year was over and quit my other job so that I could actually have time to date more and have a real social life for a change.

It's possible that my experience with cancer started at about this time, more than two years before I was actually diagnosed. I say "possible" because I went through pain that was almost identical to the pain from the cancer and I haven't figured out if they were related or not.

It all started with a girl. Yes, another girl that would, in the end, ultimately reject me. Looking back now, it makes sense why all of these BYU girls had to reject me. I don't think any of them would have been able to handle what was about to happen to me.

This girl was a cute and active girl from Arizona. She was a runner. I had taken her out a few times and began to like her quite a bit. She asked me if I would run with her in a 10k that would be held two weeks down the road. I thought to myself "There's no way I'll be able to run this thing without killing myself." But I wanted to impress the girl and I needed to get some exercise. So I decided to go running every night before so that I could get into shape and do the 10k without looking like a complete wuss. I wanted to show her that I wasn't just a nerdy engineering student. I was athletic and could get up and do a 10k without hardly training.

That night I started my "training." It went well. Not too painful. I think I ran 2 miles. The next night I started running and was feeling strong and more confident. I easily finished my planned two miles and then decided to do a little more. I figured I needed to be able to run at her pace… about 7:15 per mile, so I got out the stop watch and started my next two miles. The third felt ok, although, my legs were beginning to ache pretty badly. The final one was rough, but because I am so competitive with myself, I pushed through the pain from my burning legs and kept on running uphill the whole way back to the house. I sprinted the last block uphill, walked a little, stretched a little, and then went inside and treated myself to a home-made strawberry smoothie before going to bed. I felt tough, like I still had it in me until the next morning when my leg hurt so bad that I struggled to make it up the stairs to campus.

I had this throbbing, achy pain in my right leg at the top of the fibula. It felt like I had pulled something except that the pain was in a place where there are no muscles to be pulled. The pain didn't go away for almost a month until I was able to go home for the summer. I ended up not running the 10k and the girl left me for another guy. I felt pretty humiliated running into her on campus and having to explain to her why I was limping around all the time.

By the end of the semester I was sick of dealing with girls at BYU and ready to get started on my internship at Fluor. The minute I finished my last final I loaded up my little green car and made the marathon drive back to Sugar Land with my roommate Jordan.

11 SUMMER INTERNSHIP: MAY 2006 – SEP 2006

After dropping Jordan off at the airport I suddenly realized my bitter-sweet summer situation. I was going to work a great job, make lots of money, and sit around on my butt all summer, bored from not having any friends at home.

I started work the next week. My first week on the job, I ended up sitting around in a cubicle with nothing to do. I would probably do about one hour of work in a 9 hour work day. It drove me crazy! I felt so worthless. My conscience was eating away at me because I felt like I should be as productive at work as I had been the past three grueling years of school. It turned out that working at Fluor was just like that sometimes. As an intern, there wasn't much for me to do, but they kept me around anyway just in case something popped up. Well, finally something popped up after a couple of weeks. I started doing fairly simple Excel work to produce datasheets for the company. This work kept me semi-busy for about a month and a half until they moved me to my first project – designing a refinery that was to be built in Kuwait. My excitement about the project was shot down after my first week of, again, sitting around with hardly anything to do. To keep myself entertained and feeling productive I would ask people around the office if there was anything I could do to help them. This usually resulted in mindless chores like helping the secretaries organize their file cabinets. Finally they moved me to another project where I finished up the last month of the summer. This project was for the expansion of a refinery in Louisiana. They kept me pretty busy and I made some good friends.

The social life that summer started out really slow, but ended great. At first I didn't know anybody in Houston other than my family and some of the "adults" in my home church congregation, called a "Ward." Thank goodness Mandy was around that summer. She kept me entertained and I had a lot of fun hanging out with her. We played a lot of soccer with the Latinos downtown. I went to church in the same ward that I grew up in a few times until I realized that I needed to just suck it up, get out of my comfort zone, and go to the young single adult ward to try to make some friends that I could hang out with for the summer. The usual quest for cute girls was also a motivating factor. I don't remember a whole lot about my trips to church in the singles ward though. There weren't a whole lot of exciting experiences. I do remember, however, that the people in the ward were a lot of fun. Everybody had a career, or at least a full time job, and lots of money to spend on fun activities. It wasn't uncommon for a big group to go to an Astros game or to a play, or something, for weekday church activities. People had the time and money to do almost whatever they wanted. This was completely different from the poor student wards that I attended at BYU.

Making the move to Sugar Land ended up being the best thing that I could have done for my spiritual health. Before leaving Provo, I was so caught up in trying to act like a goofy, funny, college guy. I was always being sarcastic, making inappropriate jokes, and using semi-foul language. I knew that I needed to make changes, but I just couldn't. I had too much fun joking around with my friends and ended up kind of relying on that type of humor for my social life. The only way that I would really be able change and be more of the person that I was inside was if I up and left for a while. Well, that's what I got for the summer. A chance to leave all of that stuff behind and just be myself. It was great! Making the changes took a lot of work, but by the end of the summer I was able to completely cut out all of that stuff and form good habits to replace it with. Instead of trying to be a funny, cool college guy I was able to be the nice, respectful, considerate person that I was inside. It felt like a burden had been lifted once I had grown up and left the college guy behind. Making that change was so important to me. It made me happier, it made me kinder to others, and it formed me into the type of person that my future wife would want to build a relationship with.

12 THE GIRL OF MY DREAMS

One week, shortly after starting to attend the singles ward, I felt like I needed to be more involved in the activities that were provided so that I could make more friends and hopefully meet somebody to date. I decided that I should try going to the singles' weekly bible study group in my area. I showed up hoping to meet some cute girls and all that I found was a group of people, who, at that time, I thought were a bunch of weirdoes – at least some of them seemed like weirdoes. I decided to be nice and sit patiently through the lessons and activities. Maybe these weirdoes weren't as bad as they seemed. Well, it turned out that they weren't. They definitely weren't my first choice of people to hang out with over the summer, but I figured they would do for a few more months. By the end of the summer I had learned an important lesson… Just because others might be really different than me doesn't mean that I can't enjoy being around them. It especially doesn't mean that I, or anyone else, should label anybody a "dork" or a "weirdo."

After arriving and meeting everybody there I quickly came to the conclusion that there was nobody there that I would be interested in dating. My hopes were dashed until right at the end, when I was getting ready to leave, this really cute girl showed up. She was dressed very simply, wearing black workout pants and a white t-shirt. I thought that she was really good looking, but not quite the perfect ten that I had been looking for before. She came in and apologized to everybody for being late and began socializing with all of the other people there. I watched her from across the room hoping she would make it easy for me and come over and introduce herself. As I watched her go around the room and talk with different people, I was surprised and intrigued at how nice and sincere she was to all of the people there that I considered weird. This is the first thing about her that really impressed me. Normally the really cute girls were kind of snotty and wouldn't be so sincere to different people like that but she seemed to be different.

She finally made her way over to me. I thought "Great, this is my chance, she's going to come introduce herself." Unfortunately she didn't say anything; just walked right by. When she walked by the second time I knew I had to be the one to act if I was going to meet her. I stuck my hand out and introduced myself. Her name was Kelly, and I quickly found that she was full of good sarcasm and not afraid to make fun of me right off the bat. I liked a girl that wasn't afraid to joke around. We talked for a few minutes and then she left. I didn't really get to know her that well, but I talked to her long enough to realize that she was pretty cute and by far the best girl that I had met all summer. I had to go back the next week to see her again!

The next week the group met at a local park just before the sun went down. I showed up hoping that she would be there. She was late, again. Halfway through she came in with a friend and practically ignored me the whole time. I thought "Oh great, another girl that's going to play stupid games with me." I had to go out of my way to talk with her, and when I did, she would hardly leave her friend's side. After following her around a little longer and putting in a little more effort I was finally able to get a conversation going. She was really fun to talk to. We spent the rest of the time hanging out and chasing fireflies. By the end of the night I had realized that I didn't want to wait another week to see her again. I got her phone number and told her that I wanted to hang out with her sometime, but that I was going up to the lake that weekend and I would call her when I got back.

Later that week my brother, Nick, returned home from his mission in Brazil. It was so fun to see him back and to see that he was still his same old self. We all had fun listening to his crazy stories about Brazil and meeting the wooden parrot that he used to talk to when times got tough. I think it was the weekend that he got back that we went up to my grandparent's lake house The only thing I remembered about being up at the lake this time was that Kelly and I started texting back and forth about hanging out when I got back. I was texting her while we were playing games on the golf course up there. Of course I was asking Mandy what I should say. Nick tried giving some advice, which wasn't taken considering he had hardly spoken to a girl for two years. He didn't know how to handle girls yet. She ended up inviting me to go out with her and some friends when I got back.

The next night after the drive home, I met up with Kelly and two of her friends. We went to Friday's for dinner and then went to Sam's Boat (a bar/hangout) so that Kelly's friend could meet up with some guy that she was interested in. I thought it was a little weird going there, considering we don't drink, but I ended up having a really good time getting to know Kelly more.

After that night we started hanging out almost every day. It was awesome! Finally there was a girl that I was interested in that actually wanted to hang out with me. I had never really had that before. I would ask her if she wanted to do something and she would just say yes. It was amazing! No games or anything! Kelly kept a list of everything we did together up until just after we moved to Utah. She showed it to me on the drive up to Provo. I loved it! I was still in shock that she actually liked me so much. When she gave it to me I started to feel really excited and overwhelmed at the same time. I thought that our little fling might actually turn into something and that maybe she was the one for me.

This is the list that she had written down:

Jul 8-TGI Friday's and Sam's Boat
Jul 9-Church, Soccer game and myspace
Jul 10-Singles' Bible Study Group

Jul 11-Asked me to Metro Prom
Jul 12-Walk
Jul 14-Longboarding, Sweet Mesquite & Bruce Almighty (my rescue)
Jul 15-Beach and Moulin Rouge
Jul 16-Longboarding
Jul 17-Singles' Bible Study Group
Jul 18-Looked at Stars
Jul 19-Thai Basil (Bought me roses and gum)
Jul 20-Church Institute and picked up Nick's car
Jul 21-Cheesecake factory and RM at Dave's
Jul 22-Swimming
Jul 23-Dinner at Weaver's with friends
Jul 24-Family Home Evening at Brent's, talked about Utah on pier
Jul 26-Walk, talked more about Utah
Jul 27-Astros game with Dad and Mary
Jul 29-Kelly Clarkson and Hitch
Jul 31-Singles' Bible Study Group
Aug 1-Park
Aug 2-Galleria
Aug 3-Institute and Talladega nights
Aug 4-Anchorman
Aug 5-Hot tub and TV
Aug 7-Singles' Bible Study Group and TV
Aug 13-Watched TV and talked A LOT
Aug 14-Swimming
Aug 16-Longboarded to hockey game
Aug 17-Church Institute and Ben and Jerry's
Aug 21-Family home evening
Aug 22-Hung out at Swoozie's
Aug 25-Red River
Aug 26-Talked at my house
Aug 27-Stopped by the Staub's
Aug 29-Left for Utah
Aug 30-Got to Utah

Aug 31-Set up apartments and ate with Brad and MaryAnn
Sep 1-Set up apartments
Sep 2-Temple square, volleyball and soccer game
Sep 3-Church, group prayer, rock canyon park
Sep 4-Provo canyon
Sep 5-Rock climbing

I didn't realize how much we were together until Kelly showed this list to me that day. There were a few things that really stood out to me though. One night we went longboarding on the golf course. Another night we went longboarding down to the ice skating rink and back and she wiped out pretty bad. I don't think we longboarded much after that. The world cup was going on, so she came over and watched a few soccer games with me. We organized a trip down to Galveston with a bunch of friends. I was excited because we brought a surfboard. I thought it would be fun to try to surf a little, but we pulled up to the water and the highest wave was about four inches. What a disappointment. We still had fun just swimming and playing in the sand. We did a lot of hanging out together. Nothing too interesting, just things like watching movies and TV, and talking. I absolutely loved having a girl around that I was interested in who would actually spend time with me.

Kelly and I mostly hung out at night because both of us worked during the day. Usually while I was at work, I emailed and texted her to keep myself entertained since I didn't have a whole lot going on at Fluor. There was one day at work that I was looking at Google earth. I thought it was fun to look at different places around the world. While tinkering with that I started wondering about the stars for some reason. Maybe I ran into a program that let you look at stars from different parts of the world or something. For some reason though, I think I sent Kelly a text or email about stars or constellations. She replied and said she wished she knew more about them and wanted to look at constellations. Since I felt like I knew something about the constellations (I really don't) I asked if she wanted me to show them to her that week. She said yes. I suggested we take a blanket out on the golf course one night and look at them. She seemed really excited about it, which made me excited because who really wants to go look at stars??? I figured she was trying to get me into a situation that would make it easy for me to put the moves on her and kiss her.

That night I grabbed a blanket and took her to a part of the golf course that my good friends and I always used to play on when we were kids. We both laid on the blanket and we looked up at the sky for a few minutes and talked about the constellations and stuff. The problem was that it was right in the middle of the summer and it was so hot and humid and the mosquitoes were swarming like crazy! After finally mustering up the courage I leaned over her and kissed her. To my surprise, she didn't pull away, so I kept kissing her. We kissed for a couple of seconds and then she just started laughing. She stopped after a second and then kissed me again. After a few more seconds she started laughing again and I had to stop to figure out what was going on. I think she asked me what I was doing. I thought "Oh great, she didn't want me to kiss her. Now she's not going to want anything to do with me." I stopped, said sorry. She said it was ok and that she liked me kissing her. So I started kissing her again and she kept laughing. I think it was because I kissed different than what she was used to. I kept trying, but she kept laughing. It was pretty awkward for me. I didn't know what she was laughing at and I was getting self-conscious. After a couple of minutes though, she finally calmed down and stopped laughing, but by that time we were so sticky from the humidity and tired of swatting away the mosquitoes that we decided to just call it a night. What a romantic experience!

The next day was her birthday. I thought I was in trouble because half the time that I kissed somebody that I was interested in they didn't want anything to do with me the next day. It was always a tough call on what to do after kissing a girl. I would normally try to play it cool and not try to hang out with her the next day. However, if she did actually like me then I would be a jerk for kissing her and then not seeing her the next day. This time I decided to just go for it and show her that I was interested.

After discussing it with Mandy and my mom we decided that I should get her flowers. The only problem was that I had never bought flowers for a girl before. I didn't know which ones were good or which type and color to get her. My mom ended up going with me to help me pick them out. I chose these pink roses and got her a few packs of her favorite gum. I was so afraid that I was being too forward but I went through with it anyway.

I went over to her place and gave her the roses and gum and then met up with a bunch of our friends for dinner. I tried to read her all throughout dinner, and it didn't look good. She hardly paid any attention to me and I don't think she even sat by me. I was planning on possibly getting rejected when I dropped her off at the end of the night. To my surprise, however, as we were walking over to my little green car she grabbed my hand and gave me a hug. What a relief! She still liked me! I took her home and we ended up kissing for like 20 minutes in the car before we said goodnight. I didn't know what to do at this point. I hadn't been in this stage of a relationship since I was 17. Luckily she made it really easy for me to ask her out and we just kept hanging out the rest of the summer.

Just before I met Kelly she had broken up with this guy that I knew. He was a total scumbag. He was manipulative, a liar, a bad influence on her, and didn't treat her well at all. He was pretty much just an over-all bad person. Anyways, there were several times throughout the summer that he tried to stalk Kelly so that he could try to sweet talk his way into getting back together with her. Luckily, I was there to rescue her from him a couple of times.

One time he went to her work and parked his car behind hers in the back of the store so that she couldn't leave without talking to him. She called me and I picked her up from work at the front door so that she wouldn't have to talk to him. There was one night in particular that he was trying to stalk her and I was really worried about it. I felt like if she were to meet up with him and talk that she would end up going back to him. We were together at the bible study group that night and she was about to leave early to meet him. I was so worried that I would lose her that I ran out the door to chase her down and convinced her to go to a park with me instead of meeting up with him.

We sat on the dock next to this lake at the park and talked everything over for a long time. I really felt that the best thing for her to do was to get away from Sugar Land so that she could just completely remove herself from the situation with this guy. It also just so happened that I was about to move back to Provo to finish up my last year of school. What a perfect opportunity!! She could drive up with me and live in Provo. We talked about that for a while and planned everything out from where she would live to how much money she would need to make to pay her bills. Logically, it was the worst decision she ever could have made. She didn't know anybody up there, jobs were hard to find, and she was already in debt. Regardless, she felt it was a good idea and she decided to move there and drive up with us. I was so excited because I knew it would help her a lot and that it was the right decision.

However, after driving up I started to wonder what the heck I was thinking. I was scared to death. I felt like I had convinced her to move there and now felt responsible for her. What if she didn't find a job? What if she hated her roommates? What if I decided that I wanted to break up with her? I started getting a lot of anxiety. I was worried that I would feel responsible if this move didn't turn out the way I had told her it would. Luckily, though, everything worked out great! She found a job, she liked her roommates, and I didn't break up with her.

13 BYU: SEP 2006 – APR 2007

The first thing on the to-do list was to find Kelly a job. I took her to the restaurant I used to work at and convinced my old manager to give her a job there as a server. It wasn't the best job, but she would make enough money to pay the bills. I thought it was perfect. However, she never really got enough hours and hated the manager. She ended up yelling at him and walking out in the middle of a shift. He was a jerk, after all, and probably deserved it. Looking back, her telling him off should have been my first sign of her fiery personality (which I didn't realize she had until after we were married). After that we ended up getting her a job working for a friend of my good friend from Sugar Land. She was kind of like his personal assistant. She must have done a really good job there because he loved Kelly and always bragged to my friend that she was the best employee that he ever had. The only problem with the job was that it wasn't full time and didn't quite pay enough to make ends meet. Luckily I was pretty wealthy from my high paying internship and was able to make up for what she didn't have. I paid her rent a couple of times and bought her groceries here and there.

It was after she got that job that I learned all about her debt situation. I knew she had some debt because she always had debt collectors calling her phone. I think they called her about ten times a day. I never put much thought into it though until one day after paying for something I sat her down and we talked about how much money she owed. I was shocked to find out that she owed money on several credit cards. She also had several unpaid medical bills, a whole lot of student loans, and unpaid traffic tickets.

I felt so bad for her! It broke my heart to see her in so far over her head. In a way I kind of felt partially responsible for some of her debt-related grief because I had convinced her to move to Utah where she had no chance of paying it off. Luckily, I had saved $13,000 from working at Fluor and also received about $8,000 in grants for that year. I figured that I had way more money than I needed for that school year and that once I graduated I would be making plenty for a single guy. I decided that the money I had been given should go towards relieving her of some of her stressful money situation. Plus, if I ended up deciding to marry her then I would need to pay it all off anyway. I cared about her a lot and I didn't like that she had such a heavy burden constantly hanging over her head. Nobody had ever taught her about how money and debt worked. I felt so bad that such a sweet girl had to deal with such a difficult thing. I think I paid off about $4,000. It helped her a lot and it made me feel good to be able to help her.

Looking back, I feel really bad about how I behaved in Utah that year. I was so used to being a poor college kid from my previous years at school that I never really spent much money on Kelly. I had the money to do a lot of fun things with her. But, regrettably, I chose to spend more time hanging around my crummy apartment than taking her out on nice dates. I guess in a way that is a good thing though, because all of the money that we had saved while dating ended up paying off all of her debt once we were engaged and married.

Most of our dates were free activities. We drove up into the canyon a few times. We spent a lot of time hanging out in our apartments with friends. We used to play Rummikub and different card games a lot with roommates. That was a lot of fun. I did take her out to dinner here and there. We liked to go to Jason's Deli and get the Texas spud with cheese and BBQ. Looking back, I wish I would have put in the time and effort to plan more quality activities with her.

My last year of actual school was pretty uneventful. It was just school as usual except that this year I didn't have to work and take classes at the same time. This made such a huge difference. It was good because then I was able to spend more time with Kelly. The downfall, however, was that since I was spending so much time with Kelly I was worried that if I didn't marry her she would be extra heart-broken because we had spent so much time together and gotten so close. This constantly triggered the question of if I should ask Kelly to marry me or if I should break up with her. I had so much anxiety over trying to figure this out. I hated it. I worried about it constantly. I felt like I loved her, but I didn't know if I loved her enough to be with her all of the time. Then if I broke up with her I worried about her being hurt. It was a vicious cycle for me. Looking back now, it was so stupid of me to be so worried.

I was constantly starting up conversations with friends, family, married people, or practically anybody that could offer some kind of useful advice to help me with my decision. I'm sure I drove everyone crazy! It got to the point that I was calling nearly everybody in my family almost every day. They all pretty much told me the same thing… She's a great girl but it is your decision. This didn't help much. I just wanted somebody to tell me what to do!

I prayed and prayed to try to find the right answer and never got anything. I was looking for some type of feeling or confirmation that marrying her was the right thing to do. I never got any type of answer though. I was so frustrated, but looking back, I think I learned a very valuable lesson about prayer and our free agency.

I feel like God gave us the ability to choose for ourselves what we would like to do with our lives and who we would like to spend our time with. There are so many things that are completely up to us. Through the process of making decisions for ourselves and dealing with any consequences that might come from them, we are able to either gain confidence in ourselves, or learn important lessons from our mistakes. I do feel, however, that as long as we pray for guidance and follow the commandments that we have been given, God will help us along the way to keep us from getting into too much trouble from bad decisions. After finally marrying Kelly and learning these concepts, I changed the way that I prayed. I rarely asked questions like "What should I do?" Instead, I would pray for help in making the best decision and I would push forward with whatever I had decided to do. Through experience, I have found that when guidance is needed, it always comes through my own thoughts. Before I would ask myself, "Am I just coming up with these thoughts on my own or am I receiving answers to my prayers?" Now I realize that my thoughts are often influenced and are in fact the answers that I have been asking for. It is for that reason that it is so important to be able to make decisions on our own and go forward, acting on our decisions while trusting that God won't let us down.

Anyway, I got so frustrated from constantly worrying about whether or not I should marry Kelly that I wasn't taking into consideration what she wanted to do. I always felt like she really liked me a lot. We had talked about marriage a little and said that we loved each other. I was pretty confident that she was on board with the idea. But I didn't want to talk to her too much about it because if I did decide to ask her to marry me I wanted it to be a surprise for her, and talking about it all of the time would give it away.

14 PROPOSING TO KELLY

I guess it was about January when I was right in the middle of this whole stressful ordeal. By then, we had been dating for about six or seven months. I would be graduating in April and I think she was starting to wonder what she would do with her life if I headed back to Sugar Land and left her in Utah. She started making these comments about how she wanted to apply to BYU for the summer. It drove me crazy. I thought "If she applies to BYU then what about me? What about us?" It was like she didn't care whether we were together or not. Sometimes I thought she was intentionally making these kinds of comments to drive me crazy and to get me thinking about where our relationship was going. It turns out, that I was wrong. She later told me she was just making plans for her life in case things didn't work out between us.

One day I met Mandy for lunch in the food court at BYU. I started up the usual conversation about whether or not I should marry Kelly. This time though, I was feeling the pressure. I had to make up my mind soon because all of this stressing out was getting out of hand. Plus, Valentine's Day was coming up and I had no idea what to do for a girlfriend on Valentine's Day. I had never had a girlfriend on Valentine's Day before. I don't know what exactly Mandy said to me to help, but I just remember thinking, "I have to propose and it has to be on Valentine's Day." My theory was that if I proposed on Valentine's Day then I wouldn't have to go through having to think of a nice romantic night for Valentine's Day and a romantic proposal date. I could just get them both out of the way in one night! I know that's a pretty lame way to look at it, but I was really bad at coming up with the romantic stuff.

Mandy agreed to help me pick out a ring. Thank goodness she was there to help me through that whole process. She helped me to not be so cheap and to actually pick out something that looked good. Kelly and I had looked at rings before but I still needed to have Mandy around to help me make the final decision. We went to all of the ring stores in the mall several times and finally picked out something that we thought she would like. It was going to be perfect timing too. I would have the ring ready just a day or two before Valentine's Day so that I could propose when we went out that week.

I originally told her that we would go out on Valentine's Day or the day after. But when I went to pick up the ring they told me that there was a delay and that it wouldn't be ready until the end of the week. I was so annoyed. I hate lying, but I had to in order to get out of this one. So I told her I needed to study for a test on Valentine's Day and that we could go out that weekend instead. I think she was pretty annoyed, but it worked out well because she had gotten us tickets to see a band called Kalai for Friday night. I figured I could just make a romantic night out of it and propose before we went to the concert. The problem was that I had absolutely no idea how I was going to propose. In Provo it seemed like everybody had to do it in some sort of super creative and cute way. I was no good at that stuff and was so nervous because I knew that whatever I ended up doing would be transformed into a proposal story that would be told over and over again for the next several months and then remembered for the rest of her life. I was feeling a lot of pressure to do it right.

After a few days of stressing over what I was going to do I came to the conclusion that I'm not the kind of person that does over the top creative romantic stuff. So why try to be something that I'm not. I decided to just do something sweet and simple.

I bought a cute wooden pink box and a bunch of candy and cheesy Valentine's Day stuff and filled the box with it. I also bought some ring cleaner to hint at the fact that I had an engagement ring for her. That way, when she saw the ring cleaner in the box she would wonder what it was for. I was going to give her the box of stuff and keep the ring in my pocket. The plan was that after she opened the box and found the ring cleaner at the bottom she would pick up on the hint and get an excited look on her face, at which point I would drop down to one knee, pull the ring out of my pocket, and ask her to marry me. After I proposed we would leave to go to dinner and the concert. I thought it was a pretty good plan. Unfortunately, it didn't really go quite how I had so carefully planned.

I stopped by the grocery store on the way over to her apartment and bought a bunch of roses. I walked in the door and she was still getting ready... I wasn't expecting that, but knowing her, I probably should have. I made her pause on her hair so that she could open up my present. I gave her the flowers and she cut them and put them in a vase. When she went to open the box I started to get really nervous. I thought for sure she would pick up on the hint of the ring cleaner. She opened the box and went through the stuff. When she pulled out the ring cleaner she just looked at it and then put it back in the box with no reaction at all. So she hugged me and said thanks. Not knowing what to do because my hint didn't work, I said "Well I have one more thing for you." I pulled out the ring box and she looked at it like "Oh, that's nice" thinking that it was some kind of earrings or necklace or something. It wasn't until I opened it up that she realized that I was actually proposing. The moment she saw the ring a huge smile shot across her face. I had completely taken her by surprise. All she could say was "Oh my gosh, are you serious?" over and over again. I knelt down on one knee and asked her if she would marry me. I was so nervous. Not because I thought she would say no, but because I couldn't believe that I was actually proposing to somebody. It was such a weird feeling. Both of us got teary eyed right after I asked her. I was really excited to have a fiancé and also so relieved that the whole proposing thing was over with. It made me feel so good that she actually liked me enough that she wanted to be with me forever. Apart from feeling excited, loved, and relieved, I was also scared to death of what I was doing with my life. I was getting married! Everything in my life was going to change. What was I getting myself into? I think by Kelly's facial expressions, she felt the same way.

After she tried on the ring and approved of it we sat down on the couch and she gave me a scrapbook that she had made for me for Valentine's Day. We went through it and looked at all of the pictures and then realized that we were running seriously late and needed to get going. She hurried up and finished putting on her make-up and doing her hair so that we could rush to dinner. But we didn't have time to go out to the restaurant I was thinking of because the concert was about to start, so instead, we made a quick stop at the Wendy's drive through and picked up a couple of burgers on the way to the concert. We took the fast food inside and ate while we waited to get seated. I had such an awesome feeling that whole night. I kept looking at her and thinking "Wow, she's my fiancé! What am I doing with a fiancé? And how did I get so great of a girl?" It was a great night. The concert was amazing and it felt so good to have Kelly with me knowing that she would be with me forever.

15 FINISHING BYU

The rest of the semester seemed to go by really quickly. It felt so good to have that marriage decision out of the way, even though the anxiety of getting married was still nerve racking for me up until the moment we tied the knot. It seemed like the rest of the time in Provo just flew bye. We continued hanging out like we had been until finals came and it was time to pack up and move back to Sugar Land.

Everything else going on in my life was a lot of fun as well. Nick was just off of his mission and decided to live with me that year. Mandy was also in Provo for her freshman year. I always loved having brothers and sisters up there with me. Laura was there when I first started at BYU. She was fun to have around, but I didn't really see her too much. She had already been there for a year and a half and had a good bunch of friends to hang out with. It was weird because my whole life it seemed like we had similar friends because she would always tag along with me and my friends. Now, she had all of these other friends of her own that I didn't know. It kind of felt like she didn't really need me around as much as she used to. I was happy for her though and very proud of the girl that she had turned into while I was on my mission. This school year, Laura had already graduated and was living in Dallas with Eric. Nick and Mandy took her place for me though.

Living with Nick was so much fun for me. I loved it! I felt bad though because when we talked about moving in together I pictured it being a lot different than it really was. Although I really enjoyed having him around as a roommate, I think it probably would have been better for him socially if he would have lived with guys his age. Plus, I was always with Kelly and I think that kind of drove him crazy sometimes. I was always annoying him with my questions about whether or not I should marry Kelly. I loved his response though. He said "If you don't marry her then I will." Mandy was also so great to have around. I loved meeting up with her on campus for lunch. I don't remember if she bought me lunch with her student card or if we just met up; I just remember how much I enjoyed the times I had to take a break from school and be with family. Nick was the same way. I loved it whenever I saw him on campus. It was just so nice to be around people who you loved and who you knew you could rely on if you needed anything. Sometimes I wish I could be up there with Whitney because I think it would be a lot of fun to be able to hang out with her. I like to think that if I were still up there I would invite her over for dinner a lot and ask her to hang out, even though she sometimes prefers to be a little less social.

16 MOVING BACK TO SUGAR LAND

After finishing the semester in April all I could think about was how crazy it was that I was going to be getting married in June. The whole marriage thing still stressed me out a lot. I also felt like I needed to rush home and start work right away so that we could start making more progress on paying off all of the debt that she had. I ended up skipping the graduation ceremony and leaving just a day or two after I finished my last final so that I could get to work right away. I think we left Provo on a Thursday and I was planning on starting work the following Monday. We packed up all of our stuff and loaded it into my little green car and Kelly's even smaller car. I was so sad to leave my friend, Jordan. I had lived with him for three years and he still had another year or so of school to go. Saying goodbye to him was really hard. So I just hugged him and then jumped in the car and tried not to tear up on the way to the gas station. We were guys and needed to be tough around each other.

Moving away from Provo was a difficult step for me. I was leaving my friends and everything I knew to go off and start this whole new grown up life. I was such a jerk to Kelly too. I don't know how she stuck with me after that trip home. I think that going through all of these changes really triggered my anxiety problem. I spent most of the time in my good friend's car, who was already married and driving down to Houston with us. I wanted to ride with him because I felt like I needed to talk to somebody about all of this anxiety that I was feeling at the time. I didn't want to ride with Kelly because she was right in the middle of why I was having the anxiety in the first place. I felt like separating myself from her for a little while would help me wrap my mind around all of the changes that were coming up in my life. I think she ended up driving almost the whole way from Provo to Houston by herself because I was too wrapped up in my own problems. I still feel bad about that.

Things got a lot better once we finally made it back to Sugar Land. Life started to get really exciting! Kelly and I both began work and Kelly spent a lot of her time doing wedding preparation. I had this great paying job and an amazing fiancé. I finally felt like I was no longer a social outcast for not having my life in order. The anxiety had nearly vanished and everything was going great... until out of nowhere, Kelly transformed into this crazy woman that I felt like I had never met before. I think the stress from all of the wedding and work had overwhelmed her just a little. I started seeing sides of her that I had never seen before. It made me think that my sweet loving fiancé was putting on an act the whole time we dated so that she could cover up the crazy person that she really was on the inside. Well, I'm over-exaggerating a lot. She wasn't really that bad. There were just some stronger personality traits that came through that I hadn't really noticed before. It scared me at first. I thought "What am I doing? I didn't sign up for a girl that acts like this." But regardless of how crazy I thought she was getting, I was determined that she was just stressed and would eventually return back to her normal self after the wedding was over.

17 THE BIG DAY: JUN 23, 2007

After all of the seemingly endless hours of stressful preparations, the big day had finally arrived. Kelly was still a little crazy and I was going through so many weird emotions that I don't think I was acting anywhere near normal either. I'm surprised that Kelly actually said yes to me from the way I was acting. I still had a lot of anxiety over whether or not marrying Kelly was the right thing to do, even though inside I knew that it was.

All of the wedding stuff seemed to happen so fast that it was a blur. The day before the wedding I tried to relieve some stress by going and playing tennis with some friends and family. I don't think it worked very well, I was still so nervous. I wish I would have written all of my feelings down at the time because now I don't really remember anything about what was going on in my head. I must have been really scatter-brained. Luckily, my family was there to just order me around and tell me what to do and when to do it. The day of the wedding they even woke me up and helped me get all dressed up in the tuxedo that we rented. Thanks to them, everything ran smoothly for me that morning.

Kelly, on the other hand, had woken up late and was going crazy to get her hair done and get ready in time. Go figure she would be running late on our wedding day. I don't really remember much of what happened once we arrived at the temple for the ceremony. Everything went by so fast. All of a sudden we were in this beautiful sealing room surrounded by all of my family and close friends. It felt so good to be there that day. Even though I was stressed beyond belief, there was a peace there that I can't describe and I knew that what I was doing would bring me happiness. I looked around the room and saw all of the amazing friends that I have been so blessed to have throughout my life. They were all there to show their love for us and to support us through this sacred step in our lives. I absolutely loved it!

Before I knew it I was kneeling across the altar from Kelly just before the actual ceremony took place. She looked so beautiful! I could tell she was really nervous too. I know she doesn't like being the center of attention and it was driving her crazy to have everybody watching her. I looked at her so differently in that moment. I saw her as this amazing person that I was so proud of. I felt lucky and blessed to think that I would be able to spend the rest of eternity with somebody so awesome. I don't remember what all was said during the ceremony, but I do remember the strong desire that I felt to do everything I could to make her happy and be a good husband for the rest of my life and forever after. Once the sealer was finished giving his advice he said I could kiss the bride. I looked over at Kelly, anxious for our first kiss as husband and wife and I think she just smiled awkwardly and said something like "No thanks" or "Maybe later." She was really embarrassed to kiss me while everybody was watching, so I just gave her a quick peck on the lips to ease her embarrassment as everyone else in the room chuckled.

After the ceremony we went outside to take pictures with everybody that was there. It was a beautiful day! The only problem was that it was like 95 degrees outside and disgustingly humid. I was okay with the heat despite the tuxedo that I was wearing, but I felt really bad for Kelly. She was wearing a huge wedding dress with multiple layers. I immediately understood how miserable she was when the photographer asked me to pick her up and spin around. She was drenched in sweat and the dress was so heavy that I could hardly carry her for more than a couple of minutes.

After all of the picture taking was finally finished we headed back to our side of town for a luncheon. We had lunch at a nearby Mexican Restaurant... kind of a random place to have a wedding lunch, but it was a lot of fun nonetheless. It was nice to be able to hang out with close family and friends before the reception later that night. I was also glad to have Kelly's family there to support her. I felt bad that none of her family was able to be there with her in the temple. I wanted them to feel as included as possible because I know it was hard for them to miss out that morning. After filling ourselves with fajitas, Kelly and I went back to our apartment to relax for a few minutes before the reception.

We were worn out from waking up early that morning so we took a quick nap and then drove over to the clubhouse where we had the ring ceremony and reception. I thought the ring ceremony was awesome! All of Kelly's family and friends were able to make it out to support us. It was great for me because at that point I wasn't stressed out anymore. I could just relax and enjoy getting to know Kelly's family better. Our bishop at the time, who was a great friend of ours, performed the ceremony and did a great job! I think everybody on Kelly's side of the family was happy with how the ring ceremony turned out.

The clubhouse was decorated so beautifully. Everybody in the family and lots of good friends from church pitched in to make it look great. All of a sudden all of our guests showed up and formed a huge line for us to greet. It seemed like we stood and talked there forever as an endless flow of family and friends poured into the building. It was so fun to see everybody there. I was really glad to be able to meet a lot of Kelly's family and spend some time getting to know them better.

As the line died down my good friend Rob, who I have been friends with for as long as I can remember, pulled me aside and made me sit down at a table. Rob had been married for a few years and just had his second kid. He said that at his wedding he spent so much time talking to people that he never got a chance to eat anything. He went and got me a plate of food and we sat down and started eating together. The BBQ that night was so good and it was so nice of Rob to pull me aside. The only problem was that while I was sitting there pigging out on BBQ, Kelly was taking pictures with all of her family. I was so stupid. I watched them get all lined up for pictures and just thinking "Oh, that's a good one" or "I'm glad that we'll have pictures of all of her family." It wasn't until after all of them were taken that I realized I should have been in the pictures with them. So, now we have a bunch of reception pictures with Kelly and her family and I'm not in a single one. As you would expect, Kelly was just a little annoyed at me for that. Luckily she didn't realize that I wasn't there until after we got the pictures back a few weeks later.

After cutting the cake and hanging out for a while we were told that it was time for us to leave the party. We loaded up all of the presents into the car and headed home to our apartment... our very own apartment. It was so exciting! Once we got there and got everything unloaded from the car we were so exhausted that we both decided to just call it a night and go to sleep.

I woke up the next morning excited to get going on our honeymoon. I had it all planned out just perfectly!! Well, not really. I had originally planned on going down to South Padre Island for a few days of hanging out on the beach. Unfortunately, a big storm was forecast to hit the island and it was supposed to rain the entire time we were to be there. I had to cancel our hotel reservations. It worked out okay though because Kelly wasn't feeling too well at the time and wasn't up for a long car ride. Instead of driving to the beach we decided to take a much shorter trip to one of our favorite places... New Braunfels, Texas. We didn't do much there though. We stayed the night in a hotel, spent the next day at a really awesome water park, and then went to dinner at a restaurant called the Grist Mill, our favorite place to eat in New Braunfels. We had a lot of fun, but looking back, it was a pretty lame excuse for a honeymoon. I think the most exciting thing about our honeymoon was the thought that we were off traveling together and that we could do whatever we wanted because we were married! I loved the idea of being married to Kelly. I finally felt like I wasn't alone anymore. I had a new partner and best friend to share everything with. I couldn't wait to get started on the rest of our lives together.

The week after our wedding my mom's side of the family decided to rent a beach house in Galveston since they were all in town. I guess they figured it would be nice to relax after dealing with all of the stress from the wedding. Hanging out at the beach sounded like a lot of fun and Kelly and I felt left out because we weren't really invited. We were supposed to be on our honeymoon, but seeing that our plans were ruined by bad weather we decided to go down to the beach house to hang out with everybody. I think we went straight there after getting back from New Braunfels. It was a lot of fun to hang out at the beach house, but a little weird at the same time. Everybody kept making jokes about us being married and sleeping in the same bed and "stuff." We should have known it was coming though, Brad and Mary Anne always liked to joke around and embarrass us.

It was really nice to be able to hang out with my family without being stressed about getting married. With everybody's lives going in different directions it's rare for us to all be able to get together. I felt like since we were dealing with wedding stuff the whole time they were visiting I never really got to hang out with them. Going out to the beach house was the perfect opportunity for us to catch up before everybody had to get back to their normal lives.

18 FIRST YEAR AND A HALF OF MARRIAGE: JUN 2007 – DEC 2008

After the beach house it was time to get back to real life. The party was over. All of a sudden we had to figure out how to live together without driving each other crazy! I thought it was going to be easy, but was quickly proven wrong on our first weekend together as a married couple.

Kelly's dad and his family were in town for the weekend. We met up with them at Dave & Buster's for dinner and games. It was kind of weird for me at first because it was the first time that I had really spent much time with them. It was a lot of fun though. We ate dinner and then ran around and played games for a couple of hours. There was one game that we all really liked. It was some kind of trivia game where five or six people can sit down and race each other to answer questions. As I was sitting next to Kelly, enjoying the game, some girl came and stood behind me kind of in-between Kelly and I. She must have been a little drunk or just talkative, or something, because she kept talking to me and giving me hints on which answers to pick. I felt kind of awkward because this random girl kept talking to me. I didn't want to be rude or anything so I talked back here and there, but never got into any kind conversation or anything. After a few rounds I could tell that Kelly was annoyed at the girl so we jumped up and left. Well, by that time we were all ready to leave. Kelly's family went and cashed in all of their hundreds of tickets for prizes and we said goodbye and left.

Considering how much fun I had the drive home was a lot quieter than I had expected. Kelly was hardly talking and every time I asked what was wrong she said nothing and that she was just tired. So I believed her and we went straight home and went to sleep. Things hadn't improved by the time we went to church the next morning either. She still wouldn't talk and wouldn't tell me why. It was driving me crazy. We got home and she still was mad about something, but wouldn't talk. Finally I got sick of it and sat her down and made her speak. After about 30 minutes of drilling her with questions she finally burst out saying how mad she was because I was flirting with the girl at the trivia game the night before. I just started laughing because I couldn't believe that she thought I was flirting with that girl. I was annoyed that the girl kept talking to me and there I was getting in trouble for trying to be polite. It was all just a big mess. After complimenting her and trying to build up her confidence for about 20 minutes I think she realized she was being unnecessarily jealous. We still joke around about that fight every once in a while.

I quickly realized that the first year of marriage can be a little difficult. There is just so much getting to know each other and learning how the other thinks and reacts to different situations. It's funny because no matter how well you think you know somebody, once you marry them, you have to start a whole new "getting to know you" process. For me, that process involved lots of miscommunications and misunderstandings that caused all kinds of annoying arguments. It didn't matter how well we got along before, after we got married we got into little fights about all kinds of ridiculous stuff.

Cleaning was one of the silly things that we used to fight about. For the most part we always kept our place clean and tidy. Dishes were usually cleaned and the front rooms were always in order. The bedroom, however, was a different story. Kelly liked to try on a bunch of clothes while she was getting ready for the day (like any girl, I'm sure). She also liked to throw clothes into a pile after taking them off. There were always clothes scattered on her side of the room. It didn't really bother me except that every once in a while I wanted to do laundry or something and didn't know which clothes were clean and which were dirty. Well, one night I decided to pick up the bedroom while Kelly was out in the living room watching TV or studying or something. Bad decision! She got pretty mad because she didn't want to clean then. I didn't care if she helped me or not, I just wanted the place to be picked up. But she got mad at me for suggesting the idea. I thought "That's ridiculous! How can she get mad at me for wanting to clean? I'm just going to do it anyway!" So I went ahead and started to clean up the bedroom.

Well, she didn't like that at all. It really annoyed her and I just couldn't understand why. All I wanted to do was clean and I didn't care if she helped me or not. It was too late though. I had interrupted what she was doing and now she just wanted to pick up her mess so that I would stop bothering her. I felt bad that she was doing the work now so I started picking up other stuff that needed to be cleaned. That made her even more angry and she started cleaning other stuff. I then continued to pick up other messes around the house so that she wouldn't think I was being lazy. By the end of the whole ordeal we had stayed up late and spot cleaned the whole apartment. We finally went to bed around 2:00 am, frustrated and annoyed at each other.

It took me a while to figure out why she reacted that way. It turned out that she wasn't in the mood to clean at the time but felt like she should be the one to pick up her own stuff, not me. By me insisting on cleaning it for her it turned into her feeling like she had to do it at that moment. This threw off her plans and made her feel obligated to do it right then, which made her mad. From then on I always asked her if I could pick up before trying anything.

That is just a simple example of the type of stuff that we dealt with during our first year of marriage. I'm pretty sure everybody has experiences like that. There's just so much to learn about the other person and so many personal adjustments that need to be made in order to learn to get along well.

One of the biggest adjustments that I had to make was to dismiss all previous expectations that I had for Kelly and our marriage. By "expectations" I mean all of the ideas and plans in my head as to how I wanted my life to be. I wanted a wife who fulfilled everything on my perfect wife list and met all of the basic requirements that, over time, I had come up with in my head. These were mostly little things like… my wife won't be somebody that gets road rage, or, my wife is going to be clean all of the time, or, my wife is going to be as physically active as I am. However, the truth is that there is no such thing as a "perfect" wife, at least according to the standards I had set in my head. No matter how perfect I thought Kelly was at first, I had found things that I didn't absolutely love about her. After realizing this, I could either dismiss my "expectations" and learn to love her for who she was or I could let the fact that she wasn't perfect get to me and allow it to cause problems in our marriage. I chose to do my best to let everything go and ended up finding all kinds of new qualities in her that made me fall in love with her even more.

I think this concept works for everything in life. We all seem to have this mental picture of how we want our life to be. When it doesn't work out according to our plan we tend to get all upset or depressed over it. The truth is, we're not the ones running the show and things never go exactly how we want them to. However, despite this inconvenient truth, we are in complete control of how we let things affect us. This was one of the greatest things that I was taught while on my mission in Mexico. No matter how bad a situation may be, we have the ability to choose how it affects us. We can choose to be upset or angry at the things that happen, or we can choose to be happy and positive regardless. For some reason I feel like this concept is always hard for me to explain. I can't stress enough, though, how much that lesson has changed my life. I feel like after having grasped the concept it has helped me so much throughout everything I have been through.

There's one more funny fight with Kelly that stands out in my memory. Actually, I don't even really remember what the fight was all about. I think it might have been about how she was always getting home from work later than I wanted her to. I got annoyed a lot because I wanted to spend time with her after I got home from work. I kind of got my feelings hurt because she chose to hang out with the girls at work over coming home to hang out with me. I was going to play it tough though, and pretend that I didn't need her around all the time and that I was just as independent as she was.

The night we got into our argument I called her before she got home from work to see where she was and when she was going to get home. She knew that I was already annoyed at her. I decided that I would just go running to blow off some steam and stay out until she got worried about me. That way when I finally got home she would realize that she needed to be more sensitive to my feelings and be home more often to spend time with me.

Well, my plan to send her on a guilt trip backfired on me big time. I went out to the high school track by our apartments and ran as much as I could until I was too tired to go on. To waste more time I sat on the bleachers and walked around until I couldn't take the swarming mosquitoes anymore. I wanted to make sure that when I finally made it home and walked through the door she would realize how much she had hurt me, even though I wasn't really too hurt over the whole deal. I just wanted her to feel bad enough to want to change.

Well, after a few hours of wasting time I finally made my way back to our apartment. When I walked through the door I didn't get the apologetic response that I was hoping for. Instead, all she said to me was "Are you done pouting yet?" I couldn't believe it! My plan to manipulate her to change didn't even affect her one bit.

After that experience I realized that playing mental or emotional games in my marriage to try to manipulate things to go my way was not how I should attempt to solve my problems. It taught me that I needed to just be more straight-forward and express my feelings directly to her. Better communication was the key. After learning that lesson we seemed to communicate much better and had fewer pointless arguments.

Despite all of the rough patches that we ran into during our first year of marriage, life was great. I loved being married! It was so fun to be able to come home from work and have my best friend there to hang out with. We both were working at the time and had plenty of money coming in. I worked at Fluor and got home around five or six and Kelly still worked at Swoozie's and got home at all different times. After work we usually just hang out around the apartment. Typically, one of us goofed off on the internet for a few minutes while the other worked on something else that we had going on.

We made dinner together and always sat down and watched TV while we ate because we didn't have a kitchen table. Kelly's domestic side had not fully come out yet, so dinners were usually really easy meals like beef, broccoli, and potatoes with Velveeta cheese. Half the time I wasn't even that lucky. Frozen pizza, hotdogs, and sandwiches were pretty common. Every once in a while, though, she would take the time to cook something different and it was always delicious. I was always grateful for everything she did for me and I tried to pitch in with cooking and cleaning and stuff as much as I could to help even the load.

One of the more frustrating things about the first year of being married to Kelly was getting used to attending all of the holiday activities at the in-laws. I was used to having my family around and doing things with them whenever they were in town. I knew that after getting married I would have to spend less time with my family and more time with hers. I just didn't realize how much time it would actually be. She was so good at keeping up with all of her family members. She did her best to attend family functions from her real dad's family, her mom's family, her stepdad's family and sometimes her other stepdad's family. I didn't mind going to all of her family events. At the time, I really enjoyed getting to know all of them and now I feel so comfortable with them that it is a lot of fun to get together. The only problem was that it got pretty hectic during holidays like Thanksgiving and Christmas. It ended up being this huge stressful ordeal just to be able to make it everywhere each holiday. I think that was just another thing that we both had to adjust to. After the first year it seemed like holidays were easier to deal with and much more enjoyable.

There was one thing though, that always drove Kelly crazy... and that was my family. Kelly pretty much grew up as an only child and wasn't used to the chaos that existed every time my big family came into town. For a basic Weaver Christmas we would usually have all of my brothers and sisters and parents in town plus my grandparents; a total of about eleven people in the house at a time with everybody's stuff scattered all over the place. On special occasions, though, we would have two of my uncles and their families in town as well, making it more like twenty people. It was almost routine for Kelly to just disappear for hours at a time when everyone was there. She couldn't take it and would have to leave... usually to spend extra time at work or to go shopping or something. She would do anything she could think of to get away for a while. At the time it bothered me a lot, but now looking back, I just laugh. It would happen every time! At first I would make excuses to my family for her so that nobody would be offended that she didn't want to be there. But after a few holidays, everybody knew how she was and we would all just joke about how our big family would drive her crazy.

I was pretty disappointed, though, that she got so stressed out around my family. My family is one of my favorite things about my life. I have always felt so blessed to have the family that I have. Even though we picked on each other a lot growing up, I love my brother and sisters so much. When we were growing up we were all so close and such good friends and that we had so many good experiences together.

While getting to know Kelly and learning of the experiences she had growing up it made me feel so bad that she didn't have a big family like I did. I'm not saying that she may not have had the same love for her family as I do for mine. It's just that I wanted her to be able to have the additional blessing of having lots of close siblings like I do. Ever since we've been married I have always tried to do everything I can to help her get along well and learn to love my brother and sisters. I know how awesome they are and want them to be to her what they are to me. This is why it bothered me at first that she didn't like to be around them. With time, though, she has gotten used to the chaos that comes along with my big family. All of my brothers and sisters think she is so awesome and it makes me so happy that she doesn't get stressed and leave anymore.

Apart from all of the new and interesting changes that being married brought to my life, I also had to learn how to adjust to a working life as a young professional engineer. Half way through my last semester of school at BYU, Fluor made me an offer to come back down to Sugar Land to work for them full time. It was an offer I couldn't resist, and actually, my only offer, so I accepted. As I mentioned before, I started work right away to begin saving money to pay our bills. I think it weirded out my supervisors that I wanted to get started so soon. Most guys my age took a few months off to completely wind down from school before starting up work. I think I only had about five days between my last day of finals and my first day of work. On top of that, I think it was unusual to them that I was getting married so young.

I went into work my first day all prepared to start off my new career as a rotating equipment engineer (working with pumps, compressors, etc.). But when I showed up they said they needed somebody to fill in part time as a Cathodic Protection engineer. I had never heard of Cathodic

Protection before but I was willing to do whatever they wanted. So I agreed to being put part time on a project as a rotating equipment engineer and part time on a different project as a Cathodic Protection engineer. The supervisors showed me to my cubicle, helped me get my computer stuff set up, and introduced me to some of the guys that I would be working with on the rotating equipment project. After getting introduced to everybody my supervisor took me over to the Cathodic Protection group to introduce me to the guy I would be working for there.

His name was Whitt. He was one of the most interesting guys I had ever met: very full of himself, super sarcastic, funny, rude, extremely politically conservative, knowledgeable, chauvinistic, kind, caring, and a great teacher, all rolled up into one country going, gun loving guy. There are so many funny and interesting stories that I could tell about working with him, but I don't think they would be appreciated without really knowing him. He's a great guy and I learned a lot from him while working at Fluor. He always took good care of and looked out for us young guys in his group.

Work, like lots of things in life, didn't turn out quite the way that I had expected. The rotating equipment gig ended up being really boring. I made some good friends on the project I was on but never really did any work. Every day I would go into my cubicle and pretty much sit there hoping that somebody would give me something to do. At first I would go around to all of the different managers and ask them if there was anything they needed help with. They never really had much for me to do and I think they got annoyed at me asking all the time so I started coming up with ways to keep myself occupied.

I had recently started up my first 401k but didn't know anything about how to run it. I decided that I needed to learn how all of the stock market stuff worked. I spent a lot of my down time reading over stock market tutorials on the internet to try to learn as much as I could. After becoming more familiar with stocks, I opened up a fake account that I could practice trading fake money in. I have always liked organizing people together for different things, so I sent out some emails to friends and co-workers and ended up getting a big group of people to participate in a stock trading competition that I created. I made a lot of friends at work from starting that up. It was really good too because we all shared information and learned a lot together. I quickly became known as the stock guy among some of the young engineers that worked at Fluor. I had never met half of them, but somehow they knew who I was.

While I was on that project I also sent out emails to all of the young guys and girls that worked at Fluor to recruit people to come out and play in weekly soccer pick-up games that I organized. I found a local park that we could play at that was right next to the office. Every Thursday anywhere from fifteen to thirty people showed up. I even got some of the Kuwaiti client engineers to come out and play with us a few times. It was great! We all had a lot of fun and I was able to make a lot of friends by getting together every week. After a few months, though, the cold weather set in and the soccer excitement quickly came to an end. It was fun to have these "extracurricular" activities to entertain me when times were slow. I don't know what I would have done if I didn't start them because as far as actual work went, I didn't really do much more for the rotating equipment project other than simple excel work.

On the Cathodic Protection side of things, Whitt had a decent amount of work for me to do and kept me pretty busy. I was stuck though, because I liked being busy, but the more work that I did for Whitt, the more I was being sucked into being a full time Cathodic Protection engineer. I definitely wasn't planning on going down that road. The Cathodic Protection world is such a small industry. You can make good money doing it but it is so technically specific that once you get into it you pretty much have to start from scratch if you want to change and do anything else. I didn't want to get trapped in a position that was so specialized.

My plan was to get general engineering experience, earn an MBA, and then move into more managerial or business related work. Regardless of my plans I decided it was better to be busy at work doing something I didn't absolutely love than to have nothing to do at all. I decided to work for Whitt full time but to also continue with my plans of earning my MBA. Whitt always made fun of me for wanting to do the MBA stuff. To him, anybody with an MBA was just an idiot who was more concerned about cutting costs than providing quality engineering.

It didn't bother me that he picked on me for that, I went ahead and signed up for night classes at the University of Houston, Victoria branch. They had a building right there in Sugar Land only five minutes from Fluor. It was going to be great. I had convinced my friend Rob to start the program with me and we went to class together a couple nights a week. It was fun being able to go to classes at night with Rob, but I think we only had three or four classes together before I got sick and had to stop the program.

So there I was, a full time Cathodic Protection guy. The group I was in was really small. It was just me, Whitt, another funny older guy, and four other guys my age. Together we took care of the Cathodic Protection needs of all of the projects that Fluor was involved in. I became really good friends with the guys in the group. Whitt always tried to arrange as many free lunches from vendors as possible which allowed us to hang out and goof off quite a bit in a non-work kind of way even though we were still "working."

Apart from having fun at the free lunches, every year there were two big conferences that we would all try to go to as a group: The Offshore Technology Conference (OTC) and the National Association of Corrosion Engineers (NACE) conference. Both were a lot of fun. I think I went to the OTC three times and to the NACE conference only once. The OTC was a humungous event that took place at

Houston's Reliant Stadium, The Reliant Center, and the surrounding parking lots. Thousands of vendors from across the world would set up booths at this thing. It was open for an entire week, but we would only go for one day. We would spend all day long walking around and still wouldn't be able to see everything that was there. It was really interesting too because all of the vendors would bring the different things that they sold. The place was filled with huge pieces of equipment, pumps, compressors, engines, pipes, monster construction trucks, and anything else that might be needed in the oil industry. Bars and scantily dressed models were set up at some of the bigger companies' booths to draw in the engineers. It was always a crazy conference! Mostly all we really did there was go around and visit the vendors that we were working with and collect as many pens, candy, stress toys, note pads and other handouts that we could along the way. We would come back with bags full of junk that we had collected.

The NACE conference was pretty much the same thing except on a much smaller scale. It was still a big event, but nothing like the OTC. I had a lot of fun at those conferences with the guys I worked with. Overall, despite my general lack of interest in Cathodic Protection, I really enjoyed work and the friends that I had made there.

While I was off in the strange world of Cathodic Protection Kelly stayed occupied with plenty of work and school of her own. As I mentioned before, Kelly still worked at Swoozie's, the same place that she was working at when I first met her. At the time she was in charge of designing and printing all of the invitations that the store sold. She was really good at what she did. All of her customers loved her and would specifically ask for her. She loved that store and the friends that she worked with.

I wish I felt the same about her working there. I hated that place! Since she loved the store so much she would end up spending all of her time there. She always got sucked into going above and beyond what anybody asked her to do.

That's the kind of person she is though… hard working and wanting to make everybody happy. I love that about her! The only problem was that when it came to that store, those amazing qualities drove me crazy. She would often end up staying extra hours at work just to stick around and help out because the other girls were lazy and careless with their responsibilities. I got annoyed a lot because I wanted to spend more time with her when I got home from work.

Apart from late hours she had to work weekends and holidays all the time. I didn't like that either because it ended up interfering with lots of fun activities and trips that we wanted to take. We had the opportunity to go up to my grandparents' lake house several times but couldn't because Kelly had to work. There was also this time that I went camping at Brazos Bend without her because she was picking up extra shifts. I felt like she missed out on a lot of fun stuff because she wanted to work.

I can kind of understand why she got so involved in the store though. To me it was just a dumb store but to her I think it was the possibility of a future career. Kelly always complained about how she was frustrated with her life because she didn't know what to do with it. Most of her friends from high school had already graduated from college and had fancy careers. She felt like she didn't have anything going for her. She had taken a lot of college classes before we met but never stayed in the same major long enough to finish. I felt bad for her and I think she clung to Swoozie's so much because it made her feel like she had some kind of direction.

Growing up, my mom always complained about how she wished she would have finished college. She told me several times to make sure I gave my wife the opportunity to finish school, no matter what it took. So, I encouraged Kelly to keep going with her school. She didn't really know what she wanted to study so we decided she should just take the few classes that she needed to finish up her associate's degree. She enrolled and took classes while working at the same time. She did great! I was so proud of her. She worked hard and I think she made the dean's list every semester that she was in school. I wanted her to be happy and to feel accomplished and successful the way that I did with my education. I felt bad, though, because we still didn't know how we were going to finish her bachelor's degree. We talked about online classes, but there wasn't a program available that she was really interested in. It wasn't until after I got sick that everything fell perfectly into place for her to get into a bachelor's program that she really loved.

So there we were... I worked every day at my boring office job and Kelly was always busy with work and school. Life was great! Everything seemed so easy at the time. There were several occasions that I can think of where I was completely amazed by how blessed I thought I was. I would always hear stories about people and all of their problems. It seemed like everybody was struggling with something: finances, marriage problems, health problems or whatever. I felt like God must have really liked me or something, because everything was working out so well. I had never had a problem with anything in my life. Kelly and I, despite our occasional fights, enjoyed a great marriage and we were doing quite well financially. I think I received two pay increases during my first year at Fluor. On top of my overpaid salary, Kelly made a decent living at her job. Being the cheap guy that I am, I put as much of our money away in savings as I could. I still drove the old beat up green car that I had bought my first summer at BYU and Kelly, for the most part, spent very little money herself. Our income far exceeded our measly living expenses. That first year of being married we were able to pay off nearly all of our debt and put away a lot of money in savings. We felt so blessed that our lives were going so well. Looking back, it's a shame to think of how blissfully oblivious we were to all of the major changes that were about to take place in our lives.

At the beginning of 2008 I had the chance to go to a NACE conference in New Orleans with the guys that I worked with. We drove down early one morning and spent the day walking around and visiting with some of the vendors that we knew. We were having a good time, but by the end of the day, my feet and right leg were getting really sore from all of the standing and walking. That night we went to one of the vendors' parties and hung out on the second floor of one of the buildings on Bourbon Street. We threw beads down to the pedestrians below, even though it was a normal weeknight and everybody was fully dressed and sober. By the end of the party my leg was aching and I decided to go back to the hotel with the other married guy in the group while the rest of them went out to the bars and casino all night.

We spent the entire next day walking around at the conference again. By the end of the day my leg and feet were hurting so bad. I was getting really annoyed at still having to be there so I convinced the guys to leave a little earlier than expected. My leg was aching almost the entire drive home. The pain was so similar to what I had felt before when my leg hurt after running. I couldn't explain it. After a few days of resting however, the pain went away and life returned to normal, at least for a week or so.

I struggled with my leg hurting on and off like this for the rest of 2008. It was a deep aching feeling on the outside of my right knee. I was pretty active with the soccer pickup games at the time and just figured it was related to some type of sports injury. When my leg hurt, the simplest solution I could think of was to rest it for a couple of days. And that usually made the pain go away, but only for a week or two. When the pain came back I would rest it again. This worked pretty well for a couple of months until it started hurting even while I was resting it.

By that time the soccer games had died off and I wasn't playing any sports so I figured I needed to stretch it out more or get into better shape. So I organized weekly sand volleyball games that summer with some other friends. Every Saturday about 6 or 7 of us got together to play. It was a lot of fun and we were actually starting to get pretty good and have competitive games. The volleyball games didn't solve the problem with the pain in my leg. It seemed to help my leg some weeks and hurt it other weeks. I couldn't figure out what was wrong with it.

By the end of the summer the pain had progressed to the point that instead of hurting for only a couple of days and feeling good for a week or two, it was hurting for a whole week and feeling good for a week. On top of that, the pain was beginning to wake me up in the middle of the night. It was really starting to bother me. Between my leg pain and the overweight couple that walked around on the squeaky floor boards in the apartment above us, sleep was hard to come by. The pain was really starting to affect my everyday life. I realized that I couldn't fix it on my own and that I needed to do something about it and have it checked out. But the Weaver family reunion up in Utah was just a week away. I planned on going to the doctor as soon as I got back.

The family reunion was a whole lot of fun. I felt bad for Kelly though. I knew how she got with the chaos from my family. I was so nervous about how she would react to having to be stuck in the car for the twenty-four hour drive up to Utah. There would be no escaping for her. I thought by the time we got back she wouldn't want anything to do with my family again. It seemed to work out okay though.

We were both excited to get to Provo and have the chance to see some old friends from when we both lived there. We arrived in Provo in the afternoon after the seemingly endless drive. We spent the rest of the day visiting BYU and relaxing for the hike up Mt. Timpanogos that was planned for the next day. We woke up the next morning and drove up the canyon to where we would start the hike. We met up with some of my uncles and their families and took some pictures before getting started. This was the first real outdoorsy type thing that I had ever done with Kelly and I was interested to see how she would do. I thought it would be a tough hike but that she could make it all the way to the top with us without a problem. I was wrong. She didn't really care to try to make it to the top. I was there for the challenge but she was there for a nice social walk with the family, and I think mostly because I wanted her to.

We started the hike and Nick, Mandy, Whitney, and the rest of the go-getters almost immediately rushed out of sight. I wanted to run off with them so bad but felt it would be best to stick back with Kelly and the rest of the slow group. I thought I would be bored but ended up having a really good time spending time with Kelly. Plus we got to take some cool pictures together in the mountains that we'll always have to remember.

About half way up, though, Kelly and the slow group got sick of hiking and decided to turn back. I wanted her to keep going so bad because I knew how awesome it would be at the top, but she just wasn't interested. So I ditched her and continued up with a couple of my uncles and cousins. I loved being up on the mountain with all of the Weavers. I love how active and athletic everybody is on the Weaver side of the family. There's almost a sense of pride to be around all of them and to know that you're one of them. I really had a good time hiking up the rest of the way with them. The only problem was that they seemed to be a little more used to the altitude than I was that day. After all, I did go from sea level to 11,749 feet in less than two days. Right when we got to the steep, more dangerous part of the climb I started to get hit with altitude sickness. I was getting so weak, kind of dizzy, and it was getting really hard to think straight. I thought "Oh man, this isn't good! If I take a wrong step I'll roll all the way down the cliff and probably won't survive." But I pushed through and kept going, determined to make it to the top.

Just before reaching the top we ran into Mandy and Whitney. Whitney was having a really hard time with the altitude sickness too and had started to lose it emotionally. I took care of her though and did my best to make her feel better and help her up the rest of the way. It felt so good to finally make it to the top. I really wished Kelly could have been there, but realized that it was probably best that she turned around when she did. It turned out to be a really scary and difficult hike. On our descent we slid down a huge glacier and hiked through beautiful scenery with lots of waterfalls. By the time we reached the bottom the sun had gone down and we were so dirty and exhausted. We ran the last half mile or so because we were so excited to be down. It had been a huge hike and I was really lucky that my leg didn't start acting up while we were on the mountain. I would have been in big trouble!

After hanging out in Provo we drove up to Logan to meet up with the rest of the Weaver family for the reunion. The Weaver reunion was fun, as always. We spent part of the day hanging out at my uncle's house playing volleyball and eating good food. The other half of the day was spent at a park where we played games and hung out. I was really glad that Kelly was there with me. It felt good to be at the reunion and to actually have a wife with me. I was excited for everybody to meet her and see how awesome she is. Despite all of the chaos from the huge Weaver family, I think she had a good time.

The next day we went to the local pool with the whole family. That was a weird experience for all of us Texas Weavers considering we grew up with a pool in the back yard! I think it cost $5 to get in and the place was packed. Everybody there looked like they were so excited to be able to swim. It was fun to be with the family, but the water was so cold that I couldn't stand to be in for very long. I ended up sitting on the side a lot with Kelly watching my cousins go crazy on the diving boards. That night we ended the reunion by going up into some campgrounds in the mountains, cooking a big dinner and telling stories around the camp fire. It was sad to say goodbye to all of the Weaver family but we moved on, excited for the next part of our trip.

That night, our whole family drove over the mountains to my other aunt and uncle's house on Bear Lake. It's always so fun to get together with them. They are both so kind to all of us and I always feel like they enjoy having us around. Their house up there is awesome too…right on the lake and next to the mountains. It's beautiful up there. We spent a lot of time driving around on the four-wheeler and gator. Some of the other Weaver cousins also came to spend the day boating and swimming out on the lake. The lake is fun to swim in because the water is so clear. The only problem is that the water is so cold that I can't stand to be in it for more than just a few minutes. I think the water was 62° that day. I'd much rather just hang out in the boat than get in for skiing or anything. It was so fun to be able to be up there and just relax with the family. Everybody was there except my sister Laura and her husband Eric. I wish they could have come too!

Sadly, that was the end of the trip and it was time to start the long drive back to Texas. We said our goodbyes to everybody and headed out. Once again I felt sorry for Kelly… the car ride home landed right on her birthday and she had to celebrate it somewhere in the deserts of southern Utah crammed in the back of a minivan with my family. She had been such a good sport the whole time but I could tell she was extremely ready to get away from us when she got home. After a long week of vacation we finally made it back to Sugar Land and were ready to get back to normal life.

Before we knew it, it was time to move out of our apartment. We looked at different places to move in to but never really liked the idea of living at any of them. So Kelly came up with something I hadn't even considered before… buying a house. It was so weird! We were thinking of buying a house! How did my life get here? I still felt like a dorky teenager on the inside. I couldn't be buying a house. It seemed like the next logical step in our life though, so we decided to go for it. Going out and looking at houses with her was so much fun. I loved the idea of having our own house that we could make just the way we wanted. I was excited to take that next step in our life together. We looked for several months but never found anything that we really loved. There was always something wrong… it was a bad location, or too small, or too expensive. We were running out of time to search too. Our lease was almost up and we still hadn't found a place.

Right in the middle of trying to decide what to do, my friend Rob came up with an idea. He lived in some town homes that were near my parent's house and the one next door to him was for sale. He was interested in getting into real estate, so he offered to buy the place with his dad and let us rent it from them. I was a little afraid of moving in next to them at first. Kelly and I kind of enjoy our alone time and I didn't want to risk things getting weird with our friends if boundaries were crossed too often. But we ended up deciding that it would probably be a lot of fun living next to them and would allow us to save a lot more money for a down payment on a house when we moved out. We moved in and spent a lot of time and energy remodeling the place. We really liked the time that we had to live there. It was fun to have our good friends next door and we really enjoyed being back in the church congregation in which I grew up.

19 CANCER DIAGNOSIS: DEC 2008

Sadly, the rest of my life has mainly revolved around me being sick. It's quite painful to write about all of the memories and emotions from my seemingly never ending battle with cancer. I do it, though, because I feel like it has been one of the most important things to happen to me in my life. I want to share my experiences, feelings, and the many things that I have learned so that Kelly, my family and other loved ones will not feel so bad for me and will be able to better understand and remember the eternally positive things that have come from it.

I have to add that sometimes I really feel strongly that my getting cancer is something that Kelly and I were both aware of and willing to endure before coming into this life. I feel that God played a huge role in setting everything up to make this difficult journey as comfortable as possible for us. Everything just seemed to line up too perfectly for it to all be a big coincidence.

All of my dating experiences seemed to be rigged for failure all so that I could eventually meet Kelly, the one I was meant to go through this with. The internship that brought me to her was practically thrown at me. I got the job without even wanting to apply for it! I was able to easily convince Kelly to make an uncharacteristic move up to Utah when everything logical seemed to suggest that it was a bad idea. The move worked out great for her and we were able to continue dating and eventually get married. My only job offer ended up being just minutes away from where Kelly and I grew up and where all of our family and close friends lived. I received three pay increases in the year and a half that I was with the company, making my salary a lot higher than it should have been. This allowed us to save enough money to live comfortably despite all of our extremely high medical bills. None of the houses that we were looking to buy felt right, which led us to move back into the church congregation that I grew up in where we have been swarmed by so many amazing friends that are eager to help us with anything we need. And probably most importantly, the place we ended up living in was only a mile away from my parents who have helped us so much with everything that we have been through.

I feel that God blessed us enormously and I don't know how we would have been able to endure such a difficult trial if he had not so perfectly set all of these things up for us. Everything was put into position for me to begin the most trying experience of my life.

Unfortunately, the problems with my leg had not improved after the family reunion. The pain was more intense and more frequent. I went to an orthopedics doctor who told me that the problem was sciatica, or a pinched nerve. This made sense to me because the pain would often throb up and down the whole length of my leg. He told me to take some steroids and do some physical therapy. I took the steroids, but decided to skip out on the physical therapy. I didn't really get the concept of paying to go and have somebody watch me stretch and exercise. I figured I could just do the physical therapy part on my own. Another month or so passed by and things only got worse. By this time I was taking crutches to work because it hurt so bad to walk on it. The pain started waking me up at night. I had to go downstairs and sleep with a heating pad in this big comfy chair that we had to get any relief. Kelly didn't realize how much agony it was causing me at nights until one night she came down and found me rocking back and forth on the couch in pain. She spent hours some nights rubbing my leg to try to help me with the pain. It was then that I started to see her differently and realize how amazing she really was and how much she cared for me.

There was one night in particular that the pain was unbearable. I decided to try out the pain killers that my doctor had given me. I took the maximum recommended amount but didn't realize that I should have eaten food with them. I was so sick when I woke up to go to work the next morning. I went upstairs to get ready and almost threw up. I was determined to not use my vacation days though, so I decided to go in anyway. It was only a 5 minute drive to work, but it only took about two minutes for me to realize that I was really drugged from the pills and in no shape to be driving. Somehow I survived the rest of the drive, hobbled up to my cubicle, and started to check emails and messages to see what I needed to do for the day. After about ten minutes I realized there was no way I could make it through the day. A couple of the guys in my group had to drive me and my car home and put me to bed. It was kind of a funny story at the time, but now looking back it seems more depressing than funny.

I went back to the doctor and told him that I wanted to try the physical therapy this time. He agreed and told me that if it didn't improve that I needed to see a Neurologist. I tried the physical therapy (which ended up being kind of pointless, as anticipated) and still didn't see any improvements. I immediately made an appointment with a neurologist who visited with me and then scheduled an appointment for me to come in and have my nerves tested to figure out if there was any nerve damage. By the time of the next appointment my leg had started to swell a lot. I could start to feel a knot in the back of my knee. It was November and to help with the swelling and pain I would sometimes sit out by the pool and soak my leg in the freezing water. When I went in to see the neurologist he told me I needed to see another orthopedics doctor.

Luckily, while I was there at his office, Kelly called me up and told me that her mom was at an orthopedics doctor that morning and had randomly put me down for an opening that they had that day. I rushed over, had some x-ray's done and was told that I needed to get an MRI. The MRI was scheduled for the day after Thanksgiving. That

Thanksgiving was a bad one. We had dinner over at Kelly's mom's house with all of her side of the family, which was good, but the pain was so bad that I ended up spending most of the time by myself, rolling around on the floor in one of the back rooms. From then on, the pain was so intense that I was hardly able to do anything. I had the MRI done and was immediately called back with the results. The doctor told me that it looked like some kind of mass and that I needed to see a tumor specialist named Dr. Marco. At that point I wasn't really nervous about anything. One of my good friends growing up had a tumor behind his knee and only had to go through a simple surgery to have it removed. I figured my problem was something like that. But the pain was so bad that I didn't really care what the problem was. I just wanted it fixed so that the pain would go away.

We met with Dr. Marco a day or two later where he was to tell us all of the bad news. Kelly and I were waiting in the examination room after just being told from the PA that it looked pretty ominous. He had told us that it was most likely cancerous and that, worst case scenario, I would lose my leg. Hearing that news suddenly sent everything into slow motion. All I could think about was the idea that Kelly might be stuck with a one legged guy for the rest of her life. I started to cry a little but then decided that I should try to force back the tears before Dr. Marco arrived. When he finally came in he explained to us that it looked like a cancer and that we needed to get more imaging and a biopsy. He also explained again that if it were cancer, it was probably something called Ewing's sarcoma or Osteosarcoma, both curable cancers with the worst case scenario likely being that I would have to lose my leg.

They rushed us over to the imaging department of the building that we were in so that I could get another MRI and a CT of my chest done immediately. I think it really started to hit me while I was there in the waiting room. I wasn't worried about doing chemo, or dying, or anything like that.

I was just so worried about what all of this would mean for Kelly. It broke my heart to think that because of my problems, she would have to be dragged along through everything and then possibly have to be stuck with a one-legged guy. I cried on her shoulder in the waiting room and apologized to her over and over again... something that would become all too common throughout the upcoming years. She assured me that she was fine and that we should still try to stay positive about whatever the outcome of the scans was. The next steps were the biopsy and another meeting with Dr. Marco to discuss the results.

Meeting with Dr. Marco and being rushed to do scans was too overwhelming to really process what was going on. Life altering information was just thrown at me with no time for it to sink in. The emotions and anxiety were too much to absorb. It completely shut my brain down. I spent the rest of the night in a weird nightmarish trance, not knowing what to think and even questioning if it were all really happening.

The next couple of days were when things really started to set in. I went in to work, in horrible pain, and had to discuss everything with my friends there. I tried to be strong and confident on the outside, but inside I was struggling and couldn't believe what I was telling them. Luckily work was slow and I had plenty of time to look up information on the two cancers that I might be facing. I realized that doing that kind of research ended up being a mistake. I read a lot of scary things involving bad cure rates and horrible outcomes. I quickly learned not to research my cancer on the Internet. There's too much information out there that is outdated or inaccurate, so I spent the rest of my time trying to learn about amputations and prosthetics.

My mind has always run off of worst case scenarios. I always try to hope for the best but prepare for the worst. If an amputation was the worst thing that I could be facing then I felt like I needed to prepare myself mentally for it in order to help everything settle down in my head. I read about the different types of amputations and prosthetics and read stories about some of the amazing things that amputees are able to do. I tried to find positive things that would make me feel like I could do it if I needed to.

Then I sat for what seemed like hours and tried to think through what it would actually be like to not have a leg. I knew I would have no problem doing sports and other activities with a prosthetic. If other people did it, so could I. But how would it affect everyday things like showering or doing work around the house? How would I be accepted socially? How would it affect my marriage? Trying to find answers to these questions and process all of it was too much to handle. I nearly broke down in tears a few times in my cubicle. After a few days, though, the thought of possibly becoming an amputee became a little easier to handle even though I was still in shock over everything. I still couldn't believe this was happening to me and couldn't make sense of why I might be going through all of this in the near future.

The days before going into the biopsy I think I prayed harder than ever before in my life. I thought back on all of the miracles in the scriptures and the miracles that I had seen on my mission. I knew that God was fully capable of fixing this so that the biopsy results would come back negative for cancer. I knew that God hears our prayers and I knew that he would always be there for me, especially in situations like the one I was stuck in. My prayers definitely were not lacking in "faith" or at least the type of faith that I understood at the time. Plus, I figured, why wouldn't God heal me? I'm a faithful church-goer and a pretty good guy. And I felt like I had so much potential to do so many good things in my life that he needed to heal me so that I could be around to help in his work. There was no doubt in my mind that it was possible and plausible for me to be healed. But despite all of my prayers and faith, the biopsy results showed that it was in fact Ewing's Sarcoma, an extremely rare pediatric bone cancer.

I couldn't believe it. The miracle that we had been praying so fervently for never came. This is about where everything I thought I knew and understood about faith, God, prayer, etc. was completely turned upside down and thrown out the window. I just didn't get it. I had seen miracles in my life and I knew they were possible! My thoughts immediately turned back to the experience I had on my mission where my companion and I witnessed a girl being miraculously healed of cancer. I knew that God could do the same for me, but he didn't. My miracle never came and it didn't make any sense. My spirits were knocked down, but not out yet. I still wanted to figure out why the miracle never came and why I had to go through all of this. I was determined to push forward and try to understand how all of the puzzle pieces fit together.

Thankfully, in our following visit, Dr. Marco taught us about the disease in a way that gave us confidence that we would be able to beat it. He told us that Ewing's Sarcoma is a curable cancer with relatively high cure rates. The odds were in my favor. I would just have to do about ten months of intense chemotherapy and a surgery and then I should be fine. I left his office that day thinking "Ok, I can do this." Kelly and I both felt good about being able to beat this challenge together. It would be a minor set-back in our journey through life, but we could take it.

Everything changed a little, though, when I got home from class and walked through the front door of my parent's house. We had already explained everything to my parents over the phone on our way home. I walked up the stairs and found my family sitting around on the couches trying unsuccessfully to hold back the tears. When my mom saw me she broke down and rushed over to me and gave me a big hug. I felt so bad. I hate seeing my mom or anybody else in my family cry. More than that, I hate being the reason that people are crying. I've always tried to live my life in a way that would make people happy. It was so uncomfortable and painful for me to be the cause of so much sadness. Again, I felt especially bad for Kelly because I knew she had to be having just as hard of a time even though she was so good at hiding it with her tough outer shell. I still felt confident and optimistic but I saw that some fear and sorrow had set in on my family. I had a feeling that the same sentiment would probably show through in all of my close friends and everybody else that cared about me.

Dr. Marco had made appointments for me the next day with an oncologist that he thought we would like. His name was Dr. Beinart and he worked at the Methodist Hospital, downtown in the medical center. He had trained at MD Anderson and assured us that he would use the same treatment plan that they used. We felt pretty comfortable with him and decided to go ahead and keep him as my doctor. He was eager for me to start chemo by the end of the week. The next few days were spent in the hospital doing follow up doctor's visits, blood work, chest x-rays, heart scans, bone scans and a minor outpatient surgery to have my power port installed in my chest. (A power port is a central line that is placed under the skin and allows chemo to be infused directly into the jugular vein). Everything happened so fast that it seems blurry to look back on. Before I knew it, it was Friday, and we were in the hospital being checked in for my first round of inpatient chemotherapy.

20 SO THIS IS WHAT CHEMO IS LIKE
COCKTAIL #1

One round of chemotherapy was designed to last three weeks. I typically checked in on a Friday around noon and received chemo until Tuesday morning when I would be released from the hospital. I would have to return to the hospital for a white blood cell boosting shot on Wednesday. Ten days after receiving the chemo, generally the next Sunday night, my immune system would practically disappear and I would sometimes run a fever and have to be admitted back in the hospital for a few days of antibiotics to fight off any infections that I might have in my body. By the end of my second week into the cycle I would usually be mostly recovered, leaving me five to seven days of feeling pretty good before I had to go back in and start the next round. The plan was to do six rounds of inpatient chemo, surgery, another four rounds of inpatient chemo, and then four rounds of outpatient chemo; a total of 42 weeks of chemo and about 4-5 weeks to prep for and recover from surgery. It was a daunting treatment plan but we still felt confident that we would make it through and be okay in the end.

Upon checking into the hospital on Friday I would be admitted and introduced to this little room that was in serious need of remodeling. The hospital rooms on the cancer floor were fitted with only a hospital bed, an IV pole, a nightstand, a tiny bathroom, and a chair that would fold out into a cot for a guest to sleep on. It was good enough for a patient and one guest. The problem was that I frequently had Kelly, my parents, and sometimes a handful of other visitors to accommodate. We would squeeze as many chairs in as we could and sometimes people sat on the bed with me. Typically, after arriving to the hospital room, the nurses would access my port and draw blood to see if my blood counts were good enough to receive chemo. We would then have to wait sometimes hours before they were able to get started with the treatment and hook me up to the chemo. My first regimen consisted of three different types of IV infused chemo meds. For anybody who knows or cares about chemo meds, I was given a few of the more heavy duty chemo meds: Vincristine, Adriamycin, and Ifosfamide. The first night the only side effect that I could notice was a little bit of chemo-brain. Chemo-brain is really hard to describe. It's like your ability to remember, concentrate, think, and process what is going on gets really foggy. A lot of times it's like you're so wiped out mentally that you just kind of shut down a little and stare off into space. It comes with a slight headache and makes it difficult to focus your eyes on anything. Being mentally "out of it" kind of ruins your social skills and makes it hard to communicate. The further into my treatments, the worse it would get. By the time I would get to leave the hospital it would be so bad that it almost felt like I was watching a movie of my life as it was happening. It's really weird and hard to explain what it is like. All I know is that didn't like it.

I would usually wake up the next morning (Saturday) to much worse chemo-brain and some minor nausea. By the end of the second day though, the nausea would be fully set in. Food no longer felt good going down into my stomach. Things started to taste really strange and not much was appealing. It would often take me five or ten minutes of analyzing the hospital menu before being able to decide on something that sounded good enough to eat. Liquids started to feel really slimy in my mouth which would sometimes make drinking a chore. The slimy feeling and the weird tastes in my mouth would usually last about a week and a half. It would really be annoying after the nausea had gone away because I would want to eat and need to drink a lot but things would still taste and feel weird in my mouth. Apart from the strange problems with my mouth and stomach, all of the chemo and different medicines that went into my body would start to come out in my urine and sweat and smelled horrible. I could smell the medicines seeping out of my skin. I don't know if other people were able to smell it, but I sure could. It was really annoying! I could taste it in my mouth and smell it all over me. I couldn't get away from it. The nasty smell of the medicine and sweat combination didn't do well for my stomach either. While in the hospital I often tried to hold my breath the whole time I was in the bathroom so that I wouldn't get sick from the repulsive smell. It usually took a few days after being home from the hospital before the medicine smells would go away but the taste in my mouth would bother me for about a week and a half.

Somebody would always be with me at the hospital while I was getting chemo, usually Kelly or my parents. We spent most of the time watching TV, goofing off on the Internet, or just hanging out. Well, it was more like my family spent most of their time watching TV and hanging out. I mostly just laid there and slept. Sometimes we would play games or put together puzzles that were in the waiting rooms of the hospital. Kelly and my parents would always encourage me to get up and walk around to get me out of bed and keep my muscles going at least a little. I would try to get out of bed and walk a couple of laps around the chemo floor at least three or four times a day. On day two, it was still fairly easy to accomplish this. I was pretty tired but still had a decent amount of energy.

Sunday was always a little worse than Saturday. By then the nausea had gotten more intense and the fatigue more severe. By this point I not only disliked food, but dreaded it. I would have to force food down because I knew that if I didn't eat the nausea would only get worse. I would get so tired. I started to feel like I had stayed up all night long after doing a full day of strenuous physical labor. All I wanted to do was lay there and sleep.

Monday, the last day of actually receiving chemo, was way worse than Sunday. I didn't know how it could get worse, but it did. I was more nauseated than before, more tired and had much worse chemo-brain. I slept most of the day and forced food down when I could. By Monday night it would feel like I had been trapped in my tiny hospital room forever. I was so worn out and sick from all of the chemo, but so restless from laying down for three days straight that it was like I was in some sort of zombie state where I was too tired to move but unable to sleep. I spent a lot of time going in and out of sleep and rolling around in my bed.

After a long night of trying to sleep but being woken up every hour or so by nurses and CNAs, Tuesday morning would finally arrive and I would get to start to prepare to go home. Unbelievably, Tuesdays would be even worse than Mondays. I felt worse than I ever had before in my life. However, the sickness was nearly trumped by the excitement of getting to leave the hospital and get out into the real world. I would always be so thrilled to be able to get out of the hospital that smiling and joking around was really easy. After being in there for almost four days I could hardly stand the wait to get out of there. The nurses would always have so many things that they would have to do to make sure that I was in good enough shape to be released from the hospital. Finally after waiting on the nurses for what seemed an eternity and signing all the release forms I was free to go. Kelly would load me up in a wheelchair with a barf bucket and all of our stuff and haul me down to the patient pick-up area to be driven home.

It's interesting what being trapped in a small space for a few days will do to your perspective on everyday things. Everything looked so amazing each time I was wheeled outside into the open air. Colors seemed so vibrant and everything seemed to be moving so fast. Looking at everyday things, like birds, trees, cars, and people was exhilarating. Every time I left the hospital it was like I was entering this whole new environment that I had never experienced before. I don't know if the chemo-brain played a role in this or if it was just that I had been trapped in there for so long that everything seemed new again. Whatever it was, I loved it. The only thing was that the whole experience was really hard to enjoy because most of the drive home from the hospital was spent staring blankly into my barf bucket in intense concentration to try to keep myself from throwing up. My stomach was so sensitive to any bump in the road or change in direction. Luckily I have an iron stomach, which was probably developed during my time living in Mexico. I hadn't thrown up since I was twelve and had endured two years of food poisoning, stomach infections, and bad water in Mexico without ever throwing up. The chemo, however, was definitely a major challenge to my stomach.

After arriving at home I would slowly and carefully make my way out of the car, up to the house, into the bedroom, and straight to the bed. I would walk very carefully, taking baby steps and focusing intensely so that I wouldn't lose my balance and fall over or throw up all over the floor. After the long trek from the car to the bedroom I would lay down on the bed and spend the rest of the day trying to sleep and forcing down food when I could so that I wouldn't get more nauseated.

The exhaustion on Tuesdays was so extreme it was unbelievable. While I was in the hospital receiving chemo and the first few days after getting home I tried to drink as much as I could to flush the poison out of my system as fast as possible. This helped a lot to reduce the side effects but also made me have to go to the bathroom all of the time. Normally this wouldn't be a problem, but considering how exhausted I was on Tuesdays it made the 10 foot trip to the bathroom a huge ordeal. Just to roll over in bed from one side to another wore me out. When I had to pee I would slowly lift myself up to sit on the side of the bed. Just sitting up would wear me out so much that I would have to spend a couple of minutes just to catch my breath. Once I caught my breath I would sit there for another minute or so to mentally prepare myself for the long journey over to the bathroom. After baby stepping my way over to the bathroom and back I would feel completely worn out and lay straight back down to go to sleep. Apart from getting up to use the bathroom I would try to get up and walk around the house as much as I could… usually only once or twice on Tuesday and then more often on the days after. The exhaustion was at its worst on Tuesdays and then seemed to improve daily until about day nine of the cycle on which I would have only about 70% of my normal energy back.

Things seemed to improve a little on Wednesdays. The most difficult thing about Wednesdays was that I had to return to the hospital to get a shot that would help my white blood cells recover more quickly from the chemo. I still felt pretty horrible on Wednesdays. The drive back up to the medical center was not much better than the drive home from the hospital on Tuesdays. In some ways it was worse. For some reason they always scheduled my appointment for the shot "early" in the morning. I say early, but in reality it was around nine or so. During the days of the cycle that I was really exhausted I would typically sleep in until eleven or twelve. Waking up at eight fifteen while feeling as tired as I did felt like waking up at four in the morning after having only slept for a few hours. I would have to baby step my way back to the car, ride to the hospital with the barf bucket in my lap, and get wheeled up to the cancer floor just to get a tiny shot in my arm. After receiving the shot I would be wheeled and driven back to the house where I would baby step my way back to the bedroom or couch in the living room so that I could rest and nap for a while. The whole process took about two hours and was absolutely miserable every time. It was like a repeat of the drive home from the hospital except that there was no excitement about being able to leave and get a change of scenery.

After getting home from the hospital, sleep was so amazing. There were no nurses around to wake me up all the time and it was such a great escape from all of the physical and emotional problems that I was going through. When I slept everything would go away and when I woke up I would feel great for a minute or two without nausea or fatigue or anything. For a minute or two I could forget about my cancer and feel like a normal person again. Being able to sleep through most of the physical side effects was a major blessing! Plus, I think having almost an entire pharmacy of different medicines in me created some really weird dreams. Unfortunately, one of the anti-nausea meds that I was on made it really hard to fall asleep. That combined with having to either eat or go to the bathroom about every hour and a half usually made sleeping pretty difficult. Most of the days right after getting home from the hospital were filled with lots of short naps, lots of laying around on the couch, watching TV, or goofing off on the computer.

Since I was always so tired, most of my small frequent meals were brought to me when I was in bed or on the couch for the first day or two of being home from the hospital. Eating was so miserable, even with the confusing regimen of anti-nausea pills that the doctor had me on (Zofran, Reglan, Compazine and Decadron). Just the thought of putting anything into my stomach made me feel sick. I had to do it though because the longer I would go without food in my stomach the worse I would feel. Eating was a necessary evil! The challenge wasn't to find something to eat that would taste good. It was to think of the food that would bother my stomach the least. This turned into an annoying guessing game for Kelly and my mom. Every few hours they would come in and tell me "Okay, it's time to eat something. What do you want?" They would then list off anything they could think of that might be appealing to me: yogurt, fruit, quesadillas, grilled cheese sandwich, macaroni and cheese, a smoothie, ice cream… anything that crossed their minds. To which I would reply "No, no, no, no, no" and then sit and stare at the floor for a couple of minutes to try to get the thought of all of that food out of my mind. Sometimes it would really annoy me how persistent they were at making me eat. Somehow, though, there was always one random thing that seemed like I would be able to keep down. Kelly and my mom were thrilled to have me finally make up my mind on something and were willing to go anywhere to get me food that I was willing to eat. This eating game would go on for a few days after coming home from the hospital until the nausea would eventually wear off to the point that eating was more tolerable.

Once eating was not so much of a problem it became a game to see how many calories I could get in me. Plus it would feel so good to be able to enjoy food again! I would usually lose some weight during the days I was really nauseated. Once the nausea went away I felt like I had to play catch up to try to gain all of my weight back. I was a skinny guy to begin with and couldn't afford to lose any more weight. So once I started feeling better I would eat almost anything and everything that was put in front of me.

The few days of me feeling good, having energy, and wanting to eat however, were short lived. On about day nine, the Sunday after getting out of the hospital, my blood counts would drop and all of my energy and appetite would practically disappear. Chemo is designed to kill all of the fast dividing cells in your body. Cancer cells are usually fast dividing cells, which is why chemo can be effective at killing cancer. However, all of the other fast dividing cells in your body get wiped out as well. This includes hair follicles, stomach, intestine, mouth, throat, and esophagus cells, and bone marrow cells. Your bone marrow makes your blood cells (red blood cells, white blood cells, hemoglobin, and platelets) which only live about ten days or so, at which point they die and are replaced. When the chemo kills your bone marrow, you stop producing new blood cells until the bone marrow recovers. This results in a period of time in which your already existing blood cells die off and there are not any new ones to replace them with. Simply put, the number of blood cells in your blood drops and causes all kinds of problems in your body. When your red blood cells and hemoglobin are low you get really tired and don't have any energy. When your white blood cells are low you pretty much have no immune system and are extremely vulnerable to any type of infection. A common cold can be a serious problem. When your platelets are low you run the risk of bleeding uncontrollably from practically any part of your body, internal or external. By days ten, eleven, and twelve of the chemo cycle all of my blood cell counts would drop and I would feel miserable again... exhausted and nauseated. The exhaustion and nausea weren't as bad as when I just got home from the hospital, but they were bad enough to make life really uncomfortable again. This would usually go on for a few more days to a week depending on what type of treatment I received for it. Sometimes my blood levels would drop so low that I needed to get red blood cell or platelet transfusions. It would be really annoying when I would have to go back to the hospital to get a blood transfusion. After being at the hospital for five days in a row, having to go back for any reason was extremely frustrating. Despite my frustration, the blood transfusions would always make me feel better and help me recover faster. By day fifteen or sixteen of the cycle my blood would usually be nearly recovered and I would have about five or six days of feeling good before having to go back in for the next round of chemo.

21 ROUND 1: DEC 19, 2008

My first round of chemo was a major eye opener as to how long and miserable of a process the whole treatment plan would be. I had no idea that going through chemo would be so difficult physically, mentally, and emotionally. Dr. Beinart was eager for me to start chemo right away and didn't think it was a good idea to wait until after Christmas. My leg was in so much pain that I didn't really care when I started. The pain before my first round prevented any fears of what I might be facing from setting in. I was so engulfed in the severity of the pain that I was experiencing that nothing else really crossed my mind. I was almost excited to start treatment because it would just get me that much closer to getting rid of the pain and becoming a normally functioning person again.

I had so much support from family and friends during my first round. It just so happened that it started the same day that Nick and Mandy flew in from college for Christmas break. They, along with Whitney, my parents, and of course, Kelly were right there with me through the entire round.

We checked into the hospital on December 19. After being admitted and checking into my room, one of the first things that the nurses did was give me a shot of morphine in my IV to help with the pain. That was my first time to ever get such a heavy duty pain killer. Man, did it work well. Not only did it help with the pain but most of my memory of the first couple of days of suffering in the hospital was erased.

During that first day in the hospital Kelly and I had Nick, Mandy, Whitney and my Parents to keep us company. Actually, they mostly kept Kelly company because I was practically passed out most of the time from the morphine. I do remember though, that there were so many of us there. We were like one big happy family all in one depressing little hospital room. Kelly laid on the bed next to me while a couple of people sat on the end of the bed, a couple of people sat on the pull out bed and somebody else sat in a small chair that we borrowed from another room. It was really claustrophobic. I don't know how Kelly survived in there with so many people. Even though there was really nothing to do in the hospital room we still had fun joking around and spending time with each other. It's always so fun to have all or almost all of my family together, no matter what the circumstances. I spent the rest of that day napping and hanging out with my family until it was time for them to go home. Kelly set up her tiny bed to get ready to go to sleep but ended up cuddling with me in my hospital bed where we eventually fell asleep and slept peacefully... at least until the nurses woke us up for their routine patient check-ups.

When I woke up the next morning the first thing that I noticed was that the pain in my leg had magically disappeared. We were told that Vincristine can damage nerves and we think that the first dose of it killed off my nerve completely because I woke up that morning and the pain was gone. It was such a relief to not have any pain. After months I finally got a break from it. The only problem was that the pain was replaced by another issue called "Drop Foot." Drop foot is the inability to lift the ankle or toes upward. I couldn't walk normal anymore. When I walked I would have to lift my knee extra high to keep my toes from dragging on the ground and tripping me. It looked pretty goofy. The doctors told me that there is a chance the condition could reverse itself with time but that it would most likely be permanent. Somehow, it didn't really bother me at the time. I would take drop foot any day over the pain that I had been going through. Plus, I had heard stories of people overcoming damaged nerves. I figured that if they could do it, so could I. I was confident that I would be able to overcome the drop foot with time and some hard work. A physical therapist came in and fit me for a brace that I ended up wearing for the rest of my treatments. It was uncomfortable and annoying but it made it easier for me to walk and helped me to look more normal.

After the excitement of my new pain free leg had worn off I started to notice the side effects of the chemo a little more. I had started to feel fairly sick and I was introduced to the strange world of chemo brain. My brother, Nick, came up that day and brought my acoustic guitar. I tried to play a little but it was really hard to focus on anything. It turns out that playing the guitar with chemo-brain was a little too difficult for me. I let Nick play instead.

By the end of the second day in the hospital I was too exhausted to do much of anything other than stare blankly at the TV. I ended up sleeping most of the rest of the round to escape all of the miserable side effects that had set in. I was so out of it that I can barely remember the visitors that came to see me. When I got home my family would say "It was so nice of so and so to come up to the hospital to visit you." I didn't even remember that they had come to visit me. It took me a few days of being home from the hospital before my memory of all of the visitors started to come back. The sleeping continued for the next two days until it was time to go home. Sleeping was about the only thing that really helped me feel comfortable.

After what seemed like an eternity it was finally time to be released from the hospital. I had to struggle to endure the drive home without throwing up, then I had to make a deceivingly long trek from the car to the house. I was probably a sight to see, hobbling along with my crazy unwashed hair and goofy drop foot walk. Making it to the bed I was finally able to rest without all of the beeping pumps and nurses popping in every hour or so. I still felt absolutely horrible though. I laid in bed that first Tuesday of being home feeling like my body could shut down at any moment. I was more exhausted and sick to my stomach than I ever could have imagined. I thought "How am I ever going to make it through 10 months of this. I don't even know if I can get the courage to make myself go in for round two." Thankfully, all of the comforts of being at home made dealing with my physical state a much less daunting of a task.

It was so peaceful to be able to be at home. There was a big enough bed for Kelly to lay with me, a comfort that I had forgotten how much I really enjoyed. I couldn't believe that she slept on that little pull out bed every night that we were in the hospital. I felt so bad for her, but so loved that she was willing to make that sacrifice for me without complaining. I laid in bed with my brother and sisters gathered around to offer their help in any way they could. I could see a little fear in some of their eyes as they watched me in the horrible shape that I was in. I felt so bad to be the cause of them feeling that way. I tried to relieve some of their worries by joking around and putting a smile on my face. After all, the physical side effects were only physical and couldn't bring my spirits down. I still had the ability to choose how to let this cancer stuff affect me, no matter how miserable I was. I was determined to stay happy and try to enjoy the time that I had to spend with Kelly and my family.

As much as I loved being out of the hospital, being home from the hospital was really nerve-racking. Everything was so new and we didn't know what to expect. It was really scary sometimes. We were fine while I was in the hospital because we were surrounded by nurses who knew exactly what was going on and what to do if something went wrong. Being home and all on your own, though, is a different situation. Chemo causes so much havoc on your body. Once at home I started getting all kind of weird side effects: I could see my pulse in my eyes, my muscles and bones would ache, I would have strange mental images when I closed my eyes, my dreams were really strange and realistic, I had an extremely fast heartbeat, palpitations, insomnia, achy teeth, swollen gums, mouth sores, sore throat, and all kinds of bowel problems, to name a few. We had no idea if the side effects I was experiencing were "normal" or if they were something that I needed to worry about. Naturally, we worried about all of them and made lots of phone calls to the nurses at the hospital. Every time we called them they would just say something like "Oh yeah, that's perfectly normal." It was shocking that there were so many things going wrong in my body and that it was all "normal."

It would have been really helpful to have known somebody who had already gone through the same chemo that I was receiving. We could have gotten advice or tips that would have helped with knowing the side effects before starting and we would have been more prepared for what was happening. Unfortunately, that was a luxury we didn't have and we were forced to learn through experience. I've since learned that the first round of any chemo regimen is always the most difficult because you don't really know exactly what to expect. Usually after the first round though, you know what's normal and have learned tricks that you can use to make the next round more bearable.

As I mentioned before, eating was such a miserable chore that had to be done in order to keep me from getting more nauseated. It was funny because the longer I would go without food in my stomach, the worse the nausea would get. It was really hard, though, because it was so horrible to force food down at any time for the first couple of days after being back home. Kelly and my mom got so annoyed that I couldn't ever make up my mind on what to eat. Most of the foods that I chose were softer, soothing things like yogurt and smoothies. The only thing was that there are no calories in those kinds of foods. I needed something to help me recover from the torture my body had been through. Apart from the yogurt and smoothies, I think one of the first things that I said that I might be able to force into my stomach was a junior bacon cheese burger from Wendy's. They were so shocked and thrilled when I finished the whole burger. They complimented me like I was a little kid by saying things like "Wow, good job! You ate the whole thing!" Despite feeling like a small child, I felt like I had just made a major accomplishment. This kind of childish treatment continued for several rounds to come and turned into something that we would always joke around about.

I got out of the hospital on Tuesday the 23rd and was able to rest and regain some strength for a couple of days before the big Christmas morning with all of my brothers and sisters. Sadly, that year I missed going over to spend Christmas Eve with Kelly's family. They always throw such a great Christmas Eve party. They have door prizes, white elephant, a trivia challenge, Christmas carols, presents and lots of food. It would have been my third year to go. I finally felt comfortable around all of them and really enjoyed spending time with them, especially at Christmas. Kelly went without me and returned with gifts and goodies for me.

I knew that Christmas day would be long and exhausting for me so I decided to go to bed a little early to try to get as much rest as I could. I knew I wouldn't be able to sleep in and that I wouldn't want to nap all day and miss out on all of the excitement. It turned out to be a great Christmas. I was too worn out to do much more than sit on the couch the whole time, but even still, I really enjoyed being around everyone and watching everybody open gifts. It was also nice to have Kelly off of work for the whole day. Christmas season was always super busy for Swoozie's, where she worked. The store was closed on Christmas, though, and I got to have her for with me the whole day!

Long before finding out about my cancer, the whole Cassell side of the family had planned on coming to Houston for my grandparent's anniversary. They, along with my parents, my brothers and sisters, and Kelly and I, made a total of 20 people hanging out at my parent's house for just about the whole time that my counts had dropped. Having so many people in the house at one time only added to all of the chaos that seemed to be going on from me being sick. We were so paranoid about me catching some type of infection that we all used hand sanitizer every few minutes. On top of that, I think my mom, Kelly, and my sisters cleaned and sanitized the house a few times a day.

Fortunately, I was so worn out that I pretty much just locked myself in my parent's bedroom for half of the time that everybody was there. I was too tired to come out and visit with everybody. I felt really bad for Kelly though. That was a really stressful time for her. She was so worried and concerned about me. She wanted to be there with me at the house to take care of me but, as expected, was going nuts because there were so many people around in the house. I knew how she got when my family came into town. This time was way worse, though. There were twice as many people as normal and she couldn't escape because she wanted so bad to stay and take care of me. On top of that, there was definite tension building up between her and my mom. I am Kelly's husband and she felt like she was the one that needed to take care of me. On the other hand, I am also my mom's son and my mom wanted to be there to take care of me also. It turns out that having two stressed and emotional care givers around to take care of one person who is mentally out of it is not a good idea. Kelly got so frustrated at my mom over lots of little things. For example, my mom would come in and ask me what I wanted to eat. While she was preparing the food, Kelly would come in and ask the same question. I was too out of it to say "Oh, my mom is getting something," so I would just repeat whatever my mom was making. Kelly would run off to prepare my meal and my mom would come in with my food. By the time Kelly had made what I asked for, I was already eating what my mom had prepared. Stuff like that happened all the time too. She would go to pick up a prescription only to find that it had already picked up by somebody else. It would drive her crazy! I have to admit, though, that most of the problems that they had were my fault. A lot of it could have been avoided if I were better at communicating between the two. It was so hard though! I was so chemo-brained that it was lucky for me to communicate at all. I think Kelly eventually broke and we decided to go back to our town home as soon as I was feeling well enough.

Being at our town home was so nice. The peaceful, quiet atmosphere was such a great change from all of the noise and chaos that was going on at my parent's. It was only a day or two of being there before I noticed that my hair was starting to come out in the shower. At first it was just a few more hairs than normal. Each day, however, it would get significantly worse. After a few days I was able to grab and pull chunks of hair out that would leave small bald spots on my head. Losing my hair was a lot more emotionally difficult than I thought it would be. Before it happened, I just figured, "I'm a guy. I don't mind being bald. Then I won't ever have to do my hair " Once it started falling out, though, it was like the whole cancer situation immediately became a reality. It made me feel like I had no control over anything anymore. My body was falling apart and my life was turned upside down and there was nothing that I could do to stop it. It was such a debilitating feeling. I got out of the shower and sobbed in Kelly's arms. She was such an amazing source of comfort for me. She was the only one that felt comfortable enough to cry to. She was tough enough to handle it and return my tears with smiles and encouragement. She handled everything so amazingly! I was too afraid to cry in front of my family because I knew how much it hurt them. They would often just break down and cry with me. I didn't like that because I didn't feel like having a pity party. Sometimes I just needed to break down and then get over it and move on. That's what Kelly helped me with.

There was one time, however, when Kelly wasn't around to make me feel better. I broke down in front of Mandy and my parents in the back yard. I was so irritated and angry. I felt like part of it was genuine emotion and part of it was caused by being too overwhelmed from all of the physical and emotional distress that I was going through. I was so angry with my life. I wasn't angry at God or anything; I was just angry at how things were turning out for me. I wanted my normal life back. I was already sick of having to deal with all of this medical stuff. I hated that that my life was falling apart. I hated that I was so dependent on the help of others. I hated that I was causing so much sadness and pain to family and friends that cared for me the most. My anger built up until I picked up something in the back yard and threw it across the deck and then broke down in tears. My parents and Mandy quickly followed. Whenever they started crying I felt like I had to be the tough one to make them feel better. How I wished Kelly was there with me to make me feel better.

With my hair quickly falling out, we arranged for family pictures to be taken one last time before I lost it all. The pictures turned out alright even though I feel like I looked like a skinny, pale, sick guy. That night we went back to my parents' house so that I could shave my head. I was really nervous about cutting all of my hair off. I didn't want to keep having to go through the emotional distress of watching it fall out in clumps in the shower, so I figured cutting it off all at once would make it a lot easier to go through. Kelly, Laura, Nick, and Mandy were all there to help me through it. Thank goodness they were there too. They all joked around throughout the whole haircut, providing much needed comic relief for me. Even with all of the jokes and good company I still found myself holding back tears. After Nick had shaved it off we were all pleasantly surprised at how well it turned out. This was relieving to me because I really didn't want Kelly to be embarrassed of me if I ended up looking really ugly as a bald guy.

The day after shaving my head the whole family went out to eat at the Aquarium to celebrate my grandparent's anniversary. I felt really pathetic! Not only did I look sick like a cancer patient, but now I needed special attention. I couldn't walk well with my brace on and my back was partially thrown out from walking too much the day before. I had to be dropped off at the front of the aquarium and walked through the restaurant with family around me to make sure I wouldn't fall over from being so weak. It was pretty depressing to all of a sudden lose so much of my independence. After we made it to our table, though, I was able to have a really good time joking around with my family. We laughed so hard at how much grandpa ate that night. After eating appetizers, he polished off a mountain of a platter full of all kinds of fried food that was piled on top of a bed of French fries. It was one of the un-healthiest looking plates we had ever seen. Somehow, he had no problem finishing off the meal with a huge slice of cheesecake. We still laugh when we think of how much he ate that night.

After what seemed like forever, all of my family left, my blood counts returned back to normal, and I had almost a full week of feeling well enough to get together with friends and try to maintain my normal life. It was so nice to be able to spend some of my time with Kelly and nobody else. As much as I enjoyed being with her though, I felt like I should try to hold on to my work life and get back to work.

I tried to work as much as I could during my good week. My first day back in the office I went in with my crutches. It nearly wore me out just to walk from the parking lot to my cubicle. People that I had never talked to came around to ask me how I was doing. I guess word had spread throughout our part of the office that I was going through chemo. It was either that or the fact that I was now a bald, pale-looking sick guy. After socializing a little with the guys in my group I decided I better get to work to catch up on everything I had missed. After just a few minutes though, I realized that I had no business going into the office that day. I only lasted about an hour before I had completely lost all of my energy and decided to go back home to rest. The rest of the week I think I went in for just a few hours a day. I ended up doing a lot of my work from home on the laptop that they had given me.

As word of my cancer and treatment plan began to spread throughout the church and among friends and co-workers, I began to see that everybody dealt with my having cancer in a different way. There were very few who handled it well right from the start and they all seemed to have one thing in common. They had all gone through some kind of horrible family experience at some point in their life: major illness, disability, death, etc. There is something about people who have made it through these types of things that makes them different. They're more understanding, more compassionate, and more charitable. There was a connection with them that I didn't even have with my best friends. I knew that they understood what I was going through and it was a great comfort to have their support at that time.

Everybody else seemed to handle the situation differently. It seemed like all of a sudden, cancer was all that some friends would talk to me about. Some friends wanted to dig into my emotions to try to understand what I was going through. Others pretended like it wasn't even happening and tried to joke and change the subject whenever I brought it up. Some were really sad and others were unrealistically confident that everything would turn out perfect for me.

This was really hard for Kelly and me. Sometimes we felt alone or like we couldn't hang out with our friends because they were all acting weird. We just wanted them to be there for us. To help us when we needed help and to listen to us when we needed to talk or vent, and to just be normal friends the rest of the time.

For the most part, though, people were so kind to us and always offered to help in any way they could think of. Sometimes they made me feel like I was some sort of celebrity or something. It was like everybody wanted to come and say hi to me and offer to help. We are very grateful for all of the support that we received.

Another annoying social issue that we had to deal with was that all of a sudden, everybody had an opinion as to what I should be doing to help treat my cancer. We were told by all types of people, both friends and strangers, that it was imperative that I change my diet, exercise more, rest more, take herbal supplements, take more vitamins, meditate, change my thinking habits, see different doctors, get treatment from a different hospital, and read pretty much any book that had anything to do with anybody having cancer. It happened all the time. I always appreciated their concern and desire to help, but it drove us crazy when they would keep bringing it up. Sometimes I just wanted to tell them "I'll try your thing if I want to, please don't pester me about it all the time!"

These kinds of social nuisances along with all of the crazy side effects of the chemo made round one an absolute killer. During the worst of my physical side effects I didn't think that there was any way that I could make myself go in for another round. Luckily, a few days of feeling well and getting back to normal life is really great at fading away some of the memories of how sick I was. I was still dreading going back for round two on Thursday night, enough so that I broke down and cried like a baby because I didn't want to do it again. But after surviving round one I felt like I could do it again and push forward with my treatment plan.

22 ROUND 2: JAN 9, 2009

Before going in for round two we decided that we were going to be prepared and bring everything possible to make it as fun and comfortable as it could be. We brought extra pillows and blankets so that we wouldn't have to use the ones at the hospital. We brought our laptop and a whole bunch of movies to keep us entertained. We both brought several changes of clothes and Kelly brought all of her hair and other girly stuff. I think after everything was packed up we had a few bags full of stuff. We had to get an extra-large wheel chair to haul all of it up to our room.

Round two was a lot different from round one. We recognized a lot of familiar faces up on the cancer floor. Knowing a lot of the nurses took the emotional edge off of going in again. This round I wouldn't have my brother and sisters to keep me company and provide comic relief. They had all returned to their normal lives of school and work. My parents would come in on the weekends to hang out and help give Kelly a chance to escape from the hospital, but for the most part it was just Kelly and I.

The first two days before I got really sick Kelly and I spent a lot of time just hanging out and watching movies. In a way it was kind of nice to be able to spend so much time with her. It was almost like being on a date... a really twisted date where we were both confined to a small room and I was forced to get sick. Nevertheless, I really enjoyed the time that I got to spend with her. I always loved it when she would lay in the hospital bed with me and cuddle until we fell asleep. Unfortunately, she would usually wake up from so many nurses coming in and move to her tiny pull out bed. Also, it was pretty hard for both of us to sleep in those little beds when I had so many IV tubes all over the place.

My parents were so nice to come up and spend time in the hospital on their weekends. I know it was difficult for my mom sometimes. She gets so restless that it would drive her crazy to be trapped in one place for so long with nothing to do. She and Kelly went on lots of walks to explore all of the different areas of the enormous hospital. My dad was perfectly content to sit and read or watch TV in silence while I laid there sick. I am so grateful to them for all that they did for Kelly and I, especially for giving Kelly a chance to get out and spend time with some of her friends. It was always good for her to get out of the hospital for a few hours where she could pick back up on parts of her life. I, however, was trapped in there the whole time with no escape. I couldn't even leave the floor because one of the chemo meds would burn me if it were to come in contact with my skin.

Again, like with round one, the longer I was hooked up to the chemo, the worse I felt. I was so exhausted from the chemo that it got to be really annoying to have to get up to go to the bathroom so much. Because there was so much fluid being pumped into me and because I was drinking so much to flush out the chemo, I had to go to the bathroom about every hour to hour and a half.

There was one night where Kelly and I ran into a funny situation when I needed to get up to go. Usually, Kelly would wake up when I needed to go so that she could help me get to the bathroom and back without any problems. Sometimes I would be really weak and we were afraid that I might fall over and get hurt if I tried to go to the bathroom by myself. It was kind of a challenge to walk with my drop foot and pull the IV stand while feeling dizzy and weak. Well, there was one night in the hospital that Kelly decided to take a sleeping pill to help her sleep better on her little pull out bed. As usual, I woke up in the middle of the night and had to go. I called out her name to wake her up so that she could help me but she never replied. After calling her a few more times she eventually sat up and said "I'm awake,

125

do you need to go?" I told her that I did and she just sat there and stared at me blankly. Remembering that she had taken a sleeping pill, I explained to her that I needed her to take me to the bathroom. She stared a little more and then laid back down to go to sleep. I thought to myself, "Oh great, this is going to be a pain in the butt." I reached over and shook her and said "Kelly, wake up! I need your help!" She finally sat up and started walking over to the other side of the bed so that she could help me. There was something funny about the way she was walking though. She was really wobbly and had to hold on to the bed to keep her balance. She got half way to my IV stand and then sat down in another chair in the room and fell asleep again. I really needed to go by then and was starting to get frustrated. I yelled at her "Kelly, snap out of it, I need you to help me." She woke up, stood up, and almost stumbled as she made her way over to my bed. I was so frustrated but couldn't help laughing at how goofy she looked. She was so drugged by the sleeping pill and had the funniest care free look on her face. I then realized that having her help me would be more dangerous than me going alone. I made my way to the bathroom, took care of my business, and came out to find her asleep in my bed. I think I just scooted her over to let her sleep next to me the rest of the night. We decided that she shouldn't take any more sleeping pills while I was getting chemo.

Going to the bathroom so frequently was really turning into a nuisance. I was so sick of having to get up all of the time. My solution to the problem was to simply drink less water. It made sense. I was already getting so many fluids from all of the bags that were hung on my pump that I didn't think I really needed to be drinking so much so I started to cut back. Bad idea! They told me that I needed to drink a lot to flush out the chemo but I didn't realize how much of a difference it really made. After a day of not drinking quite as much I started to get really sick. The nausea was so bad. I could hardly eat anything and it became really difficult to even drink anything. I nearly threw up every time anything went into my mouth. This made brushing my teeth extremely difficult, but Kelly didn't care and made me do it anyway. I always go so annoyed at her when she made me brush my teeth in the hospital because it always made me want to throw up. I didn't realize that I was getting so sick because I wasn't drinking as much. I thought that being that sick was just typical of a second round of chemo. By the time Tuesday rolled around and we were able to leave I could hardly move because I was so sick. It was horrible.

That night, after getting home from the hospital, I didn't feel much better. I woke up in the morning to go to get my shot and threw up in the trash can that was next to the bed. I hadn't thrown up since I was in middle school and immediately remembered how unpleasant it was. After throwing up I thought "Oh good, now I should feel better for a while." But I only felt a little better for about fifteen minutes and then threw up again. We grabbed the barf bucket and rushed back up to the hospital hoping that they would be able to help me feel better. Miraculously, I made it through the whole car ride without barfing again. Kelly and my mom wheeled me up to the cancer floor where I threw up again in my little pink bucket. They quickly gave me my shot and then hooked me up to an IV with fluids and anti-nausea medicine. After getting fluids for about an hour I finally started to feel a little better. We made our way back home where I could rest and start to recover from round two.

A day or two later, Kelly had to go in to the hospital for a procedure of her own. A few months before I was diagnosed with cancer, Kelly found some moles that ended up being melanoma. She had to go in every few months to get checked for abnormal moles. Well, at the last check-up she had they found a few that looked really bad. One of them was on her back and two were on one of her toes. The one on her back was easily removed in the doctor's office, but the ones on her toe had to be removed with an outpatient surgical procedure. She went in one morning and came back in the afternoon on crutches with her foot all wrapped up. The pain killers knocked her out, making her really groggy and fun to pick on. I was too sick to do anything and Kelly was unable to walk. Both of us were stuck on the couch and had to be taken care of for a couple of days. We were such a pathetic sight. I think we must be the youngest couple in the world to both have cancer. Luckily, my parents were there to help us out. Again, I don't know what we would have done without their help with everything.

Well, after a few days of recovering we thought I had successfully made it through round two. That was until my blood counts dropped. Around day 10 of the treatment cycle (I think the Sunday after getting out of the hospital) my white blood counts were expected to drop to almost nothing. We were told to check my temperature a few times a day to make sure that I wasn't running a fever from any infections. We were told to call the doctor on call and prepare to go in to the emergency room if I ever had a temperature above 100.5. We were always on the edge of our seats every time I took my temperature. The last thing we wanted was to have to return to the hospital because of a fever. Well, when Sunday rolled around I started to get really sick again. I started to have really bad nausea and completely lost all of my energy again. This happened during round one but it wasn't near as bad. That night we checked my temperature and it was above 100.5. We called the doctor and were instructed to rush immediately to the hospital.

Once we got there I was admitted and wheeled back up to the tiny rooms of the cancer floor. I couldn't believe how weak I was. The nurses rushed to check my blood so that they could start to treat me. They hung bags of antibiotics to fight any infection that I might have. After getting my labs back we found out that all of my blood counts were completely wiped out. I was given two units of platelets and two units of blood to help bring some of my levels up a little bit. I laid there in the hospital bed while the platelets were being transfused. I had never been so sleepy in my life. I couldn't hold my eyes open. I fell asleep and remember waking up almost not knowing where I was. I had never been so out of it before in my life. I thought that maybe I was close to dying because I was so wiped out. It was a really worrisome time for all of us. We were all a little scared for my life. Deep down though, I didn't feel like it was time for me to go yet. It turns out that the reason I was so tired and wiped out was because they had given me Benadryl in my IV as a pre-med for the platelets. That stuff completely knocks me out and makes me sleepy for hours.

After getting the red blood and platelet transfusions I felt much better. I felt like I was almost ready to go back home. There was just one problem… my white counts were still too low. There is nothing that they can do about the low white counts other than sit and wait for them to recover on their own, which usually takes several days. It was really depressing to find out that we would have to be trapped in the hospital again for a few days to make sure I was safe to return home. Every morning they would check my blood to see what my white count was. I couldn't leave until they were back into the normal range. Every morning we hoped that they would miraculously spike up so that we could go home. It was so frustrating to be stuck in the hospital again, especially since I was feeling relatively normal after having received the blood transfusions. It felt like we would never be able to leave. At least when I was in the hospital for possible infection I was able to leave the cancer floor and walk around the rest of the hospital. This gave us a little entertainment but got old really quickly once we realized that most of the hospital looks exactly the same. Finally, after about four days of antibiotics and blood checks, my counts were high enough to go home. We were so excited! We packed up and returned home and were able to have another whole week of me feeling well enough to lead a relatively normal life.

I don't really remember what all Kelly and I did during this good week. It was always just so nice to be able to return to our town home and have time to spend with each other. When we were at home during that week it almost felt like nothing had changed. I think that meant more to us than any exciting activity that we could think of doing.

I tried to return to work but, again, found that it was a little too much for me. I just didn't have the energy or mental capacity to put in a full day. Luckily, there wasn't a whole lot going on and I was able to work on my laptop from home and still fulfill all of my responsibilities.

This round I had completely ditched the crutches and was able to move around more and be more independent. I wanted to be able to go run errands and go places on my own. The problem was that I couldn't drive a car with my right foot. I tried it with and without the brace on and I just couldn't get the movement in my ankle that I needed to drive safely. I decided that I would just have to learn to drive left-footed. It was pretty difficult at first. Every time I tried to brake with my left foot the car would come to a screeching halt and stuff inside the car would fly everywhere. I made a few laps around the neighborhood and eventually got the hang of it. After a few days of practicing I was able to drive again and gained back a little of my independence. It felt really good to be able to do things on my own again.

It was always during my good week that we had to deal with all of the social side effects of being diagnosed with cancer. We wanted to get back to normal life and that meant hanging out with friends and being around people at work and church. It was just so hard sometimes to deal with how awkward people were around us. So many people were so kind and loving to us! I know that they had good intentions and just wanted to show that they cared and were willing to help if we needed anything, but I think they just didn't know what to say or how to act. I often wished that people would just say, "We're here for you. Let us know if you need anything." Instead they would ask all these questions... "So, how are you feeling? What are the doctors saying? How was this last round?" I had to tell the same story over and over again which got really old really fast. It seemed like every casual acquaintance would rush up to me asking me the same things. Since my hair had fallen out and I looked like a cancer patient, I would also have complete strangers come up to me and ask the same questions. On top of that, word of me having cancer had gotten out to a lot of my friends that no longer lived in Sugar Land. I had friends from high school, my mission in Mexico, and college all calling me wanting to know the whole story and how I was doing.

Maybe I was being unfair because sometimes I felt like my close friends weren't really around when I needed them. There were times when I wanted to have deeper, more emotional conversations with them, but for whatever reason whenever I tried that it just didn't go very well.

All of the attention and questions became overwhelming. It drove Kelly and I to be really anti-social sometimes. I found myself screening phone calls and hiding at home when I would normally want to go out with friends. At church we tried to sit in the back and leave before anybody had a chance to talk to us. I started to be really short with people, both friends and strangers, to avoid having to tell the same story over and over again. I didn't like being like that. I'm normally a pretty social person and enjoy talking with people. Now, everything had changed. I sometimes felt very alone even though everybody wanted to talk to me and spend time with me. All I really wanted to do is spend time with Kelly and my family, because we were all in the same situation together and we all understood, for the most part, what each other was going through. Being at home with them seemed to be the only way that life could feel normal.

Luckily, we came up with a couple of ideas to help relieve some of these problems. Kelly started a blog which worked wonders as far as not having to repeatedly explain everything that was going on. People could just read our updates and then they wouldn't have to ask so many questions. We also unofficially named our friends Rob and Jess, to be our official spokespeople. People ended up going to them a lot to find answers to questions instead of coming to us. They, along with a few other close friends ended up assuming this role. I know it probably got annoying to them too sometimes, but it helped us out a lot.

The reality of my situation had finally set in after successfully completing two rounds of chemo and officially looking like a cancer patient. I was right in the middle of this. There was no getting out of it. Before the biopsy and during the first two rounds my family and I had prayed like we had never prayed before. All of our friends and family members, who are good, faithful people, were praying for me. I felt like I should have been taken care of and that having to be treated for cancer should have been prevented. Where was my miracle? How was it possible that so many prayers could be made on my behalf and none of them were answered? I spent a lot of time searching the scriptures to try to find answers. I spent even more time in deep thought trying to make sense of everything. When I wasn't in conversation with anybody or directly occupied with anything, I was analyzing my situation and how it fit in with everything that I had learned about God and my purpose for being here in this life.

My first realization was that life isn't like all of the happy stories that you always hear and read about. People like to hear good positive stories, happily-ever-after stories about miracles and good times. They are good for us because they give us hope, make us feel good, and help us to stay positive about things in life. But a lot of times, especially in religion, the good stories are all that are ever mentioned. If somebody is going to tell a story about a person rising up from poverty and finding wealth, they are going to tell about the most amazing success story that has ever occurred. If somebody is going to tell a story about a miracle, they'll tell about the most miraculous thing that anybody has ever heard of. Telling these extravagant stories is fine because they do give us hope and help us to realize that things can be better or that miracles can happen. But I have learned that stories with these outcomes are the exception, not the norm.

In reality, tragedies occur all the time. Nobody is immune from pain, heartbreak, suffering, or death. Even the miraculous stories in the scriptures contain tragedies that are usually overlooked. We just focus so much on the good that we forget that hardships are just a part of this life. I have found that it is a lot less emotionally and spiritually crushing if I am realistic and understand that real life rarely turns out like the fairy tale stories that I have been told since I was born.

When my situation didn't turn out like all of the amazing stories, I was hurt, depressed, and my faith and hope were challenged. I couldn't understand how the principles behind these stories didn't apply to my situation. In a way, I had come to a crossroads. My knowledge of faith, prayer, God, and miracles didn't fit in with what was really happening in my life. Could it be that all of this religion stuff is just a bunch of lies? Or am I not really understanding the principles correctly? I was going through a serious test of faith and I had a choice to make. I could either choose to reject everything that I had learned about religion or I could choose to attempt to figure it all out and try to re-learn everything.

I think at this point it is easy for people to reject their faith. There are a lot of thoughts that can easily creep in and take hold of your mind if you aren't careful. At times I felt like there was a good chance that God didn't exist, because how could he let this be happening to me? At other times I felt like God did exist, but that he had betrayed me and that he wasn't keeping up with his part of the deal. There were times where I felt like anger towards God was trying to set into my heart.

I would bet that most faithful church-going people who are faced with a situation like mine probably have similar feelings. I've heard plenty of stories where people kind of fall apart spiritually after being diagnosed with cancer. Bitterness sets in and they have a really hard time dealing with the difficulty of treatments and life in general.

I understand that it is difficult to go through that kind of mental or spiritual pressure. But it all comes down to a personal decision: Either let those feelings set in and give up, or stay positive and try to push forward and figure it out. I made sure to press forward. I had seen God's hand too much in my life to be able to deny his existence. I figured there had to be some kind of reason for me to go through all of this. I planned on figuring out what it was.

23 ROUND 3: JAN 30, 2009

Before starting round three we met with my doctor to discuss how the chemo was going. While talking with him we found out that having your blood levels as low as mine were can be a dangerous and life threatening situation. My doctor decided to lower the dose of the chemo to help prevent my counts from dropping so low again. I was mainly concerned that if the dose were lowered that it wouldn't be as effective at killing the cancer cells in my body. He assured me that everything would be fine and that we were good to start round three on schedule.

Going in to the hospital for round three wasn't quite as scary and dreadful as it had been before. By this time we had made pretty good friends with all of the nurses and other people that worked on the cancer floor. I think they all liked us because we were so much livelier than the other people that they took care of. After all, we were about 50 years younger than most of the patients on the floor. I was the easy patient, too. They didn't need to change my diaper or feed me or anything like that. Kelly and I just kind of took care of ourselves and tried to make the best of the situation. We figured since we had to be trapped on the floor for so long we might as well make friends and try to make it as fun as possible. We were always joking around with the nurses and giving the food runners a hard time. Knowing everybody and being able to joke around and have fun really took the edge off of having to go in to get chemo.

We felt really comfortable on the cancer floor with all of our new friends. Kelly was so funny. I think her being bored while I was sick made her nosey or something. It didn't take long for her to figure out where everything on the floor was and how to get to it. She was always getting into the nurses stuff and would try to help them out when they were busy by getting everything for me on her own. At first she was just into unimportant things like pillows, blankets, the coke and snack drawers, but as time passed she started getting more and more comfortable with trying to do the nurses job. It didn't take her long to start messing with my IV pumps and tubing. Every time my pump would start beeping she would go over to it and start pushing all of the buttons to try to fix the problem. Before I knew it I had to start keeping an eye on her to make sure she didn't mess anything up. She loved learning about how all of the medical stuff worked.

Having the dose lowered that round made a big difference in the way I felt. After being hooked up to the chemo for a day or two I started to notice that I wasn't as sick as I usually was. Don't get me wrong, I still felt horrible, but the edge was taken off a little bit. The nausea wasn't quite as bad and I seemed to have a little more energy. It wasn't quite as difficult to force food down like it normally was. That didn't mean my appetite was any better though.

The hospital food was getting worse and worse every day. When I first looked over the menu during round one I was so impressed and almost excited. It seemed like there were so many things to choose from and I could pretty much have as much as I wanted.

The food was pretty good at first. By the end of round one we had pretty much tried everything that looked appealing. Unfortunately, there were only a few things on the menu that I would try more than once... hamburgers, pizza, turkey, mashed potatoes, some pasta, a few desert items and most of the drinks. By the end of round two we knew what we liked and had already ordered the same items a few times. By round three we were sick of almost everything that they had to offer and were always looking for anything to eat that wasn't on the hospital menu.

This was difficult for me because getting food somewhere other than the hospital meant we had to spend money. I was still super cheap at the time and eating out all of the time was getting really expensive. At first Kelly just started making trips down to the cafeteria where all of the hospital workers ate. The food there was better than what they gave the patients. But after that got old we resorted to leaving the hospital to get something to eat. I would have been more comfortable spending the money to get food except that every time Kelly's car left the hospital we had to pay about nine dollars in parking. Sometimes things would work out well and my parents would bring us something to eat when they came up to visit. Other than that, we were dishing out quite a bit of money just to go get fast food. Luckily, Kelly wasn't as cheap as me or I would have just starved myself to death in the hospital.

For the most part, round three was pretty uneventful. After doing two rounds, things had sort of become routine. I think we had a visitor or two, but it was mainly just Kelly and I with some visits from my parents on the weekend. Kelly and I, again, spent our time joking around and watching lots of TV and movies. It's hard to believe, but I really enjoyed the time that we spent together in the hospital. All we really did was sit around and talk and watch TV. I loved it when she would climb into my hospital bed and cuddle with me. It was like her being close to me would make all of the physical discomfort so much more tolerable.

Kelly and I loved to pick on each other. We had fun because it was so easy for her to pick on me when I had chemo brain. We laughed a lot because I did and said a lot of stupid things. Sometimes I would say things that didn't make any sense at all and she would just stare at me with a look on her face like "I don't know what the heck you're talking about." After thinking about it for a second she would realize that she was never going to make sense of what I was trying to say and she would just start laughing. We had a lot of fun and grew closer together even though we were both kind of miserable being trapped in the tiny hospital room.

There was something about me being sick and needing her help that really strengthened our relationship. I thought our relationship was relatively normal before getting into the whole cancer mess. We loved and cared for each other but also had occasional arguments and got annoyed at each other. I think that almost all married couples argue and get annoyed at each other. It's normal. Learning to work through these "bumps" in marriage makes us better people with more patience and a greater capacity to love and serve others. The problem with most of these "bumps" is that they are usually caused by really silly things. Things like forgetting to run certain errands, not wanting to do chores, or running late to events. Having to fight cancer together really changes your perspective on those types of things. All of a sudden the stuff that we used to argue over became really insignificant. It wasn't a big deal if the dishes didn't get cleaned right away or if we were late to church. We were more concerned about each other's well-being than all of the trivial stuff that we faced every day. We hardly ever disagreed on anything and were always happy to be together.

Kelly was always so caring. She would do everything that she could to help me feel better or make me more comfortable. Before I was diagnosed I knew that she loved me but I had no idea that she loved me enough to go through everything that I caused her to go through. She was constantly taking care of me. She pushed me around in the wheelchair. She helped me with my medicines. She made meals for me and convinced me to eat. She even slept on that tiny pull out bed every night that I was in the hospital when she could have gone home. She always went above and beyond anything that was asked of her and she did it so lovingly and with a smile on her face (most of the time). Her actions showed me how much she really loved me.

Sometimes I would just sit and watch her in amazement and think to myself "I can't believe she actually loves me." I felt so unworthy to have such an amazing wife. I was a pathetic sick person that could hardly do anything for himself. She was this beautiful independent girl that had so much going for her. She deserves so much more than to have to spend her time and energy taking care of a guy in my situation. Apart from not being able to take care of myself, I felt like I was an embarrassment to her because of the way I looked and walked. I always wondered how it would affect her because I knew when we went out in public people were thinking "What in the world is she doing with that guy?" It never fazed her though. She was always happy to be with me and willing to do anything for me.

The way she helped me and treated me made me want to be just as good to her as she was to me. I couldn't do much, but when I was able to, I would try to help her with anything I could. I always wanted to show her how much I appreciated everything that she did for me. This mutual service toward each other helped us to grow together in ways that we never would have been able to if I hadn't contracted cancer. And that, in a way, made some of my suffering at the time seem worth it.

Having a lowered dose of chemo allowed me to recover much quicker at home. I was still extremely sick and miserable, but the nausea wasn't quite as intense and I had more energy to get up and move around the house. I was getting better at enduring through the suffering. When my counts dropped we worried so much that I would get the dreaded fever, but fortunately it never came. Before I knew it I was heading straight into my good week.

This round I had more energy to go into work, but the recession had set in and there wasn't much for me to do. I was easily able to do everything on my work laptop from home in just a short amount of time, leaving me tons of free time to fill. Unfortunately we didn't really have anything planned for my good week. One day I was bored and wandered around the garage in search of something to do. I noticed a bunch of BB guns sitting in the corner rusting away. Nick and I used to shoot them all the time when we were in high school but they hadn't got much use since then.

I figured they could provide some kind of entertainment for me. So I pulled out a bunch coke cans and my sisters' old toys and set them up around the back yard and started shooting away. My family and I spent the rest of the afternoon hanging out in the back yard and playing with the BB guns. It wasn't anything too exciting, but we still had a good time.

This round there was a much bigger issue than being sick that I had to deal with... Valentine's Day! I hate Valentine's Day! Well, I don't really hate it. I'm just no good at coming up with romantic ways to impress girls. The first Valentine's Day I ever had a girlfriend I avoided it by proposing. I figured no matter how bad I screwed up the Valentine's Day events, proposing to Kelly would make up for it. It was a good thing I proposed too, because I don't think the Wendy's drive through would have gone over too well without a ring to distract her.

My second Valentine's Day was about seven or eight months into our marriage. It didn't go very well either. I thought about different things that I could do to impress Kelly, but they all seemed so corny or too expensive or too difficult to carry out. I think all I ended up doing was surprising her with a bunch of candy and roses and then taking her out to dinner. It was a pathetic attempt but it seemed to work ok.

I don't really remember what Kelly got me. It turns out that Kelly dislikes Valentine's Day almost as much as I do. It's not that she doesn't like attention or showing that she cares for me or anything. It's just that it stresses her out and she would almost rather not do anything than have to deal with thinking of something for me. We had discussed several times the idea of not doing anything for each other and just going out on a normal date, but all of the guy friends that I knew wisely warned me against taking that route. I felt like I had to do something for her, especially since she had been doing so much for me.

As much as I wanted to do something great, it just didn't work out. The holiday fell right in the middle of the week that my counts were low. I was too sick and exhausted the week or two before Valentine's Day to really go shopping or plan anything. I know I could have planned further ahead, but let's face it, I'm just not good enough at that either. I ended up running to the store while she was out on Valentine's Day and picked up some more candy and roses for her so that she would be surprised when she got home. It only worked ok because I was still sick from chemo that Valentine's Day and she thought it was nice of me to get up and go out when I was sick. Since I was sick we planned on going out to dinner during my good week.

We went to the Cheesecake Factory for our Valentine's date and somehow I ended up doing something that made her a little mad at me. I don't remember exactly what I did, but I'm pretty sure it had something to do with my runny nose problems. You see, when I lost my hair from chemo I didn't just lose the hair on my head, I eventually lose all of my hair, starting with my head, then my face, then my nose and then the rest of my body, and finally my eyebrows. When the nose hair fell out, during round two, every time I ate or drank anything my nose would start running and dripping everywhere. Most of the time I couldn't even feel it and sometimes it would drip onto the table or into my food. Well, whatever I ate that night made my nose run like crazy and she didn't like it one bit.

24 ROUND 4: FEB 20, 2009

Another good week flew by and it was time to go back in for the next round. I felt like I was starting to get this chemo stuff under control. My life was forming a new normal. I was getting used to this whole chemo lifestyle. I counted time in three week periods instead of weeks and months. Everything that we planned was according to my chemo schedule. The rounds of chemo were starting to fly by and my memories of being in the hospital began to blend together into one big foggy chemo-brained daze. I don't remember much of what happened in round four because it was all kind of the same as the round before. But there was one random thing that did really stand out, and that was how I became a movie star.

Well, not really. There's a group called CanCare that is a non-profit cancer support network who sends representatives to hospitals to visit with and help cancer patients. They happened to be filming a video for their website while I was there in the hospital. A whole camera crew came in and set up on the cancer floor. It was pretty exciting, considering what normally goes on there. The crew wanted to interview some nurses and take some video of a patient who had the energy to be able to hold a conversation and look relatively normal. The nurses immediately pointed them my direction and we filmed a short segment of me pretending to talk with a CanCare representative. At the time, I thought it was pretty misrepresenting to pick me as an example of what a cancer patient is really like. I think I was in the best shape on the whole floor. The rest of the patients were a lot older and sicker looking and hardly had the energy to get out of bed. I did not think I looked like the typical cancer patient. Regardless, the film was made and we waited anxiously to see how it came out. When it was finally posted online we were all really disappointed. I was only shown for about two seconds and my voice was covered up with corny music. I had been ripped off.

The night, after being filmed, Dr. Marco came by to give us the results of an MRI and CT scan that I had done the day before. They came in and told us that the scans looked good and that the tumor in my leg had shrunk from the initial size of a mandarin orange to about the size of a walnut. In the initial scans, there was so much inflammation that they had a hard time determining exactly what was tumor and what was normal tissue. By round four, the inflammation had gone down and it was easier to tell exactly where the tumor was and what kind of options we would have for the upcoming surgery. Unfortunately we got another dose of bad news. The tumor had shrunk in size, which is good from an oncologist's point of view, however, the scans showed that it had previously grown from the top of the fibula into part of the tibia. In order for the surgeon to be able to remove 100% of the tumor, he would have to cut out the top portion of the fibula and remove a good part of the knee joint. The best options that they could give me for surgery were a complete knee replacement or an above the knee amputation.

This sounds like a no-brainer... do the knee replacement, right? You would think so, but after learning more about what all they would have to do to cut out the tumor, having a knee replacement looked almost as bad as having an amputation.

This wouldn't be a normal knee replacement. In a normal knee replacement they are able to go in and remove just the knee joint. When cutting a tumor out of a knee, they have to cut out the diseased bones, along with any muscles, nerves, or blood vessels that might be anywhere near the tumor. Removing blood vessels would create all kinds of circulation issues which would likely cause swelling and pain. Removing nerves would create a lot of numb spots throughout the lower part of my leg and would cause permanent drop foot. I would have to wear a brace for the rest of my life. The surgeons could attempt a nerve graft, where they remove a portion of nerve from my good leg and use it to replace any nerves that they cut out of my bad leg, but there would only be a 10% chance that it would work. There would also be a chance that cutting nerves out of my good leg could cause permanent nerve damage and create similar problems in my good leg. Removing muscles would take away some of the strength and flexibility in my leg, which could make it difficult or impossible to straighten my leg out all of the way. They would also probably have to do a skin graft which I've heard are a pain in the butt and leave your skin looking kind of deformed. A knee replacement doesn't last forever either. If I was active, and I planned on being active, I would have to get the joint replaced about every ten years. Plus, I know people with hardware in their body and they always end up having pain or swelling problems where the hardware is. On top of all of these issues, there would still be about a 15% chance that the cancer would return in my leg. If it were to return, having all of the metal in my knee would make it difficult to spot a tumor until it were bigger and more difficult to treat.

The amputation would be a much simpler surgery. They would just hack off my leg to get rid of the cancer. If I were to choose the amputation, there would only be about a 5% chance of the cancer returning. The bad part is I would be an amputee and have to wear a prosthetic for the rest of my life... I think the crappiness of that option is pretty obvious. All of the stories you see on TV or read about in magazines about the amazing things that amputees can do paint a pretty picture of the life of an amputee. But when I was first diagnosed I did enough research and deep thinking to understand that there's nothing pretty about missing a limb. Sure, prosthetics have improved so much and now allow amputees to do so many more types of activities than ever before. I mean, there are amputees that finish Iron Man competitions. That is truly amazing, but can they jump out of bed and go to the bathroom at night without crutches, or take a normal shower without having to perform a balancing act? Nope!

Being an amputee would be horrible, but at the same time, the knee replacement didn't sound like a very good option either. While discussing the options with the surgeon my analytical mind kicked in and all of these questions rushed through my head. Questions like, How much more mobility would I really have with a messed up leg than with a prosthetic? How much more pain and discomfort would I have with a messed up leg than with a prosthetic? Would I be more active with a messed up leg than with a prosthetic? What types of activities could I do with a prosthetic that I wouldn't be able to do with a messed up leg? What kind of conveniences would I miss with a prosthetic?

Immediately after the surgeon left I looked over at Kelly, searching for some kind of support or guidance or something. I wanted to talk to her to see what she felt about everything. As we went over what we had discussed with the surgeon, a wave of emotional questions starting shooting through my mind. How will my choice affect Kelly? Will she still love me if I only have, at best, a deformed, less functional leg? Will she have to do extra work around the house that I'm not able to do? Will I be a burden on her? Will she be embarrassed of me? Will she regret marrying me? If we have kids, what will they think of me? Will I still be able to raise kids? These types of questions haunted me for the next several weeks.

Which surgery option to choose was as much her decision as it was mine. The outcome would affect her just as much as me. It would be selfish of me to make that decision without her being on board with it. I just wanted so badly for her to still be happy with me and love me after all of this was over. I felt like I would be able to continue living a happy life with either option and that she should be the one to make the final decision. I know how she hates making decisions and that she would never make this big of a decision on her own, so I really tried to get as much of her opinion as she would give me so that I would make the choice that she felt most comfortable with. Of course I wanted to help her understand and analyze all of the long term advantages and disadvantages that I could foresee in each option so that she could make as much of an informed decision as possible.

As for me, I think I had mostly decided which option I wanted to go with that night in the hospital. I felt like the amputation would probably be the best decision for me even though the thought of actually going through with it scared me to death. In the middle of all of the fear and anxiety I felt a sliver of comfort and confidence that I would be able to handle any challenge that might come along with missing a leg. Throughout my life I have always been so active and involved in sports and outdoor activities. That was what I loved to do. I knew, though, that my happiness in life wasn't based on those types of activities. I could still choose to be happy, regardless of what types of activities I would or would not be able to do. That choice might be a little more difficult without a leg, but I felt like I would still be able to overcome all of the negative things and focus on the positive.

Even though I felt somewhat comfortable with the idea, I was still in shock that I was actually considering having my leg taken from me, and that I would be giving it up voluntarily. What was I thinking? Was this really happening to me? It was another moment that was so far from reality, so hard to comprehend and process that everything kind of slows down and puts you in this weird mind numbing trance. The same thing happened to me when I was first diagnosed and lasted for several days. This time the trance only lasted about a day, probably because I had already researched everything about losing a leg back when they first told me that it was a possibility. After I snapped out of the trance I came to reality and realized that we would have to do a whole lot of research and deep thinking to take everything into consideration before making a final decision for the surgery. We had to let Dr. Marco know which option I would be choosing before the end of my 6th cycle... that gave us about five weeks to get it all figured out.

This round we actually had something planned for my good week. Well, kind of. Laura was coming into town to visit and we were going to the rodeo to see Brad Paisley the day before starting round five. I loved that Laura and Eric lived in Dallas and were able to drive down and visit every once in a while. Laura was finishing up medical school and would come down to visit almost every time she got a couple of days off (which wasn't very often). I have really grown a lot closer to her since they have been coming down to visit so much. It has been a lot of fun for me to see how much she has grown up over the years. When I left for my mission in Mexico she was a bratty teenager, but when I got back she had really matured and turned into a really sweet girl. I didn't get to see her much when we were both at BYU because we were both so busy all of the time. Now when she comes to visit we can just relax and hang out like when we were in high school except its much better because we've both grown up and don't annoy each other anymore. I'm really proud of the person that she has become and happy to see her fulfilling her dream of becoming a doctor.

Anyway, the rodeo was going on during round four and we were excited to get out of the chemo routine and go do something different. For anybody who isn't from around Houston, the rodeo is something that is put on once a year and is a big event. It's not like the kind of rodeo that you would find in a small town. It's like the world championship of the rodeo people. I'm not a cowboy or anything, but it's still a lot of fun to go. They hold the event at Reliant Stadium in downtown Houston and it isn't just a rodeo. They bring in a huge carnival with all kinds of games and rides. They have a livestock show with all kinds of animals and other farm and cowboy stuff for people to experience. They have all kinds of booths set up for vendors to sell anything from country crafts to pick-up trucks. There's tons of food, mainly BBQ, Tex-Mex, and weird things like fried candy bars and pizza on a stick. The actual rodeo part is the biggest rodeo in the world. The best part, in my opinion, and the reason everybody goes to the rodeo, is that every night there is a different concert with all kinds of big name artists ranging from teen sensations like Hannah Montana to classic country stars like Alan Jackson. The whole thing lasts for about two and a half weeks and brings in hundreds of thousands of people from all over the place. It's really a lot of fun and brings a lot of culture into the big city.

This year Kelly, Laura, my mom, and I were going to see one of our favorite country singers, Brad Paisley. I didn't really know how I was going to survive the whole night. I was still kind of recovering from the chemo and didn't really have a lot of energy. On top of that it was difficult and tiresome to walk much with that annoying brace on my leg, and there was a lot of walking to do. The brace gave me blisters and was really uncomfortable if I wore it very long. Luckily, the handicap parking pass cut out quite a bit. After parking, though, we still had to walk all the way to the other side of the stadium to where the food and livestock show was set up and then inside the stadium for the concert and back to the car. It was a lot of walking for a normal person but a really long hike for me. After looking at a bunch of farm animals and eating Kelly and I's rodeo regular, the corn dog and sausage on a stick, we finally made it to the stadium. I was exhausted and happy to rest for a while. The concert was awesome and we all had a really good time together. By the time we made it back to the car and home I was so wiped out. It was really good to get out of the house and do something fun before having to go in for chemo the next day.

During that round I spent a lot of time in the hospital and at home trying to wrap my mind around everything that was happening to me. My life had been turned upside down. It was like one day I was living this dream life where Kelly and I had everything going for us and the next I found myself always sick and in the hospital, breaking down in tears more than ever before in my life, and so dependent on Kelly and others around me. How did I get here? Where did my perfect life go? It was really depressing to think of how badly our situation had changed. On top of all of these thoughts, now I was having to figure out whether or not I should have my leg amputated. Could I actually handle going through with an amputation? What surgery option would make Kelly the happiest in the long run? There were so many things to take into consideration and so much to learn before being able to make this decision.

Apart from these mind bogglers there were even bigger issues that I was working through… faith and prayer. I still didn't understand exactly why God was allowing this to happen to me when I had lived a good life, had plenty of "faith," and prayed like crazy for a miracle. Over the past couple of months these topics occupied my mind for hours every day. I often found myself sitting there staring blankly in deep thought trying to find a way for it all to fit together. I prayed a lot for guidance and help in figuring it all out. My parents seemed to be going through similar experiences. We spent a lot of time discussing gospel principles and trying to make sense of what was happening to me. It became common for dinner conversations to turn to faith and prayer.

After so much pondering I finally started to understand faith and how it applied to my situation. I knew that I had "faith" because I had seen miracles before in my own life. I had even seen a girl miraculously healed of cancer on my mission in Mexico. I knew, without a doubt, that it was possible for God to rid my body of this disease before I was even diagnosed. But when my treatment started and I still wasn't healed it really threw me for a loop.

After much thought I finally came to the conclusion that I didn't really understand what faith was all about. The problem, I think, comes from the multiple meanings that we apply to the word faith. We use it to describe different things like an acceptance of a principle, a trust in someone, or a knowledge that something exists or is possible. I was focusing my thoughts and energy on the wrong meaning of the word. What I had at the time was a knowledge that it was possible for me to be healed. I called that knowledge "faith" that God could heal me.

But I was hardly taking into consideration what God's plan for me might be. Did he even want me to be healed? Maybe he had something to teach me through this whole cancer experience and I would eventually be healed by the doctor's treatment plans. Maybe I was needed on the other side for something and I wouldn't be healed at all. I wasn't focusing on what God might want for me. I was only focusing on what I wanted for myself.

I now have learned that faith has a lot more to do with a trust in God and his plan, or will for us, than a belief or knowledge that something is possible. I learned that no matter how strongly I believed something, for example, that I could be healed, it wouldn't happen unless it was God's will. And I have learned how important it is to strengthen my faith, or trust, in God and his plan for me.

Having this improved understanding of faith has really helped me a lot in dealing with being sick. It has provided a comfort that couldn't be found from other sources. Instead of being frustrated at God for not healing me right away, I have tried to understand his plan for me and been able to see many blessing that have come from me being sick. I have a stronger faith in God's plan for me and I know that everything will work out better for everyone if his plan is fulfilled, even if that means I don't survive the cancer.

25 ROUND 5: MAR 13, 2009

Kelly and I decided to sleep in after our long night at the rodeo the night before. We always tried to get plenty of sleep before going into the hospital for chemo. While we were at the hospital we didn't get a lot of quality sleep. Most nights we stayed up until two or three in the morning goofing off and watching TV. Night time was when the nurses and CNAs came into our room the most. Every hour or so, somebody would come in to check my medicines or take my vitals. Plus, there was always something wrong with the pumps, causing them to beep annoyingly all night long. Once morning would come things would slow down and we would have more peace and quiet. We figured we might as well stay up late and sleep in all morning. The food runners liked to pick on us a lot for this. Every morning they would come in and wake us up and tell us we had to order breakfast before it was too late. We would order the usual pancakes, eggs, sausage, and juice and go straight back to sleep. They would wake us up again when the food arrived, and then again about an hour or two later when they had to pick up our trays. Sometimes they would even have to wake us up to tell us it was time to order lunch. We were always just so exhausted from staying up late and being up all night. So when it came time to go back into the hospital for another round we made sure we were well rested.

After our long morning of sleeping in we finally packed up our things and made our way up to the medical center. We checked in and headed up to the cancer floor and had an amazing surprise waiting there for us in our room... two empty hospital beds! It was awesome! It was like we had checked in to some kind of honeymoon suite or something compared to the other rooms we had been in. For the first time, Kelly would be able to stay overnight in the hospital without having to sleep on the tiny little chair-bed. Plus the room was bigger and there was extra space for any visitors that might stop by. We were thrilled!

Having now completed four rounds of chemo we dreaded my sick days and tried to get as much time out of the days of feeling good as we could. Usually when we checked into the hospital the nurses would draw my blood and then make us wait hours before giving me the treatment. Sitting in the hospital waiting to start seemed like such a waste of time when I was feeling so good. They didn't really like for us to leave after checking in, but it was so depressing sitting there for so long on the cancer floor of a hospital just waiting to get hit by a long weekend of chemo. So we decided that from then on we would take advantage of that time by sneaking out of the hospital and going out on the town. It was rare for me to have an appetite so I wanted to use it and squeeze in one last good meal before the upcoming days of steady nausea. We went to a nearby restaurant and filled up on some good old Philly cheese steaks and then walked around some girly shops that Kelly wanted to visit. It felt great to return to the hospital with a stomach full of non-hospital food. When we got back we confessed to the nurses where we had been and told them they wouldn't be able to trap us there in the future. I think they just laughed and told us to next time just let them know we were leaving.

Having the larger room was really nice because Laura was staying in town for the weekend. That Friday night Laura and my parents came up to the hospital to spend some time with us. It was really fun to have Laura there. She gets almost as stir crazy as my mom sometimes and had to have something there to entertain her. She ended up finding a puzzle somewhere and started putting it together on the floor in the middle of the hospital room. I love doing puzzles and tried to help her out, but once the chemo brain set in it got really difficult to get any of the pieces to fit together. All of the cut up images on the pieces just made my eyes hurt and gave me a headache. My mom, for whatever reason, had recently got into knitting… an unlikely hobby for such an active, stir-crazy woman. She spent a lot of time in the hospital that round practicing her skills with the yarn and needles. My dad, as usual, sat in one of the hospital chairs and quietly read a book for most of the time he was there that weekend. Kelly, although she had a whole bed to herself, spent a lot of time over by my side or lying with me in my hospital bed. She was so good at making all of the bad go away even when I felt the worst. She always made me feel happy and loved. I don't know what I would have done without her.

Kelly spent a lot of time, as usual, playing with all of the medical equipment and nurses things. Every time the nurses did something to me she would watch intently and then turn to me and smile with a look in her eyes like "Wasn't that cool?" I think that round was extra interesting for her because Laura was in town and could answer all of her medical questions. It was obvious that Kelly loved all of the medical and nursing stuff. We all kind of joked around about how she liked to tinker with everything. Finally my mom said something that we all should have said a long time ago… "Kelly, you should go to nursing school." It was a perfect idea. She had been complaining for such a long time about how she didn't know what she was going to do with her life. This was something that she could really get interested in and enjoy. Plus, Kelly has always liked helping and taking care of people. Nursing would be the perfect job for her. She would get paid good money to do something that she has always enjoyed. We explained all of this to her but she was pretty hesitant about the whole idea. We had talked about doing nursing school a long time ago but had decided that it would be too expensive and take too long to finish. We were more interested in having kids than starting an intense two year university program. Now that our life was on hold I figured it would be the perfect time for her to start a program like that. I think she was a little intimidated by such a difficult challenge. I don't think she felt like she could actually do it. I knew how smart she was, though, and that she was a hard enough worker that she could get through it no problem. We all really tried to encourage her.

After a lot of persuading, we got her gears going enough to get interested in the idea. By this time, our nurses had become good friends and did so much to help us emotionally and physically. Kelly really liked the idea of being able to help others as much as our nurses helped us. She wanted to make a difference in people's lives. The next few days were spent on the Internet researching every nursing program in the area and figuring out what she would have to do to apply and get started. Before we knew it she had found out which schools she would want to apply to and which tests and prerequisites she would have to take to get in. She had most of it figured out and was pretty set on the idea by the end of the round.

It made me so happy for her to find a program that she was genuinely interested in. When I first met Kelly I thought she was awesome, but she had a lot of self-esteem issues from the jerks that she had dated before me. I felt so bad for her that she had no clue how truly amazing of a person she really was. Fixing that has been one of my personal goals ever since we started dating. I have always tried to build up her self-esteem as much as I could in any way possible so that she could be happier and have more confidence to do all of the things that she didn't feel she was capable of doing. Her being 24 and not having finished college was a major setback in her personal progress. Now she had a plan to finish and felt like her life was finally going somewhere. I could tell from her eyes when she talked about it that she was excited and determined to finish and that being a nurse was something she could really feel proud of. Deep down her confidence was growing and I absolutely loved it!

The rest of the time in the hospital was just like the other four rounds - miserable. I finally made it home and was able to rest without being constantly interrupted by hospital workers. Every time I got home it was like I was coming back from a long vacation or something. Everything about the house was so comforting. It just felt great to be home. I was recovering just fine and hoped that maybe this round I would start feeling good sooner and have a long good week. My hopes were shattered, though, when my counts dropped and I started to run a fever. We had to rush back to the hospital again! It was so devastating to Kelly and me every time I checked my temperature and it was over 100.5°. It really ticked us off that we would have to leave my parent's comfy house and return back to the tiny, depressing, hospital room. I was so sick of having IV tubes coming out of me. Going back and getting hooked up to them again was the last thing I wanted to do. Luckily, every time we arrived to the cancer floor our moods were brightened by the friendly smiles and jokes of our nursing buddies. That round I was given a blood transfusion and a few days of IV antibiotics before I was able to leave.

There was kind of a funny situation that came up while I was there in the hospital. The day before the fever started I noticed a small rash starting to form down in my crotch… where you don't ever want to get a rash. It was interesting to me because the rash started out as just a small red area. I didn't even know what it was at first and it didn't bother me at all. With no immune system, though, it started to grow like crazy and, within a day or two it had morphed into this big, blistering, painful, itchy, pain in the butt! Usually when you get admitted for a fever the doctors want to search every square inch of your body to try to find the source of the infection. I was hesitant to tell my doctor about it when he asked if I was having any problems. He, of course, wanted to closely inspect it to see if it was causing my fever. I dropped my shorts, he took a look, and said… that's really strange looking, it looks kind of like herpes. I couldn't believe it. I didn't think there was any way I could have herpes. Kelly was devastated because now she thought that maybe somehow I got it from her (even though that wasn't really possible) or that now she would have herpes too. She was really nervous and I had to calm her down a bit and let her know that everything would be fine no matter what the outcome was. He wanted another opinion or two so he sent in doctor after doctor to come and inspect my crotch. Each time I dropped my shorts and got the same reaction… that's weird. It looks kind of like herpes, but I'm not sure. Finally a doctor came in who dealt more with these types of problems. She had me drop my shorts again and quickly responded with "I don't know what they're talking about. That's not herpes. It looks like a fungal infection." She gave me a bottle of anti-fungal cream and told me to keep the area well ventilated until it was gone. How was I going to keep my crotch well ventilated? The other problem was that the rash was so bad by then that the skin would rub off when I tried to apply the cream. It was a really annoying and uncomfortable situation. I spent the next several days laying around in my underwear and walking funny to keep anything from rubbing down there. At last the rash went away about the same time as the rest of the chemo side effects, and I was able to enjoy another week of feeling good before going back for round five.

The decision to amputate my leg or not continued to press our minds. Time was running out for us to make up our minds and we still didn't know what we wanted to do. Well, I still felt like amputation was probably the best choice for us, but I didn't want to tell Kelly that I was going to choose that. I wanted her to be on board with the idea 100% before making any final decisions. She still didn't know what would be best for us to do. I think that she wanted me to do what I wanted to do, regardless of her opinion, which sometimes made it difficult to get input from her. We talked a lot about the upcoming surgery and how we thought it would affect our lives in the future. We would stay up at night going over all of the good and bad parts of each option. It was so hard, emotionally, for me to try to process everything that I would soon have to face. The thought of becoming an amputee hurt so much. Dealing with all of the physical discomfort of going through chemo plus having to withstand all of the emotional torture that the thought of surgery was putting me through was just too much to handle. I don't remember too well, but I'm pretty sure I spent quite a few nights crying to Kelly over how hard everything was. I wasn't too afraid of the physical changes that would take place in my life. I was afraid of how I was going to be accepted by others and terrified of how Kelly would accept me. I was scared that she would be embarrassed of me and maybe regret marrying me. I wanted her to be happy with her life more than anything I wanted for my own life. The thought that my illness would affect her life so much tore me apart inside. Nevertheless, that was the situation that we were stuck in. Our lives were going to change forever no matter what we chose to do. The challenge was just to make the decision that would work best for both of us.

We had the idea of going to meet with a prosthetist to find out what being an amputee was really all about. We wanted to see the different types of prosthetics and learn what their capabilities and limitations were. Once we got there my engineering mind kicked in and I became fascinated with how they worked and the technology that was used to design them. I thought the different legs were pretty cool. It was fun to look at everything, but a little overwhelming to think that I might have to use one of them someday.

I found out that the type of amputation you have is what really limits you the most. People who have their legs amputated below the knee are still able to do most of their normal activities because they still have their knee joint. Without a knee there are a lot of simple things that you aren't able to do. The prosthetics are built with a knee joint but it won't bend on its own. Because of the location of my tumor, the surgeons would not be able to save my knee. I would be stuck with the bad type of leg amputation. Even still, I truly felt like I would still be able to do whatever I put my mind to. It was just a matter of putting in lots of hard work and practice. Plus, I am really coordinated and athletic. I felt I could pick up any activity just as well as any other amputee could. I just hoped that I wasn't being overly confident.

After having nearly completed five rounds of chemo, all of the expenses from doctor's visits, hospital stays, lab work, and prescription medicines were really starting to add up. I was a cheap guy and always tried to make sure that Kelly and I were bringing in more money than we were spending. But it was getting really hard to do that. I was on disability pay and Kelly had to cut back so much on her hours to take care of me all of the time. We had to pull out of our savings every month just to pay for all of our bills and it was killing me. I felt like I needed to make more money to preserve our savings. I called up my boss and started to bug him for work., but work was nowhere to be found. By then, the recession had caused the price of oil to drop so much that a lot of Fluor's projects were being cut. People were getting laid off left and right and Whitt was doing everything he could to keep our little Cathodic Protection group together. Any available work was given to the full time guys to keep them from being laid off. As for me, I would be safe from the lay-offs if I stayed on disability. So whenever I asked for work he just said "Keep hiding on disability." Even though I wanted the extra money, I was okay with not having to go into work when I wasn't feeling great.

Without any work to do on my good week I had tons of free time and very little to fill it with. I practiced trading stock, made excel spreadsheets, watched TV, and when all of that got old and boring, I just sat quietly on the couch in thought and tried to wrap my head around all of the things that were going on in my life. I had a lot to think about… how to make more money, what I was going to do for the surgery, and more importantly, how all of the spiritual stuff that I had learned in my life apply to my drastic situation.

After figuring out faith (for the most part) I was really starting to question prayer and what its point was. I mean, we had prayed and prayed and prayed that all of this would just go away, but it never did. And it wasn't just my family and I praying either. Once word was out that I had cancer, it seemed like everybody was praying for me and adding me to their prayer lists. Somehow I ended up on prayer lists all across the US and even on a couple in Europe. But what good did it do me? I still had cancer and was possibly going to lose my leg. What was the point of all of those prayers?

I thought a lot about those questions during my initial treatments. What I realized was that God did answer those prayers and my own, just not the way that I wanted them to be answered. It took a little retrospective to be able to see how they were being answered. Looking back and analyzing my situation I realized that I had been extremely calm considering everything that I was going through. I think that normally being diagnosed with cancer and starting treatments that did all kinds of weird things to my body would cause me tons of anxiety and stress, but for whatever reason, I was usually at peace with my life.

It really seemed amazing once I thought about it. I wasn't ever really stressed, I was never depressed for more than a couple of days, and I never complained about anything or had pity parties. I just felt comforted a lot. After realizing that, I felt strongly that it was in part because of all of the prayers that were offered for me.

Knowing that my prayers were helping me to be more at peace didn't make it any easier to deal with the fact that I wasn't being healed. I was still upset by that. But after better understanding faith I realized that my prayers lacked the right type of faith. I was asking to be healed because I knew it was possible for God to heal me. But I was hardly trusting in God that he would do what was best for me. I know that he answers my prayers, but he isn't going to give me anything that will harm me or deny me the opportunity to receive important teachings or blessings. I realized that while praying I need to try to be more aware of his plan for me and keep the things I asked for within my understanding of what his plan is for me. But this can be hard because I may not always know God's plan. I think that is where the phrase "Thy will be done" comes into play.

While I was re-learning these gospel principles I spent a lot of time analyzing other things in my life. I thought about how I had been living and what type of person I really was inside. Was I the type of person that I knew I needed to be? Was I living the type of life that I knew I should be living?

Back when life was "normal" for me I felt like everything was going well. I thought I was a pretty decent guy. I always tried to be a good person. I attended church every week and volunteered for service opportunities when I could. But there were certain things that I knew I needed to improve on that had always been difficult for me. For example, I liked to be sarcastic and joke around a lot. I don't think there's anything wrong with joking around, but my jokes mostly involved making fun of other people. This was something that I knew I shouldn't do, but it was often so fun that it was hard to stop.

Another problem that I had was that when I heard of people being sick or going through hard times I didn't really care too much because I had never been through anything hard and didn't really understand what they were going through. Sometimes I would even criticize others for being "wimps" or say things like "well they deserve it" when I heard of some people's stories. I was too critical and sometimes judgmental of others and their actions or decisions.

I never used bad language, but sometimes I would talk in a way that wasn't really genuine. I think that the way we communicate, both verbally and through body language, reflects our true character. People often use their language or the way they carry themselves to portray a certain image of how they want to be seen, even though it may not be who they really are inside. I sometimes struggled with this, using "fake" swear words here and there, or carrying myself like I was smarter or more professional than I really was. This type of behavior was sometimes spiritually exhausting because it was like I was in an internal struggle from living a lie. At the time I didn't even realize that I was doing this to myself, but looking back, I can see how spiritually damaging that simple behavior issue was.

Now, after three or four months of chemo I noticed that I was a different person than who I was before I was diagnosed. My experience with having cancer and being so sick and miserable from it had humbled me in a way that would not have been possible otherwise. All of a sudden I was the person going through the crappy experience that everybody was talking about. I was that person who walked funny and I would be that person for the rest of my life. Now, I was the person that I would have joked about or made fun of.

I suddenly understood anybody who was different in any way or going through any type of hard time, even if they had brought it on themselves. I knew how difficult the trials in life could be and I felt sympathy for anybody who was struggling. I was now able to see the positive in people and situations instead of always noticing the negative. I had gained a general respect and acceptance of others despite their differences or perceived shortcomings. I think these changes in character naturally made me want to be more sincere with myself. I stopped trying to carry myself as someone other than who I really was inside. I no longer used poor language or made inappropriate jokes. It even turned me off big time when friends or television shows used off-color language and jokes.

I noticed that I was a different person inside and it was great! I no longer had to deal with the internal struggle of knowing that I needed to change, but not being strong enough. The changes that I had experienced had given me somewhat of an inner peace and made me so much happier with who I was. I still wasn't anywhere close to being perfect, but was very happy with the progress that I was making.

The changes that had taken place with my character not only lifted internal burdens but improved my self-esteem and gave me much more confidence. Before I was diagnosed I wasn't exactly shy, but I was often hesitant to talk with random people that I didn't know. I was fine with introducing myself and meeting people when I needed to develop a relationship with somebody, but when it came to random people that I would run into in everyday situations, I pretty much just kept to myself and tried to stay out of the way. Now I was different. I wasn't afraid to talk to people. I enjoyed sharing smiles and starting friendly conversations to try to help brighten others' days. I wasn't afraid to go out of my way to help others.

The self-esteem and confidence that I gained helped me look at people and situations in a whole new way. I loved the new perspective that I had on life and the new person that I had become. At the time I didn't make the connection that these positive changes in my life that brought me happiness were related to the cancer that I hated so much and wanted so badly to just go away. But now I see that these were just the first of the many blessing that I would receive from this whole nightmarish experience.

26 ROUND 6: APR 3, 2009

Before starting round six Dr. Beinart told us that he wanted to lower the dose again so that my blood counts wouldn't drop so much. I was excited to have the dose lowered again because it would make the chemo easier to tolerate, but I was nervous that lowering the dose would reduce its effectiveness. Dr. Beinart reassured me that everything would be fine so and we pushed forward with the treatment.

This round was going to be a bitter-sweet. We were so excited because after this round I would get an extra two weeks of feeling good to fully recover before the surgery. The bad thing was that the rounds of chemo were starting to fly by and this was the last one before I had to get my leg messed up or removed in surgery. We were really starting to get scared about the surgery and we still hadn't decided exactly which option we would go with. We had to let the surgeons know before the end of the round, which meant we had to get it figured out quick.

As we were waiting to be admitted to the hospital with a wheelchair loaded up with all of our stuff I noticed a crowd of people gathering around one of the fountains in the lobby of the hospital. Now that we felt like hospital regulars we had to be involved in whatever was going on. We did some investigating and found out that the Houston Astros were setting up for some kind of benefit and would be giving out free stadium hot dogs. I'm always excited about free food so I grabbed a hot dog before heading up to our room and started scarfing it down. It was surprisingly good; much better than the food in the hospital. Once we made it up to the room I had a great idea. We should go stock up on free hot dogs so that we wouldn't have to eat off of the hospital menu. We went back down and explained to them that I was a cancer patient and it was difficult to eat and that it would be nice to have some extra hot dogs on hand for the upcoming round of chemo. People are always willing to help out a nice guy that obviously looks like a cancer patient and walks funny. We walked away with five or six more hot dogs and stored them in the fridge on the cancer floor. Those hot dogs made the whole round exciting! I don't know if it was because they were free, or what, but somehow I was still able to enjoy those even when I was really nauseated. Having good tasting food made such a big difference.

That weekend in the hospital my friend Rob brought his parents and his uncle up to visit us. Rob's uncle Elwin was a below the knee amputee who lost his leg in an accident while working on his ranch. When we heard that he was going to be in town we asked if we could visit with him to ask him questions about his life as an amputee. We were still trying to decide what to do for the surgery and figured he would be a great resource for easing our concerns and finding answers to some of our questions. It was so kind of them to come up and visit with us in the hospital.

When they arrived he told us that he hadn't really shared his emotions or feelings about his amputation very much. We asked him a lot of questions like "What has been the hardest thing about it?" and "What is day to day life like?" After he answered some of our questions he really opened up to us and told us a lot of things that helped in our decision making. He explained that while he was in the hospital he had some of the same emotions that I was having. He worried about how others would accept him and how he would fit in. He was afraid that people would look at him funny and that he wouldn't be able to do lots of the activities that he loved. But most of all, like me, he was worried about how his wife would accept him. Would she still love him and would she still find him attractive?

He went on to talk about all of the positive and negative things about being an amputee; some of them I hadn't ever thought about. He explained first, that being an amputee is being handicapped.   I tried not to think of it that way because I figured it was just a matter of how much work you put into it. He disagreed and went on to point out all of the limitations that I would have regardless of how much work I did. It was a big eye-opener. He then went on to calm my worries about not fitting in.   He explained how, in his situation, nobody ever really treated him differently. Everyone, both strangers and friends, accepted him and his disability immediately and was kind and helpful to him all the time. And most importantly, his relationship with his wife only seemed to improve after the accident. They had grown closer because of hardships that they both had to endure together. This was of huge comfort to me and made me choke back a few tears in the hospital room.

But the thing that surprised me the most was his overall feeling about being an amputee. He generally explained that being an amputee really stinks sometimes and going through the adjustment was one of the hardest things he had ever faced. But despite all of the bad, the accident had caused so many positive changes to take place inside him. He was a completely different person as an amputee. He was full of love and compassion for others and more desirous to help and serve those around him. He said that the good that came from losing his leg was worth all of the hardships and that if he had the choice, he would never take it back. It kind of shocked me when he said that but I believed him. It was so helpful to hear that perspective and part of me wanted to have those same positive changes in my life. I was so grateful to him for taking the time to come and talk with us.

After contemplating the words that Rob's uncle shared with us over the next few days in the hospital I think I had sadly come to the conclusion that I needed to choose the amputation for my surgery. I just felt like it was the better option for me and would give us the highest chance of getting rid of the cancer forever. Having a lower rate of reoccurrence was really important to me because when the cancer comes back it lowers the survival rate significantly. More than anything, I wanted to always be there for Kelly. I wanted to make sure she was on board with the idea though, before telling her what my decision was.

During our time in the hospital we talked together a lot about the upcoming surgery and the things that Elwin had told us. Other than that we spent our time hanging out and having fun as usual, except this time I had lots of hot dogs to keep me going. My parents came up on the weekend, also as usual, to keep us company and to help relieve Kelly of having to be there all the time. A lot of times they would come up and let Kelly escape the hospital to go in for work or for girls' night out. It was good for her to have a break where she could get back to normal life. Their providing her with that break was such a priceless act of service. I'm so thankful for everything that they did for us in the hospital.

This round I had a little more energy to hang out with Kelly and my parents. I could really feel the effects of the lowered dose of chemo. It was great! I mean, I still felt really sick, but it was a night and day difference between the way I felt during round one and round six. This time, when I got home from the hospital I was able to do a puzzle with Kelly instead of having to rush straight to collapse on the couch for a nap. I seemed to recover pretty quickly too, and the best part of it all... I didn't have to go back to the hospital for a fever or blood transfusion. That left tons of free time to enjoy before having to go in for the surgery.

That first week of feeling good and moving back to our town home was great for some reason. I think we were both excited to get a little break from chemo. Kelly tried to return to work when she could and I continued to keep myself entertained by watching and learning about the stock market, doing dorky engineering stuff like making spreadsheets, and writing computer programs. I was always looking for business opportunities and felt like it would be important to learn how to make a website in case I ever needed one for a business that I might start. I did what I could to stay feeling productive, no matter how pointless my projects sometimes were, because it kept me from getting down and depressed about everything that was happening to me. For some reason when I was working on something and staying "busy" I felt better about myself and was able to forget about my crummy circumstances a little easier.

The other thing that always made me feel better was spending time with Kelly. And I had a lot of time to spend with her. Sometimes I would wonder if she was getting sick of me and how clingy I had become. I really hoped she wasn't. Because what would I do without her if she started to try to take breaks from me? Luckily, I think it made her feel more important and loved that I wanted to spend so much time with her. We were going through a really emotional time with the whole surgery option thing. I think by this time she had finally made up her mind and decided that she thought the amputation was the best option for me. When she learned and processed exactly what my leg would be like with the knee replacement, what capabilities I would have with a prosthetic, and took into consideration how active I liked to be, she felt like I would be happier with the amputation because it would allow me to continue to do lots of different types of activities with the least amount of pain and discomfort. It was that aspect that convinced her. She knew that I would be happy no matter what, but understood how much I enjoyed being active.

After discussing this for a few nights in a row before going to bed with tears in our eyes we had finally come to a decision. I was going to have my leg amputated in just a couple of weeks. What a nightmare! It was something that was so hard to take in and fully comprehend that it was really like a horrible dream that became more and more real each day. Every morning I would think "Only 'x' more days until the surgery." And every night I would think "Agh! Another day with my leg is gone." It was constantly on my mind and often made me break down in tears.

We still had to tell the surgeons about our choice… something that I was really hesitant to go through with. I think we ended up waiting until the very last day. I procrastinated telling them as long as I could, and when it came down to it, I couldn't go through with it. I made Kelly send the emails to confirm that I was going to have the amputation. Again, I couldn't live without her. It was just so hard to convert the idea of the amputation into an upcoming reality. Now it was going to happen.

The reality of our upcoming situation increased daily, and so did the pain that I felt emotionally. All of the worries about the amputation that I had anticipated, such as not being accepted by others and, mainly, the impact it would have on Kelly, were affecting me more and more. I was starting to feel so sorry for Kelly and what she was about to have to go through. I felt extremely guilty that her upcoming trials and difficulties in life would be because of me. I would completely understand if she wanted to leave me even though I knew that she never would. I cried a lot to her over this kind of stuff and apologized to her constantly. I just felt so bad for dragging her through everything. Not only did we have to put our lives on hold for my cancer treatments, but now we had to face a surgery that would change both of our lives forever. She, of course, was always loving and assuring that there was no need to apologize and that this wasn't my fault. I just wanted so badly to be able to give her everything that she might have envisioned in a perfect marriage and a perfect life. Things like a house, money, fun vacations, a family, emotional support, love, friendship, guidance, lots of help around the house and with the kids, and a lot of fun physical activities. By now, however, I had learned that life isn't ever perfect and there were a lot of things that I simply would never be able to give her. It broke my heart!

There seemed to be one thing that helped to relieve my anxious mind of the torture that the surgery was putting on it, and that was spending time with family and good friends.

It was really nice to have Rob and Jess in the town home next door because they were able to stop in for a little while here and there. It brought a friendly break to the emotional stress that we were coping with. They have always been such good friends for us and we are so grateful to have them around. I think my friends understood that getting out of the house would be helpful to us because it seemed like we were starting to get lots of phone calls from them wanting to hang out. Throughout this whole experience we have always been so blessed to have such good friends around to help us, even when we were feeling really anti-social.

27 SAY GOODBYE -
ONE LAST VACATION

It was perfect timing to have a lot of free time after round six. All of my brothers and sisters were flying in for one last fun week before my surgery. Plus, they all wanted to be there to support me emotionally while going through such an impossibly difficult task. At first, I was really hesitant about the idea of everybody being there for my surgery. My hesitation stemmed from the whole fear that people, including my family, weren't going to accept me after I lost my leg. I felt like it would be better if they got used to the idea of me being an amputee after seeing pictures and stuff before coming to see me in person. Kelly and my mom thought that was ridiculous and reminded me of how comforting it was to have them there for round one and when I had to shave my head. They were right, I knew I was being ridiculous. I could see how they would be a huge help during and after the surgery. I was a little reluctant, but I changed my mind and decided I wanted them to be there. They started flying in throughout the week before the surgery and ended up leaving during the week after.

I think Nick might have been the first one to make it home. He went with me to visit with a new prosthetist named Scott. We wanted to learn more details about exactly what would take place from the time I had the surgery to the time I would be ready to take my prosthetic home. Scott was a great guy. His optimism made me feel so much more comfortable with the major changes that were about to take place in my life. However, his explanation about what the surgery and the recovery would be like brought a little more reality to the situation. He told us that the femur would be cut about three inches above the knee and went on to explain how to deal with things like swelling and pain. It was so good to have Nick there with me that day. It was surprisingly comforting to see how easily he accepted the idea of me missing part of my leg and wearing a prosthetic around. Also, he was studying chemical engineering and really got into how cool the prosthetics were just as much as I did. He didn't show any sign of indifference or judgment. It built my confidence that maybe people weren't going to react the way I thought that they might. Maybe they would actually be genuinely accepting of me and the way I would look. Scott told us a lot of helpful information and tips that would make my life easier once my leg started to heal. He left us with a handful of weird looking shrinker socks and sent us on our way.

Meeting with Scott was hard. Seeing all of the things that I would have to do to prepare my leg for a prosthetic made the upcoming surgery so much more real. It began to make me start to wonder what exactly I would look like with one and a half legs. In an attempt to prepare myself mentally, I often tried to imagine how I would look. I tried to picture my leg stopping just a few inches above my knee. I think doing this type of drill helped me prepare, but it sure paid a toll on my emotions. Thankfully, Kelly was always there to lift me up and ease my mind.

At the end of the week we headed out on our last family vacation where I would have two legs. The plan was to drive out in the morning and spend the night at my aunt's house in New Braunfels, Texas where we would spend our time playing on the rivers and eating out at our favorite hill country restaurant, the Grist Mill. The next day we were going to drive up to the lake house to visit with my grandparents, golf, and play on Lake LBJ. It was going to be a lot of fun and we were all excited. However, despite the excitement of getting to ditch my chemo routine to have a fun little family get-away, the fear of my surgery was growing inside. I knew the vacation would fly by and my surgery was scheduled for two days after we got home. It was coming quickly and there was nothing that I could do to escape it!

We left for New Braunfels on the morning of May 1. When we got there, nobody was surprised to see another weird toy that Nick had brought with him. He pulled this big old home-made potato cannon, a sack of potatoes, and a can of WD-40 out of the back of the car. My aunt's house had a huge patio area that was about 40 feet above the Guadalupe river. He thought it would be fun to see how far we could launch the potatoes into the river. We had a blast taking turns firing the cannon, each time adding more fuel to see if we could launch the potatoes farther or higher. Nick was always coming up with bizarre things like that to provide entertainment. We all joked about him being a little goofy, but absolutely loved him for it.

After playing with the potato cannon we all covered up in sun screen, loaded up the cars with inner-tubes, and headed out to float the Comal River which ran straight through the middle of town. We loved floating the river. We always jump in with our tubes at the same place and then float for about an hour and a half back to my aunt's house. It is so relaxing and always brings back so many memories of my childhood. Every summer our family would make a few trips to New Braunfels just to float the river and enjoy the beautiful scenery.

This river trip was especially exciting for me. It was the first time in months that I was able to get out and do something that I really enjoyed. Swimming in the clear spring-fed river and soaking in the sun while being surrounded by tall beautiful trees and the sounds of chirping birds was such a drastic change from the mind numbing hospital room environment. I loved being able to swim and actually put my now scrawny muscles to use. Being on the river that day was just what I needed to wash away all of the emotions and fill my soul with happiness.

After the river trip we visited a small town up the road called Gruene, Texas. Gruene was a small farming community back in the day that turned into a ghost town during the great depression. Since then, it has been re-built and renovated to maintain the feel of small town Texas. It's one of our favorite places to go whenever we visit New Braunfels. Right in the middle of the town is the oldest dance hall in Texas, along with old country style general stores and antique shops that the girls love to wander through. But the real reason we visit is to eat at this restaurant called the Grist Mill. It was an old wood mill and barn located right above the Guadalupe River that was turned into a good old country style restaurant. It's a family tradition to eat there whenever we float the river. It's always delicious and satisfies the appetite that we build up from being on the river.

I felt really awkward walking around in public that night. After completing six rounds of chemo I was really starting to look like a cancer patient. In fact, I was down-right weird looking. All of my eye lashes had fallen out and I only had three or four straggling hairs on each of my eyebrows. My attempts to keep my eyebrows in tact by not ever touching them had failed miserably. Now I looked like some sort of alien or something. All of my brothers and sisters were initially shocked by the way I looked and didn't hesitate to joke around about me all weekend. I never took offense and just laughed along with them. After all, it was pretty funny looking.

The only problem was that I wasn't used to the way that everybody else looked at me. It seemed like half of the people that I walked by did a double take. I could see in their eyes that they were thinking things like "Man, that guy must have cancer or something." Or the smaller kids would have looks on their faces that said "Mommy, what's wrong with that guy?" I was kind of used to getting funny looks because of my drop-foot, but now my whole face looked weird too and I was getting even more. It kind of hurt a little even though I knew nobody meant any harm. Again I was that guy that everybody looked at funny. To top it all off, my family went picture crazy that night and now we have tons of pictures to remind me of how bad I really looked.

The next morning we hung out at my aunt's house and spent time down by the river fishing and paddling around in the canoe before it was time to head out to my grandparent's house. It was a quick drive out to the northwest side of Austin where my grandparents lived. They lived out in the beautiful Texas hill country next to this lake called Lake LBJ. My family has been taking trips out to that house my whole life. It's another big comfort spot for me that brings back tons of childhood memories of fishing, playing on the lake, and golfing on the little nine-hole golf course they have up there.

This trip the activities were about the same as they have always been. We played on the wave runner and hung out in the sun in the same place we always have... on a blanket under a big oak tree next to the lake. I went golfing with Nick and my grandpa and this time I actually tried to do well. I've always been much more interested in all of the other sports that I played to ever pay much attention to golf. Usually when I golf up there I just go to goof around with my family. But now I took it much more seriously and tried to learn as much as I could, considering that golf was a sport that I would actually be able to be competitive in after my amputation. It was a lot of fun, but frustrating because I wasn't very good.

Grandma cooked her usual Texas BBQ feast and we spent the night eating out on the patio and relaxing on the bench swings. After a couple of days of hanging out at my grandparent's house, it was time to head back to reality and the upcoming nightmare that awaited me. It is always so much fun to be up there with my family. I have bonded so much with each of my brothers and sisters during the countless number of times we have visited. This trip was extra special though. There was such a feeling of love and support from my family from their constant attempts to calm my nerves and ease my fears of the upcoming surgery.

I am so grateful that they were all able to make it down to spend time with me before the surgery. They provided a comfort that Kelly never would have been able to produce on her own.

The vacation was great. It was just what I needed to get away from all of the stress from the cancer lifestyle I had been living in. As good as it was, though, I could never really escape the constant fear of the amputation that lied ahead. The fear of the unknown from the drastic life-changing surgery that I was about to go through was just too much to hide in the back of my head.

The fun was now over. It was time to face the event that would turn out to be the worst experience of my life.

28 SURGERY PREP

We spent the day before the surgery winding down from the short vacation and getting everything ready for the stay at the hospital. We were told we would be in the hospital for two or three days after so that I could recover and get some physical therapy in. None of us were looking forward to the following day and it seemed like everybody's focus was on taking my mind off of it. That night we went out to eat as a family. I love being able to go out to dinner with my whole family. It's always fun to have everybody together to enjoy good food. This night was different though. Everything seemed really eerie to me, like there was a haze over my mind or something. I don't really think I was all there mentally. I tried to enjoy everybody's company, but I couldn't ever fully shake the anxiety that was oppressing me. As we left the restaurant the fears really set in. This was it. Kelly and I were going home to go to bed and the next day I would lose my leg!

I had tried my best to prepare myself for how difficult that night would be, but the emotions I experienced were nothing like what I had expected. It has been almost two years since the surgery and it is still so painful to think about what I went through. When Kelly and I got back to our townhome I became so heartbroken over my leg. I looked at it differently than I had ever looked at it before. I inspected every scar on it. Each one was a memory of something in my life that I felt like I was somehow losing. My right leg had been with me throughout my whole life, through good times and bad. It was there for me for all of the games I played throughout my childhood. It pushed me through all of the sports I participated in during high school. It carried me through countless miles of walking to help people in Mexico. It was there for me when I knelt at the altar to marry the love of my life. My leg had been with me through everything I had ever experienced. And now I had to say goodbye.

I know this sounds weird, but I felt like I was losing the best friend I ever had. It was like my leg was a separate being of its own. I felt a closeness with my right leg that I have never felt before with anything in my life. I wanted so bad to keep it even though I knew it had to go. When I was first diagnosed, Kelly and I joked about how my leg was trying to kill me. Now I just felt like my leg was really sick and had to be euthanized to keep the cancer from spreading. It was like I was having to put my dog to sleep but on a much more personal level. I felt so guilty for having to do it. I mean, it didn't do anything wrong. It was always there for me and just happened to get sick and now I was going to kill it.

The emotions were so strong that I started to have conversations with it in my inner monologue. I reasoned with it to explain why I was getting rid of it and I apologized over and over for what was about to happen. It was about then that I realized that I needed to try to snap out of it a little.

It was then that my thoughts turned to Kelly. I felt so bad for her. I felt so guilty for having put her into this situation. She didn't sign up for all of this when we got married. She didn't need to be married to a one legged guy with cancer. She could have been with somebody better. Deep down I knew she loved me and wouldn't want anybody else, but it still hurt to know that I couldn't be the person for her that I had envisioned being when we got married.

I crawled across the bed to Kelly to try to find some emotional comfort and to apologize to her for what I was about to do to our lives. She, of course, thought it was ridiculous that I was apologizing and said that she would stand by me no matter what happened. She held me while I cried and tried to comfort me in any way she could. I felt so bad for her because I could tell my pain was hurting her. I knew she wanted to help me so badly but just couldn't. This was something I had to go through on my own and there was really nothing that anybody could do to help.

That night, before going to sleep, I prayed and prayed for some kind of strength to emotionally and mentally endure the surgery the next day. It was already so hard and I still had the whole next morning of surgery prep to undergo. I really didn't know how I would make it.

29 ARRIVING AT THE HOSPITAL: MAY 8, 2009

The next morning I woke up and felt like I was still trapped in some kind of dream. We had spent so much time over the last few months dreading this day and now it was actually here. That night I would be stuck in a hospital bed with one less body part than I went in with. I got out of bed and jumped in the shower to start prepping for the surgery. I had to clean my leg with this anti microbial soap before going in. Such a simple task but nearly impossible to accomplish. Scrubbing my leg brought back all of the emotions from the night before. I tried my best to shut them out but ended up breaking down in the shower.

Kelly, as she did for all of our hospital stays, packed up everything she might ever need for a four day vacation. We loaded up everything and were all ready to leave when my family arrived to show their love for me and send me off. They were planning on arriving at the hospital later to be there for me when I woke up. As Kelly and I drove off I couldn't help but stare at my leg and think of what was going to happen to it. The thought of my leg detached from my body and being discarded as a piece of trash tore me apart. The surgeons wouldn't treat it with the same respect that I felt it deserved. It made me sad to think about.

Both of our emotions were on edge that morning. On the way up to the hospital we were both stressing out over little things way more than we normally would have. We were running late and it was driving me crazy. I was trying to tell her how to drive and it was driving her crazy. We were both getting annoyed at each other and it was really frustrating. After what seemed like forever, we finally pulled up to the hospital entrance where she dropped me off and then hurried to park the car.

179

I walked through the hospital doors that morning and began the worst experience of my life. I walked through the lobby and it just started to hit me. These were the last steps I would ever take with my leg. It seemed like everything started to move in slow motion as I made my way over to the elevator. I stopped to wait for Kelly and just watched everybody moving around me. I stared at all of their legs in jealousy at how easily they were all able to move around the room. That would never be me again! The fear tore me apart and the sadness pounded me. I almost burst into tears there in the lobby. When Kelly showed up she could tell that I was having a really hard time. She hugged me and held my hand as we pushed the elevator button to head up to the surgery check-in.

When we got to the desk they had us sit and wait for them to call me back. Waiting was horrible! By this time I was freaking out in my head and tears were starting roll. I had so many thoughts and worries running through my head that I basically just shut down and stared at the floor and tried my best to keep from breaking down until my name was called. Finally, they called my name and we both headed over to the reception desk.

When we got there they stopped Kelly and said "Patients only." When I heard that I completely lost it. I fell apart and cried uncontrollably and started begging them to please let her come back with me. The fear of going in to get my leg cut off was already too much to handle. I could not go through with it by myself. I pretty much just sat there and sobbed and held on to Kelly. I couldn't function at all. She had to do all of the talking for me. I had never been through a more difficult and emotionally painful experience. I wanted so badly to just walk out of the hospital but knew that this was something that I had to do for both of us. I had to go through with it no matter what. I just couldn't make myself go through with it on my own. I had to have Kelly there to help me.

After making a phone call they allowed Kelly to go with me. They took us back and put us in a small room with a hospital bed where we would wait for the anesthesiologist to come in and get started. Kelly sat on the bed with me and rubbed my arm and somehow calmed me down and made me feel better. I don't know what she said to me but she relaxed me enough for me to act like a normal person again. I was still scared to death, but her loving smile reassured me that we would be able to make it through this. Eventually the anesthesiologist came in and put some drug in my IV that completely relaxed me. It was time for the surgery to begin. I told Kelly again how much I loved her and they wheeled me off.

I can't describe how difficult that experience was for me. I didn't even know it was possible for an adult to break down as much as I did. Luckily, nobody was there to witness it. Only Kelly saw how badly I had lost it. She was there for me the whole time. But she'll never understand exactly what I went through and how bad it was. That's probably a good thing though. I still have a hard time thinking about that experience and how horrible it was for me. I know it was really hard on Kelly as well. It must have hurt her to see me in so much pain. She cried a bit also, but did her best to be the strong one for me. It was a good thing that she did too. I needed her to be the strong one for me because I was out of it. I don't think I could have made it through the whole thing without her.

30 WAKING UP TO MY NEW BODY

What was four long hours of anxious waiting for my family only seemed like a short nap for me. When I woke up from the surgery Kelly was standing by my bed holding my hand with two other people around me. Everything was blurry and confusing. I looked around and asked "Is it over?" I looked down the bed at my legs and could only see one foot poking up out of the blanket I was under. I lifted the blanket to get a better look and all I could see was a huge ball of gauze and ace bandages about where my knee should have been. My leg was gone! It was so sad to see only one leg but I was so relieved to know that the surgery was done. For the past three months I had stressed so much over this surgery and now it was over! It was like my mind was finally free from such a heavy, stressful burden and I was able to get my normal stress-free personality back. Kelly stayed with me in the recovery area until I was ready to go up to my hospital room.

As they wheeled me up to my room I knew I would have my whole family there waiting for me. I was nervous. How were they going to react to the way that I looked now? Would they be weirded out and disgusted? I hadn't been able to sit up in bed yet to see what I really looked like with one leg. Did I look horrible? Did I look like a freak? What was Kelly thinking of me right now? All of these thoughts went through my head while we were making our way to the room. When we got there though, Nick came right up to the side of the bed and caringly started joking around with me. My sisters and parents followed and, if I remember right, hugged me and asked me how I was doing. There wasn't any trace of them being weird about me having one leg. I was so relieved that my family would still accept me and love me even with one leg missing.

I had a mix of emotions during the next few hours of being in the hospital with my family. I felt relieved that the surgery was over with, happy that my family still loved me, extremely sad that my leg was gone, worried that friends and strangers would treat me differently, and scared to go through the painful recovery process. All of those emotions kind of put me in a weird mood. It was so good, though, to have my whole family there to help ease my mind. Considering the circumstances, we had a pretty good time hanging out together in that hospital room.

We had lots of visitors during our short stay there. Kelly's parents and several close family friends visited throughout the day and brought all kinds of snacks, meals, and flowers to help brighten my mood. My friend Rob brought up his Wii Fit board and hooked it up to the TV in the hospital room. We had everybody playing funny balance games on the Nintendo late into the night. We were all having a fun time and ended up getting a little too noisy. The nurses had to come in several times to ask us to keep it down. I couldn't play along with them of course but I had a lot of fun watching everybody enjoy themselves. It was the perfect activity to take the place of what surely would have been a fairly depressing night.

Waking up the next morning was a lot more difficult. The nurses rushed in at the crack of dawn and woke me up to make me get out of bed and start on some physical therapy. Opening my eyes to a new day and not having my right leg there with me was pretty hard, but not near as hard as walking around on crutches through the halls in a hospital gown with complete strangers trying to keep me from catching them stare at me. I felt ashamed of myself and wished I could have just shown them what I was like not too long ago... active, athletic, and not missing any limbs. But those days were over. This is who I am now.

As we went around the hospital for my physical therapy we passed by a full length mirror and I got my first glimpse of what I looked like without a leg. It was so depressing. I was bald, without eyebrows or eyelashes, skinny, pale, and only had one leg sticking out from my goofy looking hospital gown. I used to be a normal looking guy, fully capable of doing anything I put my mind to. Now I was this disgusting looking one-legged freak who was struggling just to make it up and down a short set of stairs used for physical therapy. Seeing myself like that was such a horrible realization that I would never be the same. I wouldn't even be a normal person again. It made me so sad. Each time we passed that mirror tears filled my eyes. I tried my best to be tough and hold back the tears around the physical therapist, but I think she noticed that I was having a hard time. After passing the mirror a few times I decided I couldn't take the emotional suffering anymore and told her I needed to go back to my room. When I got to my bed I broke down and sobbed. Of course, Kelly was there to lift me up and help me to realize that I could make it through this and that everything would eventually be ok.

At that point I decided that I was going to try my hardest to make the best of my new situation. Yeah it was going to be really depressing sometimes, and yeah it was going to be a lot of physical work, but I wasn't going to let my missing leg keep me from being just as happy as I was before I got cancer. I was going to suck it up and try to be as positive as possible so that I could get back to some kind of normal life. Plus, one of Kelly's biggest fears about me having my leg amputated was that I would be depressed all of the time after it was gone. I promised her that I wouldn't let that happen. I wasn't going to let her down. It was pretty easy to psych myself up and commit to myself to be positive and stay happy. I had no idea however how enormous the emotional and mental challenge would actually be.

31 UNDERSTANDING CHRIST

As I sat in my hospital bed that day, trying to pass the time, I thought about what I had just been through. I had willingly walked into the hospital to have my leg taken from me in order to help prolong my life so that I could be with Kelly. At the time I wanted so badly to turn around and just run from the surgery but my conviction that it needed to be done pushed me to go through with it. It was by far the most difficult internal struggle that I had ever experienced.

While I thought about that struggle and how horrible it was for me my thoughts turned to Christ and what he experienced in the Garden of Gethsemane atoning for my sins. He knew exactly how painful and difficult that experience would be for him far before going through with it. He knew he was going to be betrayed by a close friend, he knew he would experience extreme pain and discomfort, and he knew that he would ultimately die. As he entered the garden he prayed to God saying "Father, if thou be willing, remove this cup from me, nevertheless, not my will, but thine, be done." When I read those words I feel like he was dreading the upcoming experience so much and wanted to escape, but was ultimately willing to go through with it because he knew it needed to be done.

I don't want to compare myself and my experiences to Christ and his because I know what I went through was relatively nothing compared to what he went through. But I do feel like through my experience, I came to a small understanding of some of what Christ suffered. I understood what it was like to endure that internal struggle of making yourself go through with something even though you so badly want to escape it.

This meant a lot to me because it gave me such a huge appreciation for what he did for me. I understood in a way, how hard it must have been for him to go through with such an overwhelming task. I know he did it because of the love that he has for us. Having to go through with the amputation, in a way, gave me this unique understanding and love for Christ that I probably wouldn't have been able to achieve in otherwise.

32 RECOVERY

The afternoon after surgery the nurses came in and told us, "Ok, it's time to go home!" None of us could believe it. We were told that we should expect to be in the hospital for three or four days and they were kicking us out after only one. They had removed the nerve block from my leg only a couple hours ago and I had just barely got the pain under control with oral meds. I was scared to death to leave! What if I got home and they pain pills didn't work the way they were supposed to? The pain had already gotten out of control once and it was horrible. What if that happened at home and there were no nurses around to fix it? They promised everything would be fine and said we needed to go. So they rolled me out in a wheelchair, loaded me into the car, and we drove home.

It was a little scary at first being home. The pain killers worked fine but now we were in charge of changing out the dressing around my stump of a leg. Luckily, Kelly was still into all of the nursing stuff and she immediately volunteered for the job. It was ugly though. My stump was swollen to about twice its normal size and all kinds of nasty stuff was oozing from the incision. We had to change the dressing and clean it once a day for about a week or two. After a few days of being home I had to start putting on these shrinker socks that my prosthetist had given me. A shrinker sock is a sock-looking thing that goes over the end of the stump and up the rest of the leg. It is made to be really tight so that it can force out fluids to reduce swelling and size. Wearing the sock helps the limb shrink to a stable size so that it can be fitted for a prosthetic. It's really important to wear a shrinker sock because you want to be able to get away from the crutches and walk as soon as possible. But as you can imagine, wrapping a very tight sock around a very tender and swollen incision is not the most comfortable thing in the world. In fact it's really painful. I would cringe every time we forced that thing on. With time though, it became bearable.

The pain from the incision wasn't the only pain that I had to deal with after the surgery. I had another type of pain. One that everybody is always asking me about… phantom pain. Yes, it is real. It can be really annoying. Actually, for me, I would call it more of a phantom sensation. I have pain from it here and there, but for the most part it is just a weird tingling feeling. It is almost like when your foot falls asleep and you have the pins and needles feeling, except not quite as intense. I noticed it immediately after I woke up from the surgery. Except that while I was in the hospital, all of the medicine that numbed the pain also reduced the intensity of the tingling feeling. It felt like my leg was still there even though it wasn't. It was the weirdest thing. I could feel every little part of my leg but I couldn't move it. It was locked in a bent position as if the ankle and knee were both bent at 90 degrees. It still feels like it's stuck in that same position today. When I laid in bed it felt like it was hanging down under the bed and when I sat in the floor it felt like it was under the ground. It was such a strange feeling.

During recovery the sensation became a real nuisance. It seems like the swelling and the damage to the nerves from the surgery made the sensation really intense and often caused different types of pain. No matter what I did, my foot always felt like pins and needles were being poked into it. Nothing would make it to go away. On top of the pins and needles feeling, every once in a while, maybe ten or twenty times a day I would get really random pains in my non-existent leg. It usually felt like a really strong electric shock, a calf or foot cramp, or like I was being stabbed with a knife or something. Those random pains would usually come on so strong and suddenly that they would make me jump or sometimes shout out in pain. Luckily they typically only lasted less than ten seconds or so. But still, they were really annoying to deal with. Over time, as my limb healed and swelling went down, the pains and sensations became less and less intense. I still have the tingling feeling today, but I have gotten so used to it that I usually don't even notice it. I consider myself really lucky because lots of amputees have phantom pains that never go away and torment them for the rest of their lives.

Right when I got home from the hospital I spent most of my time laying around on the couch in front of the TV. I tried to move as little as possible because every time I moved it would make my stump start to hurt. The pain killers worked all right but I still dealt with a considerable amount of pain. Luckily my brother and sisters were still in town for a few more days. Otherwise we would have been really bored sitting around the house by ourselves. A good friend of mine gave me a Nintendo Wii that he had laying around his house. It was the perfect thing to entertain Nick and I since there wasn't much I could do.

Now that the operation was over and my leg was officially gone, I began to see all of the inconveniences that come along with becoming an amputee. Probably the most annoying one is that I had to rely on crutches for everything. To get around the house I could either hop on one foot, push myself around in a rolling office chair, or use crutches. I hate crutches but they beat the alternatives at the time. Having to use crutches makes everything so much more time consuming. Things like going in and out of the house and getting in and out of the car all of a sudden required so many more steps. Plus, I couldn't carry anything on my own. I had to rely on others for so many things. It was really hard to suddenly lose so much of my independence. I loved my independence and now I felt like it had been taken away from me. It humbled me to rely on somebody else any time I needed to carry something. I always felt so bad for having to ask for everything. I was beginning to see how difficult being an amputee would really be. With lots of practice I eventually got better at using crutches. Now I can do all kinds of stuff with them. I can even carry things up and down stairs. Being able to do more with them has helped me gain back some of the independence that I felt I had lost.

All of the physical aspects of the recovery were fairly easy to get through. For the most part I just needed to suck it up and deal with the pain and all of the newly found daily inconveniences. It was really just a matter of patience and endurance, two things that I had gotten to be pretty good at over the past few months. The physical recovery was a piece of cake compared to the emotional challenges that I had to overcome. It has been two years now and I'm still dealing with weird mental issues from losing my leg. And I consider myself to be doing pretty well compared to some of the stories that I have heard about other amputees. Losing a limb takes such an emotional and mental toll that it takes a long time to recover from it.

One of the first emotional issues that I dealt with as an amputee was feeling embarrassed or ashamed of myself in front of people that I already knew. For whatever reason, I felt like people that I knew were thinking "How could you let this happen to you." Deep down I knew that losing my leg was in no way my fault but I still felt like I was responsible for letting my life and my physical body waste away like it had. I think it might have been because my life had changed so drastically in such a short amount of time. I went from having everything going for me to being sick all the time and now physically handicapped. It was a really depressing feeling.

I first felt this way around Kelly, but it didn't last long because she was so genuinely accepting of me since the moment I woke up from surgery. I could see in her eyes that she absolutely did not care that I was different. It took a little longer to get over that feeling while being around my family. But after a few days of them acting completely normal around me the feeling faded and I felt accepted for who I was. The same process took place with close friends. It's like I had to be around them long enough to feel that they were genuinely accepting of me. I still struggle with this feeling every once in a while today. Whenever I run into somebody I haven't seen since before the surgery the same feelings of shame and embarrassment return. I don't know if I'll ever fully get over that feeling. It might just be something that I have to deal with the rest of my life.

As I recovered physically, I gained greater strength and mobility and I was able to go out into public more often. Going out in public was strangely exciting. It's probably because it was just a good change of scenery from the inside of our town home and my parent's house. The problem was that going out in public and being around strangers created a whole separate set of mental anxieties that I had to deal with.

The first time I really went out in public and was surrounded by strangers was just a few weeks after the surgery. Kelly's good friend from high school was getting married and we drove to San Antonio to attend the wedding. I had been out in public before, but never around more than just a couple of strangers at a time. This was going to be entirely different. There were going to be people everywhere. I was scared to death but I had promised Kelly that I would go with her.

As we pulled up to the wedding I nervously got out of the car and started crutching my way over to the building where the event was being held. I could see the crowds of people standing around waiting for the reception to start. It was my first time to be around so many people and I was anxious to see how they would react to me having only one leg. As we got closer I noticed a group of kids running around the outside of the building. As I watched them play, all of a sudden one of them stopped and stared at me. Then he tugged on his friend's shirt and pointed at me to get him to look. They both sat there and stared in complete shock with dropped jaws for a few seconds and then ran off to show me to their other friends that they were playing with. In no time I had drawn the attention of a group of kids staring and pointing, and an embarrassed father who was trying to get them to stop.

I know that the kids didn't know any better, but their reaction towards me was completely devastating. The way they all stared and pointed at me made me feel like I wasn't even human. I was just a freak object to be gawked at. It hurt my feelings more than anything else in my life that I can remember. I tried to be tough and act like it didn't bother me, but the tears eventually started forming in my eyes and I had to run inside the empty reception hall to hide. I was afraid for anybody else to see me. I sat at a table back in a dark corner and tried to hide my leg the rest of the night. When Kelly was finally ready to leave we tried to sneak out while everybody was distracted by wedding stuff. I rushed straight back to the car, eager to remove myself from any chance of another painfully humiliating situation.

That experience really scared me. It took me about a week before I was able to get over it enough to even leave the house again. I just wanted to stay inside and hide from anybody that might make me feel like I was a monster. I had to get used to it though because those kinds of experiences ended up happening all of the time.

For example, one time Kelly and I were sitting in a McDonalds when a mother and her three kids walked in. As soon as the kids noticed me they stopped walking, their jaws dropped and they just stood there and stared. None of them said a word. When their mom noticed what her kids were doing she tried to get them to stop staring and keep walking. She tugged at their arms, almost pulling them off of their feet before they would take their eyes off me. The mom tried to apologize to me and explain to her kids that what they were doing wasn't polite. But that wasn't the worst part. The worst part was that everybody else that was standing around noticed what was going on too. They were all watching the whole incident; amused by the kids' awkward response and interested in how the mother and I would react to the whole situation.

I really hated these all too common incidents. Every time kids stared at me with their jaws dropped open it was like I could almost read what was going through their little minds... "What the heck is wrong with that guy?" I didn't like being looked at like I was a freak. I didn't like drawing people's attention. And I didn't like being the center of awkward situations. All of this kind of stuff hurt my feelings and made me feel like I was some kind of monster or something. On top of that, it really embarrassed me to have people treat me that way.

One of the worst things was that I felt so sorry for Kelly. I was embarrassed for her. She was the one who was married to the freak. She had to deal with this kind of attention all of the time. When we were together I always felt like people were thinking "Man, what is that cute girl doing with that one legged guy?" I don't know how she does it, but she has never showed any sign of being embarrassed of me. She is so strong to be able to deal with these kinds of issues and never let it get to her. Again, I don't know how I would have made it this far without her.

Once I finally recovered from the wedding incident and started to go out in public more often, I really started to notice how much strangers looked at me and treated me differently. The kids would just blatantly stare and the adults would glance and try not to let me see them looking. It really made me feel awkward and kind of humiliated to see people looking at me that way.

I think these types of feelings all came from the way that I had previously felt about people who were different than me. Before, when I saw an amputee, or anybody with any kind of physical problem for that matter, I would look at them and think "I would hate to be like that" or even "Man, that's weird looking." I would feel awkward around them and almost avoid them because I didn't know how I was supposed to act. I probably thought and acted that way just because they were different from me.

Well, now, all of a sudden I was one of "those people." And if I had those kinds of thoughts about other people with physical problems then for sure other people would be thinking them about me. Deep down I know that not everybody thinks that way, but still, knowing that those kinds of thought processes exist, I had to assume that some people were thinking it about me. For all I knew, everybody could be looking at me and thinking that way, even if they showed no signs of it. I didn't want people to look at me differently. I just wanted them to look at me and see me for who I was instead of just thinking of me as that weird looking one legged guy.

Being so different from everyone else and always getting looks and weird reactions from everybody really affected me during that time in my life. I tried to avoid going out in public and hid my stump as much as possible when I did. I didn't like being embarrassed and getting my feelings hurt so frequently. Going about any kind of normal life was really emotionally and mentally exhausting. There were many nights where I broke down and cried to Kelly about how hard things were. I just wanted to be a normal person again. I wanted to be able to go through life without physical limitations and without standing out because I was different looking. I missed my leg so much. I missed my good friend! But it was never coming back. I knew that I had to just move on and try to overcome these challenges as best as I could.

I was convinced that my happiness in life was something that I could control with my attitude and choices. I wasn't going to let myself get depressed or go through life feeling sorry for myself. I was determined to overcome all of the physical, mental, and emotional challenges that I had to face, no matter how difficult they were. Having a strong will and determination didn't make my challenges any easier to overcome. Recovering from the surgery has been one of the longest and most difficult processes that I have ever had to go through. For the time being though, I just had to be patient and move on with life and try to be as optimistic about the future as possible.

33 BACK TO CHEMO COCKTAIL #2

Somehow, after all that I had been through with the surgery I felt excited to get back to chemotherapy. The hard part of my whole treatment plan was over. My leg was gone and all I had to do now to be done with cancer was to finish the last eight rounds of chemo. It also helped that we were told that the new type of chemo that I was getting would be a little easier to go through than the extremely intense regimen that I had before. It was called high-dose Ifosfamide and I only had to complete four rounds of it. After that I was supposed to move on and do four rounds of an even easier chemo called Irinotecan. I was eager to get started so that I could eventually move on with my life and be as far away from hospitals as possible.

Unfortunately, the high-dose Ifosfamide regimen was only barely easier than the first chemo cocktail that I went through. It was such a disappointment! I still had to stay in the hospital about the same amount of time as the first regimen. Each day in the hospital they gave me two bags spaced twelve hours apart. The progression of my symptoms was about the same as the first chemo regimen I went through. Day one was fairly easy, day two was a little worse, and so on until the day I was released. When I finally got to leave the hospital I was still just as physically drained and chemo-brained as before except with this regimen, the nausea was slightly more tolerable.

The improved nausea was a major plus, but there were all kinds of other crazy side effects that I had to deal with. Some of them I had experienced before, but others were completely new to me. With this chemo I quickly learned that my doctor's main concern was me getting neurotoxicity. Neurotoxicity could include anything from difficulty focusing to hallucinations. They weren't too worried about it being a long term side effect because they had an antidote that worked quickly to turn patients back to normal. The reason this gave them concern was because the patient could accidentally hurt themselves.

I was fortunate enough to not have any major problems with neurotoxicity, although it might have been cool to see what hallucinations are actually like. I did, however, have all kinds of other weird stuff happen to me.

Most · of my neurotoxicity side effects involved my inability to concentrate and focus on things. Early in the treatment it was mainly just difficult to focus on what people were saying to me. But after a couple of days it was almost impossible to hold a conversation. It was like somebody was pushing the reset button on my brain every five seconds. Every time my brain blanked out I had to think about what was just happening or what was barely said to me. After remembering what was going on I would only have a few seconds to respond before everything spaced out again. It was really weird and is difficult to fully explain. By my last night of chemo my whole body was nearly shutting down. I was almost completely unable to hold a conversation and my whole body was starting to twitch. Almost every time the reset button was pushed it was like all of my muscles went weak for a split second. This made it difficult to hold on to things and even to stand up on my own.

The neurotoxicity was kind of funny at first because my conversations wouldn't make much sense and I did a lot of dumb stuff. Kelly and I would laugh because sometimes she would ask me questions and I would just stare at her blankly, having forgotten that she had asked me something. After dealing with this for a while I started to feel really bad for Kelly and anybody else who visited me because I was really unable to converse much. It must have been especially frustrating for Kelly to stay in the hospital the whole time and not have me mentally there to keep her company. By the end of the round it got scary to start to lose control of my body. Luckily, the chemo completely wiped me out physically and I was able to sleep through most of the side effects.

Probably the most annoying thing about these rounds was the fact that I had to go through it all with one leg. Trying to push an IV stand around while on crutches isn't easy to do. And every time I had to get up to walk around I had to have Kelly next to me to hold the IV stand and make sure that I didn't fall over or anything. It was also annoying to get up to go to the bathroom with the crutches and IV stand, so I ended having to pee in the urinal bottles, which was pretty humiliating. By the end of each round I wasn't even able to go on the crutches much because I was kind of losing control of my muscles. It became dangerous for me to get up out of bed. Dealing with all of these issues always made me eager to get out of the hospital as soon as I could.

After getting home from the hospital I seemed to recover faster compared to my first six rounds. The nausea cleared up more quickly and my energy returned sooner. It was always good to be at home. But after about a week my blood counts would drop, I would have to worry about getting infections, and I would need blood and platelet transfusions. This chemo was particularly hard on my platelets which resulted in me having to go back in for lots of transfusions.

Some rounds I needed more transfusions than others. Some rounds I needed to be admitted for fever. Some rounds were extremely miserable, and some were relatively easy. Each round I went through I experienced something different and learned new things. I was beginning to see that it was all part of a process that was transforming me and making me an overall better person than I was before.

34 ROUND 7: JUNE 5, 2009

Starting this round of chemo was different than the others. I felt like I was on my way to getting my normal life back. I was up for the physical and mental challenge and ready to get going. There were definitely a few things that I was really dreading. Most of them were things like being sick all of the time, worrying about fever, etc. But probably the main thing I dreaded was losing my hair and, more importantly, my eyebrows again. They had grown back in while I was recovering from surgery and I loved having them. It made me feel like a normal person again. Sadly though, having them fall out again was completely unavoidable.

The week before starting round seven was pretty hectic. We drove up to Dallas for Laura's graduation from medical school. We had a great time despite my having to crutch around in a suit with my pant leg tucked into my back pocket (which was always humiliating). We stayed the night in Dallas and then rushed back to Houston the next morning for Whitney's high school graduation. Right after the ceremony ended, Kelly and I rushed over to the hospital to be admitted. It was stressful, but at the same time, helpful in keeping my mind off of the doom that awaited me.

After arriving and waiting to get started we found out that my surgeon wanted the stitches from my amputation removed before I received any chemo. They weren't quite ready to come out, which made it pretty painful, but we had to do it in order to stay on track with my treatment schedule. The stitches were removed, the chemo was initiated, and the torture began.

This round of chemo turned out to be probably the worst hospital stay I have ever had. I don't know what the deal was, but my phantom pains were driving me absolutely crazy. I think it must have been related to my stump swelling from all of the fluids they were pumping in me. Whatever it was, it was horrible! The normal tingling feeling turned into an extremely annoying sensation that was like my whole foot was being stabbed over and over again by thousands of needles. It was relentless and never stopped the whole time I was there. It kept me from sleeping at nights and pestered me during the days. Sleeping pills couldn't even overpower the phantom pain at night. By the end of the round I was so miserable. I had never experienced anything like it. I was more exhausted than I had ever been yet I was unable to sleep. It was almost like my fatigue turned into some sort of weird pain that wouldn't go away.

Apart from the sleeping problem, almost every time I sat up in my bed or stood up to walk around I would get these hiccup spells that would last for like 20 minutes. It was fine at first, but after having the hiccups for what seemed like three days straight, it started to drive me insane.

The hiccups, the phantom pain, and all of the other typical chemo side effects were just about as much as I could handle. By my last day I was so anxious to get out of there that I think I got up and stood at the nurse's desk and bugged them until they finished everything they had to do to let me go.

Recovering at home was pretty normal except for the new challenges that I had to deal with from only having one leg. Probably the biggest challenge was trying to make it to the bathroom and back at night while being dizzy and weak from the chemo. It was an extreme balancing act every time.

During my good week I spent a lot of my time at the prosthetic center trying to get fit for my prosthetic. Being fit is a long ordeal. First measurements of the stump have to be taken. After that, they make a cast of the stump, which is then turned into a "test socket." The test socket is tried on and adjustments are made to try to improve the fit. This step is repeated several times until the socket fits just right.

The test socket is then used to make a final carbon-fiber socket that will attach to the rest of the prosthetic leg. After the leg is attached all kinds of adjustments are made until the amputee is able to walk comfortably.

This week I went in to get cast for the socket. What an experience! I wasn't expecting to be stripped down to my underwear, dressed in strange tights, and to have plaster smeared all over my stump and up in my crotch. Luckily, my experiences from having cancer had nearly stripped me of all of my dignity so it wasn't really that big of a deal. Kelly of course, was on hand with her camera and made sure to get some embarrassing pictures of me in my weird tights. I always loved that she was able to laugh with me instead of being embarrassed by me.

That round, Kelly and I celebrated our second anniversary together. I was almost as bad at anniversaries as I was at Valentine's Days. Somehow though, I pulled this one off without her getting annoyed at me or anything. It was great! I think it helped that it fell on my good week and I was able to think straight enough to at least have some preparations. By far, Kelly's food of choice is beef. She particularly loves steak. So I took her out to a steak house and after that we just went home and hung out together. Not too romantic, but nice and simple, just how she likes it.

It was around this time in my life that about everybody I knew was aware that I had cancer and had heard through the grapevine about how miserable my treatments were. Everybody else could tell that I had been through hard times by noticing that I didn't have a leg. Well, it began to seem like lots of people had questions about what my whole experience was like. They didn't seem to care about all of my physical side effects as much as they did about my emotional and spiritual well-being. People would ask me all kinds of things, but probably the most common were "How do you stay so positive?" and "Do you ever ask yourself 'why me?'" At first I just responded with simple things, but after being asked so many times I started to really search my mind to find real answers. But finding answers to these questions was harder than it seemed. In fact, I still don't quite know the answers.

The simple answer to the "Do you ever ask yourself 'why me?'" question was easy. Yes. Of course I ask myself "Why me?" I think everybody who has ever had cancer has asked themselves that. Looking at it from a purely temporal point of view, I think "Why not me?" Cancer is just a natural thing that happens to some people. Statistically, it is bound to happen to someone, so why should I feel that it should be somebody else instead of me? Looking at the question from a spiritual point of view however, makes it much more challenging to answer. Knowing that God is in charge of my life and that I could have been healed, but wasn't, created a whole new set of questions, like "Why did God allow this to happen to me? Is it just part of God's plan for me that I get cancer? If it is, what is the purpose of me getting cancer?" I'm constantly trying to find answers to these questions, but I don't think I will get complete ones until I move on to the other side. So, until then, I just have to have faith in the fact that God does have a plan for me and that everything will work out in the end no matter what the outcome is… much easier said than done.

To the "How do you stay so positive?" question, I have to say that it is mainly my choice. I can think back on times in high school when I was going through some rough patches and I let it get to me. I felt angry, depressed, frustrated, annoyed, and almost every other negative emotion there was. Then one day I realized how miserable it was to be in a bad mood. I hated feeling that way. From then on I tried to control my emotions a little more. It was on my mission however, after I learned that I could choose how to let things affect me that I really started to manage my attitude. Ever since then I have always tried to maintain a positive, happy attitude because it makes me feel better inside. I always try to at least put on a smile for people because I enjoy making others feel happy. Somebody once told me that nobody likes being around people who don't ever smile. After hearing that, I tried to make it a habit to smile more around others. I have found that smiling has the ability to make others happier. I try to be nice to everybody and smile to help improve their day and to help to minimize any hard times that I might be going through.

35 ROUND 8: JUNE 26, 2009

Just a couple of days before going in for round eight my precious hair started to fall out pretty fast. I needed to do something about it so that it didn't fall out all over the house. I didn't want to shave it because the roots stay in your head and dry out and turn into little tiny spikes that make it painful to touch. So we decided to pull out the good old duct tape to see if it could help. And man, did it work well! I stuck a strip down the middle of my head and had Kelly rip it off. Almost all of the hair came off in one swipe. We laughed about it and took pictures and then finished the rest of my head. It was nice and smooth. I definitely recommend it to anybody going through chemo whose hair is about to fall out. Now that I had a nice, smooth head, I was ready to go back in for another round of chemo.

The hospital stay of round eight ended up being pretty uneventful except that they put us on a nicer side of the hospital that had puzzles and games in the hallways for patients and visitors to use. That was fun until my brain started shutting down and I was unable to put any puzzle pieces together. Oh, there was one out of the ordinary thing that happened while we were there. I think one of our nurses was busy or lazy or something because she wouldn't empty my urinals very often. So I just kept filling up the same one more and more until she would come in to empty it. Well, there was one time where it was pretty full and because of my mental shutdowns, I thought it would be a good idea to set it on the counter. Well, somehow my crutches got knocked over and they spilled almost an entire liter of pee all over the place. It was disgusting. I was so mentally out of it that all I could do was sit there and stare at it as it spread across the floor. I felt so bad for Kelly as I blankly watched her clean up the mess I had made. I think she got pretty mad at me too, but I was too messed up to even really care. It was a bad experience but funny to look back on.

While in the hospital I suffered through the typical side effects of the chemo that I was on. Like always, I was thrilled to be able to return home again. My time at home, however, was cut short by a stay in the hospital to treat a fever that had sprung up. Once my fever went away and my counts had recovered I was free to go home for my good week.

The main item on my to-do list for my good week was to get my prosthetic and start learning how to walk. I went in several times to have the test sockets fitted and adjusted, which was an extremely uncomfortable experience. An above the knee prosthetic is designed so that most of the weight is supported by one of the bones in your butt. So in order to make sure it fit right, the prosthetist had to shove his fingers all over my crotch and butt. As you can imagine, it wasn't very comfortable. After several tries, they got it right and went to work on making my final prosthetic leg.

When they handed over my final prosthetic, my engineering side kicked in and I couldn't help to think of how amazing it was. It just seemed so cool that a piece of technology was able to replace my other leg and allow me to regain some of my mobility. I couldn't wait to get started on learning how to use it.

Well, my excitement was short-lived because once I actually put the thing on, I realized how uncomfortable and painful it was to try to walk. I could only wear the thing for like ten minutes at a time before the pain was too much to take. Plus, it was super frustrating because when I walked it looked really strange. I limped a lot and swung my foot way out to the side and nearly fell on my face every other step I took. I realized that learning to walk would be a long and painful process.

It was around this time that the work at Fluor was really starting to dry up. I always asked them for things to do to show that I was still interested in helping out, but there was really nothing to do. One of the young guys my age had already left to find another job. Another young guy was left with all of the work, and if they started giving me things to do then they would have to let him go. So they just told me to keep on hiding out on my disability. By this time I was so wrapped up in the intensity of my treatments that I was perfectly fine with not having any work to do, so I gladly followed their instructions. Since I wasn't ever able to come in we decided to all get together every three weeks for lunch to hang out and talk about what was happening in the engineering world. I always had a good time going out with them, even when I didn't have an appetite.

Sometime during round eight Kelly started taking the nursing pre-requisite classes so that she could apply to nursing programs in the fall. It made me so happy that she was working towards finishing her degree and that she had finally found something that she enjoyed doing. But it turned out that I didn't like it so much when she was gone for classes. I kind of felt like a wuss at the time for it, but I really started to miss her when she was gone. It was the weirdest thing for me. I mean, I have always loved Kelly, but I had never missed her like that. It started to seem like every time she got home my face would light up and I would go hug her and not want to let go, even if she was only gone for a couple of hours.

It was around that time that I first started to notice that my relationship with her was starting to change. I had grown so much closer to her because of the rough experiences that we went through. It seemed like I constantly wanted to be with her. She just made me so happy and helped me to feel so loved by being so accepting of me and always helping me. I also started to look at her differently. All of the amazing qualities in her just stood out all of the time and all of the things about her that I didn't like so much were forgotten. I was starting to realize how incredibly amazing my wife and best friend actually was.

36 ROUND 9: JULY 17, 2009

This round my stay in the hospital landed right on Kelly's birthday. I felt so bad because we celebrated her last birthday stuck in a minivan driving home from Utah. This time we were going to celebrate it in a tiny, depressing hospital room. I remembered during my last good week that it was going to be her birthday and I was able to go out and buy her some presents. But I don't think I could have gotten her anything to fix the fact that she had to hang out in a hospital most of the day. Thankfully, she was able to escape to go to dinner for a couple of hours with her girlfriends.

I think once she got back from dinner with her friends she had to get to studying. Her classes were keeping her pretty busy and she usually used all of her down time in the hospital to study. When I was too out of it to really hold a conversation, she would just pull out her books and get all of her school work out of the way. It worked out perfectly. It seemed like this turned into the new routine for us. I slept in the hospital room while she had her nose buried in the books.

When I got home from the hospital and my blood counts recovered I went straight to working on learning how to walk. My body was starting to get used to the prosthetic. I could wear it for longer periods of time and it wasn't as painful. I was even starting to get a little better at making it look more normal when I walked. Things were coming along just fine, except for the fact that I would still stub my toe and almost fall all of the time. I also had to walk with a cane, which made me feel kind of funny considering the fact that older people are usually the people with canes.

For the most part I only wore my prosthetic around the house and would practice walking up and down the street. I still didn't feel completely comfortable going out in public with it, especially considering that I looked a little funny when I walked. I didn't really know what kind of reaction I would get from people and I was scared to find out.

There was one night when Kelly needed to go up to the mall for something and she wanted me to go with her. I didn't really want to go, but considering how attached I was to her, I was easily convinced to go along. I was nervous about how people would react. I expected them to all look at me funny, but to my surprise, everybody seemed pretty normal. There were lots of people that would look down at my prosthetic with a look on their face like "That's interesting." But they would only look for a split second and then move on with their business. It was comforting to me that normal people weren't going to treat me like the little kids did when I didn't have my prosthetic.

There were a few minutes while we were in the store that Kelly went into a dressing room to try things on. While she was in there I had the strangest experience. It was almost like an epiphany or something. I stood there in the back corner of the store and watched everybody move around looking at clothes and different items. They were all looking for new clothes that would make them look nice. As I watched, I started to think to myself "I'm not like these people anymore." I used to enjoy getting new clothes every once in a while so that I could look nice. But now, I could really care less about how I dressed. I didn't care about going through the trouble to find clothes to make me look a certain way. Being wrapped up in any type of materialistic stuff just seemed like such a waste of precious time and energy to me. But to everybody else, it was normal to be materialistic to some degree. At that moment I realized that I had changed and that I was different than everybody else. I had bigger issues to worry about than all of the stuff that everybody gets so wrapped up in. I was fighting just to stay alive. Everything else just seemed so unimportant.

Now, sometimes I wish people would realize how unimportant most of the stuff they do really is. I wish they could see the world the way I see it. People would spend more time with loved ones, they would be less self-centered, more desirous to help others, and spend more time doing good things to make this world a better place. Unfortunately, I think it takes something horrible like cancer for people to be able to reach the point of view that I have.

The lease on our town home ended sometime during this round and Kelly and I decided that it would be best if we moved out of the town home and into my parent's house for a while. We didn't like the idea of living with parents and losing our independence, but my medical expenses were high and my disability check had recently been reduced. We had to pull from savings each month and we didn't know how long we would be able to last until we ran out of money. If we moved into my parent's house we could save a little each month and try to build up for a down payment on a house when we were completely done with all of this cancer stuff. So at the end of the round we gathered some friends together and made the move. We put most of our stuff into a storage unit and moved into the upstairs of my parent's house. Living there ended up not being so bad. It was nice to have other people around to help take care of me and my mom was a really good cook. Plus we had plenty of space and even a nice pool in the back yard to hang out in. There wasn't too much to complain about.

37 ROUND 10: AUG 7, 2009

Somehow we had finally made it to round ten. I didn't think we would ever get here, but we did. Round ten was the last inpatient round that we would have to do. We couldn't wait to have this one over with so that we wouldn't have to spend any more nights in the hospital.

Unfortunately, though, it was a pretty rough round. I think sometime during the round we spilled another bottle of pee, and by the last night my neurotoxicity got so bad that I was having all kinds of problems. My muscles were twitching so bad that when I would stand up next to the bed to pee in the urinal my legs would nearly give out. There were a couple of times that I almost completely fell over. Kelly got mad at me every time I stood up next to the bed because she thought I might fall. Plus, my brain was really starting to have issues. I could still understand when people were talking to me, but sometimes they would have to repeat questions several times for me to answer. One time the nurse came in and asked me a bunch of questions to check out how bad I was. The first one was "Do you know where you are?" I replied "I'm in the stupid hospital" and then we all started laughing because it appeared like I was fine. But then he asked me questions like "What's eight times five?" I know that I know what eight times five is, but for some reason I couldn't think of it. I had to say "Umm... I don't know?" It was really weird. My brain was giving out on me and I didn't even realize it. Fortunately, I had already received my last bag of chemo and returned back to normal the next morning.

That last morning, before we were about to leave, one of the nurses came into my room and said they needed me for something. I thought "Oh great, now what?" I just wanted to get out of there and never return, except maybe to visit the friends I had made. I crutched over to the nurses' office and they were all in there with a big box of delicious looking cupcakes to celebrate my last inpatient round. We had become good friends and they all made me feel so loved. Unfortunately though, all I could do was smile and say "Man, I wish I didn't feel like throwing up right now." We all hung out for a few minutes and everybody but me ate cupcakes.

It was sad to say goodbye to everybody but it was so easy to leave because of how much we hated the hospital. We hugged, said goodbyes, and took off. It felt good to finally be done with that place. I was looking forward to never having to sleep in one of those little rooms again. But, sadly, I ended up getting a fever and had to go back in for a few more days until my counts recovered. So we said our goodbyes again and left for good.

On my good week I worked more at walking. I was pretty much to the point that I could wear the prosthetic almost all day long without it giving me too much pain. It was always kind of uncomfortable to wear, but I was getting used to that too. I still walked a little funny and had to use a cane to help me, but I was gaining lots of confidence. I didn't really care about what people thought anymore either. I went out into public all of the time and sometimes even enjoyed the responses that people gave me. Instead of being offended, I started to laugh when the kids would just sit there and stare at my leg in complete confusion. I loved the freedom that I felt with the prosthetic. I was able to get around more and do things that I couldn't do without it. It made me feel like I was slowly getting my life back.

Wearing the prosthetic more often also gave me lots of embarrassing experiences. I was always stubbing my toe on the ground. And every time I stubbed the toe I would have to jump with my good leg to keep from falling over. It usually looked pretty funny and it would happen all of the time. People never noticed that my toe got stubbed. They would just see me hop up and hold my arms out to balance myself. They must have wondered at what in the world I was doing.

There was one thing that I did that was really embarrassing. One night my friends from work called me up and asked me to go to the driving range with them to hit some golf balls. Before cancer, I had played several times and enjoyed it, but I always gave all of the other sports top priority because I was better at them. Now I wanted to get good at golf because I felt like it was the only sport left that I could really be competitive in. I was excited to get out and give it a try with my new prosthetic.

The driving range was packed that night. There were people everywhere. After setting up I took a few practice swings and it felt really awkward. I couldn't rotate my waist very well, I couldn't pivot on my prosthetic foot, and my balance was all messed up. Regardless, I started hitting away. The first one wasn't too bad, or the second, or the third. My friends, who weren't golfers at all, started to joke around about how I was hitting better than they were. I felt good. I was hitting the balls nice and straight and I was gaining a lot of confidence. I was starting to think "I could get to be pretty good if I came out and practiced all of the time." I was excited because I could really see myself getting into it. Right when I was starting to really feel comfortable, I took a swing and the knee joint on my prosthetic buckled and I collapsed to the ground right in front of everybody.

I was so humiliated, but at the same time, could visualize what it must have looked like to see some one-legged guy collapse on the golf course. All I could really do was laugh. I had never fallen before and didn't know how to get up off of the ground, so I had to have my friend help me up so I could finish hitting the rest of the balls in my bucket. It was such an embarrassing experience and brought me back to the reality of my new life as a handicap. I would probably fall again. In fact, this could be something that happens quite often. I might just have to get used people looking and laughing at me all the time.

Not too long after, as I looked back on that horribly embarrassing experience, I began to realize that I had gone through all kinds of humiliating experiences because of my cancer. They were experiences that had changed me in ways that probably nothing else would. I made a chronological list of all of the major ones that stood out to me the most.

My humility experiences:

- Taking crutches to work every day and not having a good explanation for it
- Getting drop foot and having to walk goofy in public
- Losing all of my hair
- Getting so constipated from the chemo that I needed help and support from my whole family
- Discussing my bowel movements with anybody and everybody in the hospital
- Showing a rash that formed in my crotch to half a dozen doctors
- Going to the bathroom in a plastic bowl knowing that my nurse friends would have to dig through it for sampling
- Getting a scrotum scan to be checked for testicular cancer
- Looking like an alien because my eyelashes and eyebrows had fallen out.
- Losing my leg (100 times worse than everything else combined)
- Having my butt and groin repeatedly groped by my prosthetist
- Kids pointing and staring at me because I don't have a leg
- Standing in the mall for the first time with my prosthetic realizing I was forever different from everybody else.
- Collapsing in front of everybody at a crowded driving range

Each of these experiences was uniquely unpleasant and chiseled away at my pride. I wouldn't say that I was too prideful before I got cancer, but I definitely had some issues that needed to be worked on. For the most part I knew that I wasn't a big deal, and that there wasn't much that was special about me, but I was proud of my degree in mechanical engineering and I probably let it get to my head too much. I thought I was a lot smarter than I actually was and I tried to make sure that other people knew that I was smart. In that process I probably annoyed a lot of people, especially my friends. I also thought I was pretty cool for making more money than most of my friends. I intentionally acted this way because I always kept my finances private between Kelly and myself, but it still got to me inside. It made me feel almost like I was better than others, even though I knew that I had just lucked out with a great job.

These issues definitely needed to be ironed out. But like anybody, it's hard to throw out pride without some kind of experience to compel you. The things that I went through definitely pushed me way further than I wanted, but they got the job done. I have been humbled more than I ever could have imagined. Now, I know I'm not that smart, I could care less about how much money I make, and I don't even use my degree. Plus I've been humbled in so many other ways as well. As a result of this I am more happy and satisfied with everything in my life. I am more grateful for everything I have. Contemplating these positive changes in my life made me realize that once again, the horrible experiences that have come along with my cancer have improved my life in ways that wouldn't have been possible otherwise.

38 THIS IS CHEMO? PIECE OF CAKE!
COCKTAIL #3

I couldn't believe it; I was finally done with all of the rounds of inpatient chemotherapy. I could almost taste the finish line. All I had to do now was four easy rounds of outpatient chemo. Kelly and I were thrilled because instead of having to spend days in the hospital we could just go to the doctor's office for treatment. Plus, the chemo wasn't even supposed to be that bad.

The new drug that I was going to be getting was called Irinotecan, nick-named "I run to the can" because of the unstoppable diarrhea that it is known to cause. Instead of getting it infused daily for a several days straight like the other cocktails, I only had to go in once a week for two or three hours, two weeks in a row. After my two weeks of treatment I would take a week off, which would complete the round. I only had to do four rounds like this and then I would be finished.

The biggest side effect of this chemo is by far the diarrhea. I was told that it would be pretty bad, but I figured I would have no problem dealing with it, considering all of my experience with it in Mexico. It wasn't supposed to knock my blood counts down either, which meant no more going in for blood transfusions. It wasn't supposed to cause much nausea, chemo-brain, fatigue, dizziness, or neurotoxicity. It just sounded like it was going to be a piece of cake and I was ready to get it over with.

39 ROUND 11: AUG 31, 2009

The first thing we noticed as we pulled into the parking garage for my first day of treatment was the fact that parking was only five dollars a day instead of twelve dollars a day. We were thrilled because parking at the other hospital was really putting a dent in our savings. We were so excited to be able to do the last four rounds outside of a hospital. We went up to the doctor's office to get started and instead of being stuck in a tiny room with a bed, I was put in an open area with a big comfy recliner.

They hooked me up and I sat and read and talked with Kelly while I was waiting for the bag to finish dripping. I was so worried about getting the runs while I was there because it would be pretty difficult to rush off to the bathroom with one leg and an IV pole attached to me. Fortunately, that never happened. But I did get really bad cramps in my stomach that made me think I was going to have to jump up and run at any moment. I also got some chemo-brain that wasn't too bad, but enough to make my brain a little fuzzy. The nausea was enough to make me uncomfortable and not want to eat much, but it wasn't that big of a deal either. Other than that I didn't really have any side effects.

After the two and a half hour infusion was complete they disconnected me and sent me home. I usually felt a little off for a couple of days until the chemo was out of my system, but after that I felt pretty good. I came back the next week and did the exact same thing. The side effects were a little worse on the second week, but absolutely nothing compared to the inpatient chemo that I did. I got a lot of bad stomach cramps and sometimes I would have to rush to the bathroom, but it wasn't very often. The third week of the round I didn't have any chemo. I just had to go into the doctor's office to have my blood checked and to make sure everything was going alright. That was it. It was the easiest chemo regimen that I had ever heard of.

The whole round of chemo only took up a few hours of only three days. It was amazing! It was so refreshing to me because it felt like I had all of this free time now and enough energy to actually do some fun things. I had gotten so much better at using my prosthetic that I was physically able to do a lot more.

I was pretty good with the prosthetic, but my prosthetist still wanted me to go and do some physical therapy. He figured they could help me improve the way I walked and teach me skills that would help me with more challenging activities. I was hesitant to go because I thought I was doing just fine, but Kelly and my mom pressured me into going anyway.

I was told to go to this place in downtown Houston that was known to be one of the best rehab facilities in Houston. I had never been to a physical therapy facility before and was blown away by what I saw when I walked through the doors. The patients there were messed up from all types of things, from strokes to horrible accidents. Some of them had decent mobility, lots of them were in wheelchairs, and some had to be brought in on hospital beds because they couldn't even control their bodies. Most of the patients worked on things like being able to move their legs again. Some were worse off and worked on things like lifting a spoon full of beads to their mouths so that they could learn to eat on their own. Some patients couldn't even move any of their limbs and were there just to be stretched.

Before going there I thought I was in pretty bad shape, but after seeing the other patients I didn't feel so bad for myself. I almost felt embarrassed by the fact that I could get around as well as I could. It was such a humbling experience to see so many people who were so much worse off than me. Every time I left physical therapy I felt so grateful for the body that I had. It was worth it for me to go just to get that experience.

While I was there my therapist had me work on all kinds of things. First my walking was critiqued and I worked on perfecting it. Then I worked on my balance by doing things like kicking a soccer ball back and forth and throwing and catching medicine balls while standing on a wobbly surface. After I had improved those skills I learned to walk up and down stairs, to step over obstacles, and to walk backwards, sideways, and toe to toe in straight lines. During my last couple of visits I worked on things like how to use exercise equipment and play golf. Even though nothing I did was very challenging for me I was still really glad I went because I had a good time and was able to improve my balance and walking which helped me in everything I did.

Now that I could get around just fine and the end of the cancer road was in sight I was anxious to get my life back. The first thing I did was try to be more social. I think during my treatments a lot of my friends got sick of calling me to hang out because I always told them I was sick. So Kelly and I never really did much. Now we could hang out with friends as much as we wanted because neither of us worked and Kelly was off of school. We started going out more to gain our friends back.

There was one night where my boss, Whitt, invited the whole Cathodic Protection group out to his ranch to hang out. Normally Kelly and I wouldn't have gone, but since I was feeling well we went for it. We had a great time and the planned activities were a great challenge to my ability with my prosthetic. We walked across this field to an old shed full of equipment. It was a tough walk for me because the ground was so uneven. When we got there Whitt started up his tractor and told me to jump on and start driving. I had never been on a tractor so it took some time and detailed instructions to figure it out. Once I had it down we drove out to another shed, loaded up some huge steel plates, and drove them out to an old tree stump in the middle of the field. We leaned the plates against the stump, went and parked the tractor, and walked back out to the tree stump where everyone had gathered. They all pulled out these guns and we spent the next hour or so shooting at a target on the tree stump. It was so much fun to be out there and do stuff that was so different from hanging out in a hospital room.

I also got more involved with my church when I was asked to be a part of the activity planning committee. I went to meetings every week and worked with friends to help organize the upcoming summer party for the church. It was a lot of fun for me to be able to hang out with friends and I loved being able to help out in the church again.

I decided to get going again on my goal to earn an MBA degree. After finishing one round of the Irinotecan regimen I felt like I should be in good enough shape to take another class. So I went ahead and picked up a class so that I could work on finishing the program as soon as possible.

All of these things that I was getting involved in made me feel like I was almost a normal person again. I was starting to feel like I would really enjoy being back in life once I was completely done with all of the treatments. All I had to do was hang in there long enough to finish up the last three rounds.

40 ROUND 12: SEP 21, 2009

It was easy to make myself go in to start round twelve after seeing how relatively easy round eleven was. I wasn't scared at all. I just wanted to get it over with. My two visits to the doctor's office were pretty uneventful. I think I had to rush to the bathroom a couple of times, but only for false alarms. One drive home we stopped by some craft stores so that Kelly could do a little shopping. The extra time spent out and about kind of did a number on my stomach. This resulted in a random stop at a gas station on the way home because the stomach cramps made me feel like I really needed to go. After that episode we decided that we just needed to rush straight home after leaving the doctor's office in case my intestines started to flare up. Other than those few issues, this chemo was a piece of cake compared to what I had already experienced.

The only other thing that I had going on my life at that time was my MBA class. I was really enjoying it and the things that I was learning. Sometimes it was a little awkward for me because of my whole ordeal with cancer. Getting to know people was a lot different than before. People would ask me how I lost my leg which would turn into me telling my whole cancer story. Or they would ask me who I worked for, which would also result in me telling my cancer story because I didn't work, I was on disability. Of course, anybody that I told my cancer story to acted awkward and didn't really know how to act or what to say. It was just like what I went through when I was first diagnosed. Now I had to go through it all over again with near strangers.

It made me wonder if I was really ready to be back in real life. I would have to deal with questions like this from all kinds of people. How would I explain all of this to interviewers? Would anybody even want to hire me or would I be too much of an HR nightmare to deal with? Then if they did hire me, how would I explain all of my problems to my supervisors and co-workers? Would they honestly consider me an equal or would they just be nice to me because I was a handicapped guy?

It kind of stressed me out and made me worried to get back into my career. I honestly didn't know if I would be accepted at all and I could see how people might consider me to be a high risk prospect since my cancer could come back and I would have to be on their disability. It made me think "What if no one ever wanted to hire me?" Maybe I would just have to stay at home and be a home-maker while Kelly went out as a nurse to provide income for our family. I knew I was being silly and letting my thoughts get carried away, but I was still worried about what I would do. The only thing I could do was stop worrying about it for now, finish up my treatments, and see what happens when I get to that point in my life.

There was one experience that I went through during that round that stands out in my mind. And no, it wasn't a good one. My aunt had given Kelly and I some tickets to go see a play downtown. We were excited to go because it would be a fun date for us to get dressed up and go out on the town. As I was getting dressed for the play my mom kept bugging me about coming outside to say hi to all of the neighbors. It was national neighbor night out that night and my parents had organized a barbeque for all of the people that lived in our cul-de-sac. It seemed like word had spread to most of our neighbors that I had cancer and they were all interested in meeting me.

After I got dressed I put on my dress shoes and walked with my cane down the driveway to meet everybody. I felt like all eyes were on me, watching to see how well I did with my new prosthetic. I was pretty confident in myself too. I walked smoothly and didn't limp or anything. I was expecting to get to the end of the driveway and have people tell me how good I was doing. But about half way down, the knee on my prosthetic buckled and collapsed to the concrete, breaking my cane and tearing a hole in my slacks.

Nothing really hurt until I looked up at the crowd and they all turned their heads to pretend like they didn't see me fall. That hurt a lot. My dad lifted me up and helped me back into the house and onto a couch. After I sat down all I could do was cry. Just when I felt like I had this prosthetic thing down I went and fell down in front of a bunch of people. I was so humiliated and discouraged. I didn't know if I would ever be good enough at walking to avoid these types of incidences. I didn't want to walk anymore that night and I especially wasn't in the mood to go to the play.

Kelly, having heard that I had fallen in front of everybody, rushed over to me and immediately started to lift me back up emotionally. She hugged me, told me she still loved me and that she would love me no matter what, and reminded me that these things would just happen sometimes and that I needed to pick myself up and keep trying. She was confident that I would perfect my walking eventually and reminded me of how good I was doing. She understood that I didn't want to go to the play, but told me that I needed to toughen up and go anyway so as to not let fear of these types of things hold me back. She knew just what to say to help me pick myself up again. We headed off to the play and ended up having a great night together.

Kelly has always been so good at pushing me to be a better person. Before, I would have considered it almost nagging in a way, because she would sometimes boss me around and tell me what I was doing wrong or what I needed to do differently. But since I had been diagnosed with cancer she has become so much more loving, sensitive, and positive. Where before she might have just said something like "I'm sorry you fell, but you need to get up and get going so we can still make it to the play," now she encouraged me to not give up and did so with a huge smile, love in her eyes, and support in her voice.

And she was like that with everything I did. Whenever I needed to take my pills, get up and move around, be a better friend, go to church, be kinder, etc., she was there to put me in my place and remind me that I needed to do better. She always did it so lovingly and usually in a way that involved a sarcastic, ridiculous threat that always made me laugh. It's just another quality of hers that makes me think she's so amazing.

41 ROUND 13: OCT 12, 2009

Round thirteen must have been pretty uneventful because I don't remember anything that happened during that round. I guess that's a good thing. Better than all of the horrible memories from my other treatments.

After a couple of weeks of walking around again I had completely recovered from my wipe-out on the driveway. Since I didn't have any work to do and was always feeling relatively good, I spent a lot of my time out and about running errands and shopping and things like that. But I couldn't drive my little green car that I had bought back in college because of my prosthetic. In fact, my prosthetic prevented me from being able to drive lots of different cars. I either couldn't get it under the steering wheel, or it took up too much room near the pedals for me to drive with my left foot. So we decided that I needed to get another vehicle.

It worked out just fine too, because my little green car had been dead for almost eleven months. The day I went in to the hospital for my first round of chemo my mom borrowed it to pick up Nick and Mandy from the airport. It broke down on their way back and ended up sitting in the driveway for months. All it needed was a battery and an alternator, but I never had the time or energy to get it fixed. Plus, Kelly and my family had made fun of me for driving that wussy car for so long that I felt like I needed to get rid of it. I ended up selling it to a needy friend of mine for only $300. I was sad to see that little car go.

By this point in my life I had been an amputee for just over six months and I was really starting to get used to it. I could do almost anything on my crutches. I was getting really comfortable using my prosthetic; it didn't bother me as much when people stared at me. I was even starting to have dreams of me having one leg.

The dreams I had where I was an amputee in the dream were always really weird. I usually wasn't wearing my prosthetic, but somehow could still walk around. A lot of my dreams started with me standing on one leg and somebody calling me to walk or run over to them. I would always look at them and think "You're crazy, I only have one leg." But their persistence would convince me to take a step on my stump. Somehow, every time I stepped on my stump I was able to hover there while my phantom sensation made me feel like I was actually standing. Every time I would be amazed and then take off running or walking. Those were the strangest dreams! I can only attribute my ability to walk with one leg to the idea that my spirit is what is running my body and still has two good legs. But who knows. Dreams are just weird sometimes.

Anyway, I think I must have stood out a lot when I went out into public with my prosthetic because people came up to me and made comments all the time. I got all kinds of strange questions and heard way more stories about amputees than I ever wanted to hear. Probably the funniest thing I experienced was when a kid on a bike saw me and rode over to my car as I was getting in. He was about eleven or twelve and was completely amazed by my leg and told me how cool he thought it was. Then as he was riding off he enthusiastically asked "Hey, how high can you jump?" I chuckled and sarcastically responded, "About 20 feet." I didn't think he would believe me but he yelled out "Awesome" and rode off with his friend.

That response was a little unusual. For the most part people liked to ask me if I was in the military, which got to be pretty annoying because when I would tell them that I wasn't it was almost like they got disappointed that they weren't able to thank me for my service. Then when I told them it was because of cancer, they usually got awkward, said something dumb, or just walked off because they didn't know how to deal with that topic.

Sadly the worst comments I ever got were when people wanted to lift me up or encourage me. Sometimes they would tell me not to worry and that I could still live a full, happy life and do anything I wanted with a prosthetic leg because they knew somebody with one or they saw something on TV. They thought this would make me feel better, but the truth is that there are lots of things that I can't do because it is impossible with my type of amputation. I'm sure they did see somebody do something amazing, but most likely, that person was a below the knee amputee. And the type of amputation a person has is a major factor in what kind of activities they are able to do. It would make me mad that they didn't have their facts straight before trying to console me. Plus, who says I needed to be comforted anyways? It made me feel like they thought that I was depressed just because I was missing a leg.

So, if you ever come across an amputee, don't assume they need your encouragement just because they have one leg. Don't try to pretend like you don't notice the prosthetic. I would say that most amputees would prefer the topic be brought up instead of ignored just so that everything is all out in the open. Simple questions like "How did you lose your leg?" are usually good. Compliments like "You get around pretty well" or "It's impressive how well you walk" are really good. I always love it when people compliment me on my walking. It just kind of makes my day.

Unfortunately, when somebody asks me how I lost my leg I have to tell them about my cancer as well, which can result in all kinds of annoying comments. I think the worst is when they ask question after question until it feels like I have told my whole story to a complete stranger. Please don't do that to stranger you run into who you think has cancer. Remember that it is probably a pretty sensitive topic for them and they probably don't want to talk about it to somebody they don't know. Another thing that really bothers me is when people tell me that I just need to have faith. They say it like they think that if I really believe I can be healed, then I will - like it is just that simple. It bothers me because they don't understand the concept that God's plan for me is what determines my fate, not how much I believe I'll be healed. But I can't give a lecture on faith to everybody that tells me that so I usually just smile, thank them, and move on with my life. Another thing you shouldn't do is tell a person with cancer that they can beat it. Sometimes, no, they can't beat it and they probably never will, no matter how hard they fight. It doesn't make anybody feel any better to try to tell them they can do something that is literally impossible. Also, encouraging stories of people being cured are only good if you have your facts straight. Don't tell somebody with brain cancer not to worry because you know a lady with breast cancer who was cured by standard chemotherapy. Every cancer is different and has its own challenges. Stories about people with other types of cancer are almost pointless to me.

So then what should you say around people that have cancer? Well, you can never go wrong with just keeping your mouth shut and offering an encouraging smile. Sometimes a simple smile can go a long way. But if you have to talk, I would say just ask basic questions and don't go into detail unless they initiate it. Be a listener instead of an advice giver. Try to end by lending simple words of encouragement like "Hang in there" or "Good luck."

42 ROUND 14: NOV 2, 2009

Round 14! We finally made it. The treatment flew by without any problems and before we knew it we were saying goodbye to cancer forever. It's kind of a tradition among cancer patients to ring a bell to celebrate the completion of their treatment. Back in the hospital during my second or third round of chemo I saw an old man ring his bell. He had the most ecstatic look on his face. Ever since then I looked forward to the day that I would be able to ring the bell. But when it came down to it, ringing the bell wasn't as exciting as it looked. I was thrilled to be done, but too chemo-brained to get much enjoyment out of a bell.

As I recovered from that last round I spent a lot of time thinking about my journey through cancer treatments and how much I had changed throughout the whole process. I felt like a completely different person than who I was when I was first diagnosed. I had gone through a major change in my character. Now I didn't make fun of others at all. I had absolutely no desire to make inappropriate jokes and was usually kind of offended when my friends did. I had completely removed myself from all forms of immorality or bad language in TV and movies. My language and the way that I talked and carried myself had improved so much. I was much more genuine with myself and no longer tried to be anyone or anything that I wasn't. My confidence had increased enormously. I had a greater love for everybody around me and I always wanted to surround myself with good people who would lift me up instead of bringing me down.

I had changed in so many ways and had become a much better person. That was really important to me because before I had cancer I knew that I needed to make these types of changes at some point in my life, but I didn't know how to get the strength to actually go through with it and make it happen. I think I just happened to luck out because my cancer experiences made it easy for me to make those changes. Since making them I have been so much happier and content with everything in my life. I hated almost everything about what I went through during my cancer treatments, but the happiness that I now enjoyed somehow made all of the misery worth it.

Having this new found happiness didn't make any of my problems go away. I still had to figure out what I was going to do with my life. My body was still plenty messed up from all of the chemo I had received and I knew that I would need several months to fully recover from that. I was just worried that now that I was finished with treatment, I would be cut from my disability. If that happened, what would we do if I couldn't find a job? I knew I would start looking for one after a couple of months because I was still kind of focused on my career and making money. I was excited to get back into that way of life.

It made me excited to think about the bright future that Kelly and I had in front of us. In just a couple of years I would have my MBA and Kelly would be done with her nursing school. We would have a pretty good combined income. We planned on continuing to live cheap and save lots so that we could eventually move into a house and have really small house payments. We would probably start a family soon after that and would be financially set to do so. I could see everything working out just perfectly and I couldn't wait to get started on making it happen.

43 AN ATTEMPT AT NORMAL LIFE
TRYING TO ADJUST

I absolutely loved not having to do chemotherapy. It was like when you're in high school and you finally get out for the summer. There was such a relief, like a burden was lifted from me. I felt like I had all of this free time on my hands. I still didn't feel 100% but I felt good enough to be able to go out and do stuff. I was super excited about life in general and was kind of looking forward to getting to 100% so that I could return to normal.

Since I had gotten to be pretty good with my prosthetic I was out and about a lot. I ran errands, shopped, hung out with friends, and played a lot of golf. I was lucky because my friend Rob had lots of free time on his hands and was able to take me out to the driving range a couple of times a week. I loved going to the driving range with him. It was always so beautiful and relaxing out there, almost like I was out on vacation or something, except just for an hour or two.

He gave me plenty of tips and helped me to improve my swing a lot. I loved the physical and mental challenge that golf gave me. I wanted to get good. Good enough to where I could go out and play with friends and be able to keep up with them or even beat them. I knew it would require a lot of work and practice, but I was willing to do it. The challenge motivated me to practice a lot. I went out with Rob whenever he could and I even practiced chipping in my back yard and putting in my living room. After a couple of months I ended up doing alright and could keep up with my friends whenever we played. It made me feel so good to still have something in my life that challenged me and that I could be competitive with.

Apart from golf, I didn't really have too much going on. Rob was really the only friend that I had that was my age and had the free time to hang out a few times a week. During the week days my life was a little boring sometimes. Kelly would go off to school and I would be stuck at home watching TV, trying to entertain myself by trading stocks, or coming up with off-the-wall business ideas. When the weekends rolled around though, Kelly and I would try to get some of our social life back. We tried to hang out with friends whenever we could get together. It was kind of weird to go hang out with them at first. We had been gone for so long that we didn't really know how to act around everybody. Plus, I was a little reserved because of lingering worries about how people would treat me with one leg. After getting together a few times, it became more natural, which Kelly and I loved because it made us feel like we had friends again.

About a month after finishing my last round of chemo I finished up the MBA class that I was taking. It felt good to be done with it and to have another class checked off. I was looking forward to taking more classes to continue down that road of getting our life back.

Another step that I finally made was buying a vehicle that I could drive while wearing my prosthetic. We had been looking for months by then and had tried out almost every kind of car that was out there on the market. It was so frustrating because my leg wouldn't fit into any of the cars that I would usually want to buy. The only types of cars that really worked for me were big SUVs and full size trucks. Kelly was thrilled about my options because she always thought I was a wuss for driving my little green car. She wanted me to be "manly" and drive a big old truck. We ended up finding a good deal on a used Chevy Silverado and went for it. I've been a truck person ever since.

Probably the biggest step we needed to take in order to get our lives back to normal was to move out of my parent's house. Now that I would be feeling better soon and getting a job we felt like we were safe enough to go back into the world on our own. I, of course, went over the budget several times to make sure it would be okay for us financially. Once everything checked out we picked out an apartment and made the move.

It felt so nice to be able to have our own space again. It reminded me of what life used to be like before I got cancer. We had our own place with our own stuff in it just the way we wanted it. I loved living with Kelly and being able to hang out with just her every night. We went back to all of our usual daily habits like cooking an easy dinner and eating it on the couch while we watched TV together. This time, though, living with Kelly was a little different. We didn't argue or disagree about hardly anything and we wanted to be with each other all of the time. We had a greater love and appreciation for each other than before and our lives seemed to be overall happier.

After being off chemo for a couple of months I started to notice a difference in my life. Something felt different inside, like there was something missing. I thought about it a lot and couldn't figure out what it was until I was sitting in church one day and realized that what was missing was the presence of the Holy Spirit in my life.

I thought a lot about the fact that all of a sudden I felt like it was missing. I guess that I had gotten so used to that feeling of peace and comfort in my life that I didn't even recognize it anymore until it left. It was the weirdest thing, because once I realized that it was gone I really started to miss it and tried to do whatever I could to bring it back. Unfortunately nothing worked. The feeling was gone and there didn't seem to be anything I could do about it. I prayed to try to figure out why this had happened and the only answer I felt like I got was that the Holy Spirit was sent to me to help me during my treatments and that it was sent because of all of the prayers on my behalf. And now it wasn't needed because I was done with my treatments.

I spent a lot of time thinking about how strongly I had felt the Holy Spirit during my treatments, and I was able to learn a lot about how the Holy Spirit works and how it had helped me specifically. When I was young I was taught that the Holy Spirit is something that is there to comfort, guide and teach us. I was taught that it communicated with us through our feelings. Feelings of peace, warmth, and love, for example. But on my mission I learned that it was a little more complicated than that. I learned that it was hard to be able to hear the promptings of the Holy Spirit and that any teachings from it usually came through a long, slow process. I realized that I wasn't really any good at recognizing promptings or teachings

Now, after contemplating the experiences that I had with the Holy Spirit throughout my treatment, I understood a lot more about how it all works. The first thing I learned is that the Holy Spirit can provide great comfort. For me, I think the Holy Spirit calmed me and gave me a greater sense of peace and well-being in my life. It wasn't a strong, overwhelming feeling like I originally thought, instead it was hardly a feeling at all. It was more of a change in my thoughts. It was like my thought process was more clear and my worries were drowned out by positive thoughts. The usual thoughts in my head that have a tendency of taking over and running wild in my mind were not really there. The controlling of my thoughts and worries are what brought me the feelings of peace and comfort.

The second thing I learned was how the Holy Spirit can teach me and guide me. I had always been taught that this was true, however I don't think I ever really understood how it worked until contemplating how the Holy Spirit had taught me throughout my treatments. Before, I thought that I would be guided or taught by feelings that I had. For example, while studying a true principle the Holy Spirit would confirm to me that it is true by making me feel a certain way. Now I see that this isn't the case, at least not for me. From my experiences, I've found that the Holy

Spirit communicates to me directly through my own thoughts. It is hard to explain, but thoughts and ideas would come to my head and would spark a new thought process. I would usually spend some time thinking about the new ideas that had come to me and at some point I would usually have a feeling of "Oh, that makes sense."

I would say that this teaching process usually takes a long time. It can take weeks just to get a piece of the puzzle that you are working on. However, it seems like the more humbled and in-tune with the Spirit you are the faster the process is. I found that the worse off I was physically and emotionally the stronger the influence of the spirit was in my life and the faster the teaching process went. At some times, when I was really having a hard time with my treatments, it felt almost like the Holy Spirit would have conversations with me. And then when I came off chemo and everything was good, I was pretty much left alone. I think it is a gift that God gives to those who are going through really hard times.

After a few months of being off chemo I started to physically go downhill. I still hadn't fully recovered from the chemo and I still had problems with nausea and weakness. It is normal to be like that for a little while after chemo, but I had been like that for several months now and I only seemed to be getting worse. I went in to the doctor's office frequently to have my blood checked. Once, when I went in some of my electrolytes were low, so my doctor decided to send me to a kidney specialist to figure out what the problem was.

After seeing the kidney specialist we found out that my kidneys had been damaged pretty badly by the high-dose Ifosfamide chemo that I had after my surgery. My kidneys were releasing all kinds of important electrolytes and nutrients that my body needed, which was why I still felt sick and weak all of the time. The doctor loaded me up with a whole bunch of pills to help replace what was being lost and

I was sent on my way. It ended up taking another few months before everything returned back to normal.

Right in the middle of dealing with the kidney specialist I was officially let go by Fluor. I had been on disability for a whole year by then and the policy was to let people go after a year. I would still get disability payments, but only until the insurance company felt I was able to work. At that point I would be cut off and would have to find work.

I figured I should start looking for a job before I got to that point. But after looking for a while I realized that finding a job would be really hard. There just wasn't a lot out there at the time. I had a couple of interviews, which didn't go too well because I hadn't dealt with work stuff for a long time and had forgotten a lot of the stuff that I used to do. Also, I felt like I needed to tell them about my cancer situation so that they were aware that I could be returning to disability if the cancer ever came back. I don't think they liked hearing that either.

I was starting to get really worried about my immediate future. Before, everything seemed so bright and exciting. I couldn't wait to get back to real life. Now I was worried that I wouldn't be able to find a job, that our savings would run out, and that I would never get to feeling better.

44 IT CAME BACK: APRIL 2010

I was out on the driving range with Rob. It was a near perfect day. The weather was awesome, the course was beautiful, I was feeling pretty good, and I was hitting the balls nice and straight. Life was good in that moment. But then, my phone rang. It was my doctor calling with the results of the scans that I did the day before. He told me that it looked like the cancer was back, this time in my lungs. There were a couple of tiny spots that he was worried about and he wanted to send me over to M.D. Anderson Cancer Center to see a Ewing's Sarcoma specialist there.

I couldn't believe it. My chances at getting back to a normal life were shot down. I was so nervous because I knew that when the cancer metastasizes to the lungs the outlook isn't good. There isn't a good treatment plan for people with lung metastases. There is no easy cure like they said there was when I was first diagnosed. All of a sudden I went from having a great day, to being worried that I was going to die sometime in the not too distant future. My thoughts immediately turned to Kelly and what this might mean for her.

I went home and cried in her arms that night. I didn't want to drag her through any more of my medical problems. I especially didn't want to die and have to leave her all alone. It broke my heart to think about what all of this might mean for her. Somehow, though, while I was breaking down, she was so optimistic and positive. The way she spoke to me to calm me down let me know how much she loved me. She easily calmed my nerves and brought me confidence to go forward with whatever treatments they might have for me.

45 WELCOME TO MD ANDERSON: APR 13, 2010

I had heard so much about MD Anderson; that it was an amazing place with amazing doctors. It had been ranked the number one cancer center in the United States for years and people came from all over the world to be treated there, but I never thought that I would ever need to go there for treatments.

As we drove through the medical center to our appointment I couldn't believe how enormous the cancer center was. It was weird to think that all of the people there were cancer patients. It was kind of a special place for me because I felt like I could probably relate to almost everybody there. They all probably had gone through similar experiences as we did and were all fighting for their lives too.

When we met with our new doctor he told us what we were already expecting, that it is hard to get rid of it when it migrates to the lungs. He wanted us to try to get onto a clinical trial first, which ended up not working out because my kidneys were so bad. After that option was closed he decided to try putting me on a standard chemo regimen for Ewing's Sarcoma lung metastases. I was going to start the following Monday and was going to be able to do the treatments as an outpatient procedure in their Sugar Land facility.

46 THIS CHEMO SHOULDN'T BE TOO BAD COCKTAIL #5

This new regimen didn't seem like it would be too bad. I was able to get it outpatient, which meant I would only have to go in for a few hours a day. Plus, the facility in Sugar Land was only five minutes from where we lived.

I was going to get three chemo drugs: Irinotecan, Vincristine, and Temodar. I wasn't too worried about the side effects because they weren't supposed to be that bad. Plus, I had already received Irinotecan and it didn't do much to me. Day one I would get all three drugs, and days two through five I would get just Irinotecan and Temodar. I only went in for a few hours a day and side effects didn't come until about a week later. On the first day I would usually have some nausea and feel pretty chemo-brained. Days two through five the nausea wasn't too bad, but the chemo-brain was still be pretty annoying. Then, for a few days after getting the chemo I would feel alright.

About four days after finishing the chemo the diarrhea would set in. Initially I thought I would be able to handle it without any problems because of all of my experiences in Mexico, but I had never experienced diarrhea like this. It was amazing how bad it was. I had horrible stomach cramps all of the time and it seemed like every couple of hours I would have to rush to the bathroom. I would even have to go in the middle of the night sometimes. Having to go all the time would completely drain me of all of my energy. I would get dehydrated and usually would have to go in to get fluids to help me feel better. It was completely miserable and it usually lasted for an entire week. After a week of dealing with the diarrhea I would start to feel a lot better and would usually have a full week of feeling good before I had to go back in.

47 ROUND 15: MAY 24, 2010

Somehow before starting this round of chemo, word had spread to everybody that I knew that the cancer had returned to my lungs. It seemed like we had to deal with the same social weirdness that we went through when I was first diagnosed. Everybody was asking about me and wondering how I was doing. People brought over lots of meals and offered to do anything we needed. Everybody was so nice to us and it was a huge blessing to have their help and support.

But this time was different than before. It seemed like very few of our friends really grasped the severity of my new situation. They all just kind of assumed that I would do some more treatment and that I would be fine. No problem. They didn't understand that there was probably a decent chance that I wouldn't make it. I don't know if it was because they were in denial or if they just were putting on happy faces and positive attitudes for us. Either way, it sometimes became frustrating to have to talk to people about my cancer and try to play along with the idea that everything would be fine when inside I knew that it might not.

Luckily, Kelly was an amazing strength to me before starting up chemo again. Whenever I was having a rough time she would always able to make me feel like everything would be alright, no matter what the outcome was. She would remind me how much she loved me, which would somehow give me the strength to keep fighting. I think it was because I wanted to continue fighting for her. She was always the motivation for me to keep going on.

We went in for my first round of treatment and were amazed at how convenient the treatment was for us compared to the other treatments I had done. The facility was five minutes from our apartment, there were practically no waits, everybody was so nice and friendly, and I only had to be there for a few hours. We absolutely loved it.

By the time I left the hospital after receiving my dose of chemo I could already feel the chemo-brain setting in. It was the first side effect that I experienced and it was depressing to think that I would be starting the whole miserable chemo thing over again. I finished up the week of daily transfusions and felt pretty awful by the weekend. Somehow this round of chemo ended up being probably the worst round I ever had. I didn't get it either. This stuff was supposed to be so much easier than the other stuff, but it completely knocked me on my butt for a week. I laid around the entire round without hardly any energy to move. And the nausea was almost unbearable. It felt like I couldn't get any food down. Finally, at the very end of the round, right when I began to feel like I was about to die, we went into the hospital to figure out what was wrong with me. It turned out that I was just really dehydrated. They gave me some IV fluids and I immediately felt better. We learned in that first round that lots of fluids were essential to making my other rounds bearable.

There were times during that round that the side effects made me so miserable that I couldn't take it. I would feel so horrible that I would break down crying like a little girl. Sometimes I would go cry to Kelly for no reason at all. She would ask what was wrong and I would just say "I don't know." It was like when my sister, Mandy, would break down and cry for no reason at all. Suddenly I understood why girls would do that sometime and it made me a lot more sensitive to them. Kelly would sometimes get randomly emotional about things and I would try to say things to make her feel better. But now I understood that she just needed somebody to listen to her and tell her everything would be ok.

She was always so good at making me feel better and picking me up emotionally. It amazed me that she was always so strong and was able to stay composed when I was completely falling apart. I never understood how, until we got into a deep conversation one night and talked about it. I learned that she just tries to live life from day to day and not to worry about things until the time came to worry about them. She taught me that there's no point in worrying about something that may or may not happen. If it happens then you can deal with it.

She taught me a lot about herself by telling me those things that day. I learned a lot about how her mind works and it impressed me that she is able to control her thoughts and emotions so much more than I am.

This round was particularly emotional for me. It was so hard to have to be going through chemo again. Just a couple of weeks ago I thought I would never have to deal with cancer treatments again. Now I was doing treatments that may or may not be successful at killing the cancer. I was facing the idea that I might not be around much longer, despite how positive we both were about being able to beat this. Trying to deal with the death issue was completely new to us and harder than anything we had previously faced.

48 ROUND 16: JUN 14, 2010

My second round of this chemo regimen was a lot easier for me. The doctor sent me home with a three liter bag of IV fluids that I carried around in a backpack. It kept me hydrated throughout the entire time I had the runs, which helped me to have more energy and less nausea. The diarrhea was still draining, but I was at least able to feel decent while I made trip after trip to the bathroom.

During my good week I had scans to check to see if the chemo was actually working at shrinking the tumors. When we went in to get the scan results the doctor told us that the tumors were being held stable. I thought it was bad news because they hadn't shrank, but be he seemed to be happy about it. He then went into this long scientific explanation of what kind of options I had and what kind of clinical trials might be available in the future. I never really understood much when he would go into detail on the science of the treatments, so I kind of shut down during our conversation. But then out of nowhere the phrase "Five year survival of 10%" popped out like a bright flashing light. I had to stop him mid-sentence and say "What do you mean 10%?" He then explained that statistically, only 10% of patients in my situation live longer than five years after diagnosis.

Right after he explained that it was like time slowed way down because a million thoughts were racing through my head at once. I knew that my prognosis wouldn't be very good, but I had no idea that I was looking at a 10% chance of only making it five years. My brain kind of shut down for the rest of the conversation because it was just too much for me to handle. Luckily Kelly was able to pay attention to whatever else he had to say.

We left his office and I don't think I even made it down the hall before I started to tear up. All of my thoughts were on Kelly and what this meant for her. I couldn't stand the idea of having to leave her all alone in life. It made me feel so guilty inside because if I were to die, all of the sadness and suffering that she would have to go through was because of me.

We got to our car and started driving home and neither of us hardly said anything to each other. I think we were both trying to hold back the tears. I knew Kelly was going through a hard time and I wanted to try to help her so badly, so I started asking her about what she was thinking about everything. She broke down and the tears rolled as she explained to me how she didn't want to have to live without me. She was having a really hard time and it completely broke my heart. I hated being the cause of her pain or suffering and I knew that this would just be the beginning of it.

As we talked about things in the car I started to think about how my family would react. I wasn't ready to break the bad news to them. I didn't want to make them cry too. So Kelly and I decided to disappear for a while and just enjoy some time with each other. We went out to dinner and were able to calm our nerves quite a bit. We talked a lot about God's plan for me and that maybe this was just part of it. We also talked about how I could be part of the 10% that makes it. We pretty much concluded that we shouldn't get so worked up over this because there were still good treatment options for me and that if I were to die from this, it wouldn't be for a while. I remembered what she had taught me and tried not to worry about it until the time came. Until then, I was going to keep on living life and try to be as happy as I could.

When we finally got done with dinner we headed over to my parent's house to break the news to them. We sat down at the kitchen table and the tears immediately started to flow. Before I could say anything my mom said "I already know." They assumed that we got bad news because we had disappeared and ignored phone calls for a while. Plus, my mom had already read online what the prognosis was for patients in my situation. She already knew what I was facing. It was such a relief to me to not have to explain everything to them.

I spent the next few days trying to absorb the whole idea that I might not be around much longer. But I couldn't. It was too difficult to process. I had to just look at it the way Kelly did. Live life from day to day and deal with things when then come. After a few days my mind had settled down with the idea that I still had no idea what might happen to me. I focused on the thought that I could be part of the 10% that makes. It was enough to keep me positive and happy. But even still, I knew I needed to make the best of whatever time I might have left, whether that be months or years.

We decided to take an extra week off from the chemo, just to take a little break and to give me some more time to feel good. That whole week my thoughts were on Kelly. Knowing that there was a possibility that I might have to leave her completely changed the way I looked at our relationship. Suddenly all I cared about was making her happy. I was willing to do anything for her. From that point on, whatever she asked me to do I would do it willingly and with a smile on my face because I would do anything to make her happy. I learned to not ever say no to her no matter how sick and miserable I felt. I think she kind of felt the same way and went out of her way all of the time to do things to make me happy. We had a mutual willingness to do anything to make the other happy.

It was at that point that our relationship really changed. My love for her has grown so much and I have gained an amazing respect for her. I look at her as a completely different person now. Almost as if she is some sort of angel. Sometimes I find myself just staring at her in complete amazement, thinking about how awesome of a person she is and how lucky I am to have somebody like her. I am so impressed at the amazing person she has become and I know with time she will only get better. Before getting married I never could have imagined having her could ever bring me so much happiness and joy. And the best thing about it all is that I don't think my relationship with her will ever change, even through death. The amazing relationship that we have built will bring us joy forever.

49 ROUND 17: JUL 12, 2010

This round must have gone by pretty smoothly because I don't really remember anything about what happened during it. I'm sure it was the usual feeling horrible and depending on Kelly for the strength to keep moving on in my treatments.

At the end of the round, just as I was finishing up my sick week of the chemo, we celebrated Kelly's birthday. Kelly is always so low key about anything that puts her at the center of attention. She hates that, but I really wanted to do something nice for her so I decided to try to throw her a low key surprise party and only invite a few of our best friends. Kelly's mom had the same idea. She wanted to make it a big event and invite everybody from her side of the family... a real surprise party. I was fine with that because I thought it would be fun to have a party with her family too. So we planned on having a small party with some friends and a big party with her family. Well, just after Kelly's mom invited everybody and made reservations at the restaurant for the party, Kelly's best friend, Jessica, called and told me she had a surprise for Kelly too. She had bought expensive tickets for the play Wicked, and wanted to take us as a birthday present for Kelly. The only problem was that the tickets were for the same night as the party that Kelly's mom had just planned. Somehow I ended up in the middle of Jessica and Kelly's mom's party plans, right during my sick week when the chemo brain was making it really hard to do any kind of problem solving.

It all turned into a big dramatic mess for me and, unfortunately for Jessica. We weren't able to go to the play. So instead we had a very low key dinner at my parent's house the night of her birthday and then the big surprise party for her a couple of days later. It worked out pretty well because after the dinner on her birthday she thought it was all over with. Having the big party a few days later took her by complete surprise. We all had a great time hanging out with all of Kelly's family that we don't normally get to see.

I feel bad for Jessica because things didn't work out the way she had planned, but we ended up having a great time later in the round. My family, Rob's family, and Rob's parents all made a trip to New Braunfels to float the river for the day. We all had such a great time even though it was kind of weird for me to go down the river with no leg. I had to crutch over to the river and then have somebody run the crutches back up to the car for me. I floated in my tube and swam around with one leg the entire time. It must have been an interesting sight for all of the people who float the river regularly. I don't think they see a one-legged guy in there very often.

After finishing the float, and somehow pulling myself out of the river with one leg, we all cleaned up and drove over to the Grist Mill for dinner. It was so much fun to be able to make that trip with that group of friends. When I was just a kid we floated the river with them all of the time. This time it was like we were just carrying on the tradition that we started when we were kids.

We had a lot of fun that round with Kelly's parties and the trip to the river. But through all of the fun we had I couldn't shake the thought that my life could be ending sometime in the near future. At this time it had been about three weeks since we found out about my latest prognosis and things were beginning to settle in my mind a little. The initial shock was out of my system and I was beginning to see life differently.

Suddenly I didn't care about a lot of the things that I used to care about. Things like having nice things and a good career or a nice house seemed so unimportant to me. It was like I immediately lost all desire for material things. I used to be all wrapped up in the whole job/money thing. I had spreadsheets that budgeted and planned out every foreseeable financial detail of my life for the next fifty years. Before, I felt like keeping up with my spreadsheets and the goals I had made were important for Kelly and I to reach some kind of financial freedom before retirement age. I wanted that so that I could be able to have the money to help others and to be able to afford for Kelly and I to go on a mission together when we were older.

Now none of that seemed important at all. All I really wanted was to have my cancer gone and to have a simple life without any complications. If I could have that I would be perfectly happy, even if we ended up never having any money and living in poverty the rest of our lives. Being healthy and with Kelly was all I needed.

Kelly felt the same way as I did and we even started to make plans on what our life would be like if I were to get better. Kelly had always wanted to move to a small town at some point in her life; something I never really considered because of the scarcity of jobs and entertainment in small towns. But now I was all for it. We were set, and still are, on moving to a small town with a simple, worry-free life if I were to ever get better.

Somehow the complete loss of desire for material things changed my life. Sincerely not caring about stuff made me feel like some kind of burden had been lifted from me. I didn't feel the constant internal nagging of my job or finances. I knew though, that if I got better I would have to think about that kind of stuff at some point, but I don't think I would ever give it the attention that I used to. I had seen the other side of life where finances have no importance and I enjoyed it too much.

50 ROUND 18: AUG 2, 2010

Round eighteen flew by without any problems either. My sister Mandy came down to spend some time with me and help me while I was sick. We had a lot of fun together during my good week. I still liked to golf as much as I could whenever I was feeling well so I took her and Kelly to the driving range with me one day. Neither of them were any good at golf but we had a great time goofing off and laughing whenever they swung at the ball and it didn't go anywhere.

Kelly and I felt it was important to spend some good quality time together whenever we could, so we decided to take an extra week off of chemo and take a little vacation. When word got out that we were interested in going somewhere we had lots of friends calling us wanting to help out by offering things like frequent flyer miles and vacation homes. We ended up deciding to go up to Utah to visit some friends and to enjoy the beautiful summer weather. A good friend from church got some plane tickets for us and Mandy's husband, Scott, said we could stay at his family's cabin.

We flew in to Salt Lake City and were greeted by my brother Nick, who took us out to lunch at a restaurant that was shown on the Food Network. Then we borrowed Mandy's car and drove down to the cabin that we were going to be staying at. The cabin was awesome and right on a golf course that was on the side of a mountain. From the back porch we could see across the whole valley. It was beautiful. But the best part was that I got to be there with only Kelly. Time with her seemed so much more precious then, and it was always especially fun to be able to do anything with her that didn't involve doctors or hospitals.

We spent the night there and then drove through the canyon to meet up with some good friends on the other side of the mountains to play a round of golf. It was so fun to be able to hang out with those guys out on the golf course. After we finished playing we headed over to their place for a barbeque with their wives and kids. We had a great time catching up and reminiscing about the past.

The next day we got together with some other friends and spent some time with my brother Nick, and sister Whitney. The day after that I played a round of golf with my uncle and then went out to dinner with him, Kelly, Nick and Whitney. It was a really simple and laid back vacation, but it was just what we needed to get a little break from all of the hospital stuff that we were used to. Through experience we learned that those little trips away from our sometimes depressing lives are able to lift us back up and give us the strength to keep moving forward.

I spent a lot of time during that round pondering God's plan for me and what he might have in store for me in the future. I had thought about this all of the time, but now knowing that there was a good chance that I might not make it changed the way I thought about it. Before I just figured that I was going through this whole cancer mess because there were changes that I needed make and things that I needed to be learned. I figured that once I learned those things I would get better and move on with my life with this new amazing perspective, able to help more people and make a difference in other's lives. I still hoped that was the case, but now understood that there might be other plans for me. Maybe I was needed on the other side for something or maybe my time in this life was just up.

It has always been hard to pray for God's will to be done when it might not be what you are wanting. It was especially difficult now because it meant I might have to leave Kelly behind, but somehow brought comfort to me in my prayers because I knew that things would end up best for everybody if everything went according to his plan. That fact felt so much more real now. I knew that if it were in his plan that I die, that in the end everybody else would be better off from it. I don't know how it would work out that way, but I know that it would. Somehow, knowing that brought comfort to the whole horrible situation that Kelly and I faced.

51 ORGANIZING THE BRENT EVENT

When the cancer returned to my lungs people were really concerned for Kelly and I and were always asking my parents what they could do to help us out. There wasn't really much that they could do because my parents and a small group of close friends were already taking care of everything that we needed. But they still wanted to find some way to help. I'm not sure who it was, but somebody came up with the idea of putting on a fundraiser for us. They spread the idea around and everybody thought it would be a great thing to do. They just had to pass it by us first.

When my parents approached me with the idea of putting on a fundraiser for us I was a little hesitant to accept. At the time I felt like we were doing pretty well financially. We still had a decent amount in savings and we still received disability checks that were enough to pay for our living expenses. We dipped into savings a little each month but we had enough for us to get by for a while. I decided to go through my budget spreadsheet anyway to double check to make sure we were financially all right. I found out that we would be all right for a little while, but eventually might need a little help in paying for our enormous medical expenses. So I accepted their request to hold a fundraiser for us.

My mom sprang into action right away and in no time had formed a committee of family members and close friends to help out in the planning. Starting sometime in August the committee started meeting at my parent's house every other week. We decided to call the fundraiser the Brent Event and it was going to consist of a 5k run in the morning, followed by a one mile family fun run, BBQ lunch, live band, silent auction and carnival type games for the kids. The planning went on for months and everybody involved put in a lot of work, but it seemed like everybody had a good time putting it all together. It was fun to get together for meetings every other week with close friends and everybody felt good about being able to do service and help out Kelly and me.

I had a lot of fun helping when I felt well enough to, but at the same time I felt really awkward about all of the attention that I was getting. I felt bad about the idea that people would be handing us money. I felt like there were so many other people out there that were just as deserving of financial help as I was. Why should I be the one that gets it instead of all those other people? But despite my reservations it was comforting to know that some of our financial burdens would be lifted through the Brent Event. To make myself feel better about accepting money I told myself that any excess that we received would be used to help others in need.

The planning pushed forward and before we knew it the Brent Event was getting all kinds of attention in the community. Word was spreading all over the place through Facebook and email, the church youth groups handed out flyers everywhere and there was even a long article written about me in the high school newspaper. All of a sudden it seemed like everybody knew about it and everybody wanted to be involved and help out in some way. So we took advantage of the situation and started putting more and more people to work. It turned out to be a great experience for everybody that was involved in the preparation and it got lots of people, especially high school kids, excited about doing service.

52 ROUND 19: AUG 30, 2010

This round Kelly started up her core nursing classes. I was so proud of her that she got into the school that she wanted to and that she was fulfilling her goals. It made me so happy to think that by finishing the nursing program she would be able to get a good job and wouldn't need to be financially dependent on me. She would enjoy her job and be able to make more than enough money to take care of herself. It took a lot of stress off of my shoulders to know that she would at least be financially all right without me.

But her starting up the core nursing classes meant that she would be busy and that I would have to spend a lot of time without her. I definitely wasn't looking forward to being without her, especially since we were always so attached to each other now. It was going to be a sacrifice for me as well, to have her finish her nursing school. I had to get used to going to all of my chemo treatments and doctor's visits by myself. We had lots of friends volunteer to help out with giving me rides, but I had to spend the majority of my time there by myself. Luckily this regimen of chemo wasn't too difficult and I was fine sitting there by myself while the poison was being infused into me.

When this round was over, I again tried to spend my good free time playing as much golf as I could. I was getting a lot better and really starting to enjoy the game. I loved being out on the course, far away from all of the medical stuff that I dealt during with the rest of my life. However my progress in my treatments was starting to affect my playing ability. By the end of this round I had been through a total of five weeks of insanely intense diarrhea. I had lost a lot of weight and now my prosthetic wasn't fitting like it should. I tried as many tricks as I could think of to keep it from falling off, but it just wouldn't stay on sometimes. This made it kind of difficult to play golf or to do anything else for that matter. I would always have to walk funny to keep it from coming off and a lot of times I would have to hold it in place as I walked. It made life really frustrating, but I figured I only had one more round to go before I would be able to stop this type of chemo and hopefully gain some weight back. I just had to be patient until then.

As I went through my treatments and all of the crazy experiences that went along with them I started to notice changes in me. I was able to change lots of things that I didn't originally like about myself. Things like how I used to make fun of people a lot, how I used to be so sarcastic, and how I used to be kind of full of myself. After having been through everything I realized that I was generally more loving of others around me, even people I didn't know. I was more sensitive to people's feelings and needs and was able to better recognize ways that I could help them. I lost all materialistic desires and escaped the grasp that finances had on me. Most importantly, my relationship with Kelly had transformed into this amazing companionship filled with so much love, respect, and admiration for each other that I never knew existed outside of fairy tales.

These changes didn't just happen overnight either. Each required lots of time and self-reflection and were often initiated by some kind of crappy experience that I went through. As each change took place, I recognized that I became more at peace with myself and that I was happier than I used to be. Now, at this point in my treatments, after I had gone through so much and changed so much I had started to see that I was happier than I had ever been before. I was still distraught over what Kelly and I were still going through, but there was new found peace in my life that in a way, overpowered any hardship that I faced. There were a lot of times when we were sad, but happiness was always quick to move in and take over.

These types of changes didn't only take place in my life, my family, several friends, and especially Kelly had similar changes in their lives that only happened because of my having cancer. I was really starting to see some of the puzzle pieces fall into place. I still didn't understand exactly why I was going through this, but I was definitely able to see so many positives that have come from it. I haven't always felt this way, but for the first time throughout all of my horrible experiences I felt thankful that I had cancer. I know that sounds a little strange, but I knew that I and my loved ones had received so many eternally important blessings that we wouldn't have received had I never been diagnosed with cancer. And I had to be thankful for that.

53 ROUND 20: SEP 20, 2010

The last set of scans that I took showed that the chemo was still effective in stabilizing the growth of the tumors. I had done four rounds of this regimen and they still hadn't grown. My doctor seemed to be pretty happy about that and told us that I should visit with a thoracic surgeon to talk about the possibility of having the tumors surgically removed. The hope would be that the chemo had killed off any cells that didn't show up on the scans and that the remaining tumors could be removed, thus leaving me cancer free. It was a long shot because it is unlikely that all of the cancer cells were killed by the chemo, but my doctor seemed to think it was a good option. I was willing to do anything to try to get rid of the cancer for good so I happily agreed to meet with the surgeon to see if surgery was a possibility.

When we met with him he explained to us all of the details about the procedure and the risks that were involved. He explained that during the surgery he would make an incision in my back, just under the shoulder blade, in order to reach the lungs. After accessing the lungs he would then feel all of the lung tissue to try to find any tumors that didn't show up on my latest CT scan. If he felt that he could remove all of the tumors that he could feel and still leave me with enough healthy lung tissue then he would make the cuts and remove them.

By looking at my latest CT scan he was able to estimate that he would probably have to take out about 30% of my lungs in order to remove the tumors. Having that much lung removed was unlikely to make me short of breath for the rest of my life, but probably would prevent me from being able to participate in heavy physical activity. The thought of losing my lung capacity made me feel like I would just become a little more handicapped. I had already lost so much of my physical abilities with the amputation that in reality losing lung capacity wasn't that big of a deal. But it was still depressing because it seemed like each step I took to get rid of the cancer was destroying my body more and more. I didn't really have much of a choice though because my only other option at that point was to do more chemo until I died. So it was an easy decision to go through with the surgery anyway. I was told to finish this next round of chemo and then return and visit to finalize preparations for the surgery.

I went through this round of chemo hoping that it would be the last one that I would ever have to do. The round went by without any problems and before I knew it I was on my way back to the surgeon's office to get my final instructions for the surgery. He told us that the plan was to operate on my left lung first, recover for a few weeks and then operate on my right lung. I was given a device to do breathing exercises with and a small pillow shaped like a bear to help me cough during recovery. He marked my shoulder where the incision would be made, told me when and where to meet for the surgery, and sent me on my way.

I was really scared to go through another surgery, especially after my horrible experience with the amputation. But at the same time I felt like I was being given one last shot to rid my body of the cancer forever. It was kind of an all or nothing move for me. Either the surgeries would be successful and the cancer would be gone or I would surely die in the not so distant future. I wasn't too fond of the option, but I had to go for it.

54 THE BRENT EVENT:
OCTOBER 23, 2010

My fist surgery was scheduled for the 25th of October. Just five days after my 29th birthday, two days after the Brent Event and a couple of weeks after finishing up my last round of chemo. They wanted me to have a couple of weeks off to make sure I was in good health for the surgery. The timing of my weeks away from chemo worked out perfectly with the final weeks of preparation for the Brent Event.

The last few weeks of preparation were pretty crazy for us. We needed to have some kind of idea of how many people would show up so that we could order the right amount of food, runners' bags, and t-shirts. But lots of people had told us that they were going to be there, but not many had actually registered for the event. We were stressing out about it so we sent out a mass email and Facebook message to tell people to start registering. From that day on we had people signing up like crazy. Every day for the last few weeks 50 to 60 people signed up each day and online donations started pouring in. Just before the event we couldn't believe how many people we had signed up. We made an estimate on how many we expected, purchased everything we needed, and got everything set up for the event.

There were so many people who showed up to help the morning of the Brent Event. We had more people helping than we had things for them to do. Kelly and I showed up just a few minutes before the 5k started and couldn't believe what we saw. The park that we were holding the event at was completely packed with volunteers and runners. We quickly found out that we had sold out of runners' bibs and people were still lining up to sign up. There were way more people than we expected, and it only got better as the day went on. After the 5k, we held the one mile family fun run. The trail that they did the fun run on was completely packed with people. The entire high school football team even came out for it. After the fun run, the live band started up and the party was under way. For the rest of the afternoon everybody hung out, listened to the band, played in the carnival games, and ate barbeque. Everybody seemed to have a great time.

I spent the entire time going around talking to all of the family and friends that I hadn't seen in so long. It was such an amazing help for Kelly and I to have so many people there to show their love and support for us. Especially since we were about to go into the hospital for my surgery in two days. It eased our minds and made me feel like everything was going to be all right.

The Brent Event turned out to be one of the best days of my life. The outpouring of love that everybody showed us was unbelievable. We were able to raise way more money than we initially expected. But the best part about the whole event was the impact that it seemed to have on the community and on everybody that was involved in helping out. Throughout the whole event there was an excitement in the air about doing service that was almost palpable. It was like donating and volunteering was the cool thing to do that day. People seemed to leave the event wanting to continue serving others in their daily lives.

After the Brent Event I really started to evaluate my life. I felt like I had lived a good life and that I was a good person, but what does that really matter? What had I done with my time here to help others and improve the world that I lived in? Not very much! I now saw things in life differently. I was so much more aware of all of the needs that people have in the world. I felt like I needed to spend more time worrying about others and less time worrying about myself. I told myself that if I were to ever get better I would spend a lot more of my time, energy, and money on serving others. The first thing that I wanted to do was set up a foundation so that I could hold Brent Events in the future, except this time I would raise money for other people who found themselves in similar situations to mine.

55 LEFT LUNG RESECTION AND THORACOTOMY: OCTOBER 25, 2010

The morning of the surgery I was pretty scared. I knew how my last surgery turned out and I didn't want to go through anything like it. I was nervous that I would come out of the operating room unable to breath or something. Kelly was a lifesaver again while we were in the waiting room. She rubbed my back, told me how much she loved me, and made me feel like everything was going to be all right.

When they finally called me back I really started to get scared and broke down on Kelly's shoulder while I was changing into my hospital gown. They put an IV in my arm and started an epidural on my back and wheeled me off to the operating room. As they wheeled me away I looked back at Kelly, wishing that she could come along with me and hold my hand through the whole thing, but she had to stay. I was on my own.

Just like before, the surgery flew by like a dream and before I knew it I was waking up in a recovery room. I felt like I could barely breath, but I was still too drugged from the anesthesia to be very scared about it. I fell back asleep and was eventually awakened again by Kelly's sweet voice. She stayed with me in the recovery room until they wheeled me up to my hospital room. When I got there I was greeted by a whole bunch of smiling familiar faces. My whole family was there to help out and cheer me up. They had all kinds of questions for me, but I couldn't really answer them. I was really out of breath and it kind of hurt to talk. I had to ask them hold off on the questions until I started to feel better.

I spent the next few days in the hospital room with all kinds of tubes coming out of me. They were all so annoying to deal with, but the worst, by far, was the chest tube that was coming out of my chest from just under my arm pit. I could feel the tube wrapped around my lung and it made it so painful to breathe and cough. I wanted them to take it out so badly, but I had to leave it in until I was ready to leave the hospital. After a few days of pain and discomfort they finally removed the tubes and let me go home.

My recovery at home seemed to go by pretty quickly. It was really difficult for me to breathe, but it seemed to improve a little each day. At first I was only able to move around the house on a rolling office chair because I wasn't able to use the crutches. But after a week or two I felt well enough to be able to get up and do almost whatever I wanted, as long as it didn't involve physical activity with my arms.

I had recovered pretty quickly and was eager to get going on the other surgery. I was scared to let too much time lapse between the two surgeries because I was horrified of the thought of the cancer spreading. So I called up my surgeon and asked them to move up my next surgery date so that I could get it over with.

56 RIGHT LUNG RESECTION AND THORACOTOMY: NOVEMBER 17, 2010

I was a little more at ease this time when I went in for my second lung surgery. I had already gone through one, and the truth was, I didn't think it was that horrible. It was still miserable, but it was definitely bearable. This time my only real worry was that I would have an even harder time breathing when I woke up since my other lung was already messed up.

Of course, Kelly was there with me to help calm my nerves before I went in. She was right there by my side as soon as I woke up. This time when I woke up I did have a lot harder time breathing. It was like I couldn't do anything but take very small, shallow breaths. It hurt so bad to breathe deeply and cough. After just a day of being in the hospital I could tell that this recovery was going to be a lot more difficult. And it was.

Everything seemed to be so much more painful after this surgery. It sometimes felt like I was constantly struggling to breathe. This time they had to put two chest tubes in, which made my life extra miserable. It seemed like there was so much fluid draining out of the chest tubes. The fluid never stopped coming, which resulted in having to stay in the hospital longer than expected. After almost a week they still weren't able to remove the chest tubes, but I needed to get out of the hospital, so they sent me home with the tubes still in me. I spent the next week or so at home with rubber tubes that came out of my side and drained into a small plastic box that I had to carry around. My recovery was long and painful and it felt like it was never going to end.

When they finally pulled the chest tubes out, I didn't even feel that much better. It was still difficult and painful to breathe and my energy and appetite were really low. My life during that time was miserable.

There was one night during my recovery where I had a very interesting dream. It started out pretty weird. I was at some type of campground just outside of a rundown city with my sister Mandy. We were anxiously waiting for something I don't remember. Then all of a sudden we had to get up and rush into the city to retrieve something from a school. It was like we were on some type of mission or something. We went into the city and did a lot of stuff that I don't really remember and then somehow the dream ended with me hiking in the forest with a friend. At that point the dream became so vivid and real. I had two legs again and I could feel the strength in them as I walked up this hill. My breathing was steady and strong. I was able to move around quickly and easily without getting tired. Physically, I felt great and was thrilled to be able to have a normally functioning body again.

Then I woke up. My body ached, I had phantom pains from my missing leg, and I could barely breathe. My reality was completely miserable. I laid in bed for a while that morning wishing I could go back to the dream that I had. Then, for the first time ever the thought came to my mind that maybe I would be happier if I were dead. My feeling that way made me feel so guilty. I couldn't believe that I was actually thinking that I would rather be dead and comfortable than with Kelly. I knew that I would miss her so much but my discomfort at that time was so great that I didn't really care. I knew that it would be really hard for her for a while, but that with time things would improve and she would be fine. The guilt I felt drove me to tell her how I was feeling. I cried and was barely able to spit out my thoughts. I thought she would be offended or upset but she surprised me. She said she understood and that she didn't like seeing me suffer, and if my passing away were to end my suffering then she would be all right with that.

Her response shocked me and helped me feel of the love that she had for me. I then realized the struggle that she and my family had been going through this whole time. It hurt them to see me suffer. Considering how much I had suffered through all of my treatments, they must have gone through a really hard time. It made me feel awful to think that I was the cause of everybody else's worries and tears.

Thankfully, I eventually recovered to the point that I was able to feel comfortable again. I no longer wished that I was dead. I was excited to get moving on with my life, hoping that it would be cancer free, at least for a while.

57 EVEN MORE BAD NEWS

A few weeks after my second surgery we went in for another set of scans to make sure the cancer was gone and to check up on my recovery progress. We hoped that the cancer was gone for good and we felt like if it were to come back, it wouldn't show up for at least a few months. But we were proven wrong when we went back into the doctor's office for the results. The doctor showed us the scans and pointed out a handful of tumors that had already grown back in my lungs and were big enough to show up on the scans.

We couldn't believe it! How could they have come back so fast? The news that they had returned immediately sent me into a mini depression. Then the doctor had to go and make things worse by telling me that at this point there was really nothing that they could do to cure me. All they could do was try to extend my life and improve my quality of life. The cancer was going to kill me and there was nothing that they could do about it. He told me I had anywhere from four months to a year, depending on how I responded to the clinical trials that they had. But there was one problem. I probably would never be able to qualify for a clinical trial because of my bad kidneys. So the doctor told me that we could get started on a different regimen of chemotherapy and hope that I respond well to it. He told me that there was really no rush to get started right away and that we could begin in January after the holidays.

58 TRY TO ENJOY THE HOLIDAYS!

I returned home from the doctor's office that day in a strange state of mind. I was heartbroken and felt so bad for Kelly, as I usually am when I get bad news, but on top of that, I suddenly felt like my life was just like this big waiting room. It was like everything that I did was kind of pointless, like I was just passing the time until I got called to the other side. I really didn't care about anything other than getting good quality time in with Kelly and being with my family.

It was depressing for my parents to hear, but I told them that this would probably be my last Christmas and that we should try to fly the whole family in. They immediately started making plans to get everybody down here. Before everybody arrived Kelly and I decided to take a small weekend vacation up to New Braunfels and San Antonio just to get away for a little while and have some time together. When word got out that we wanted to go on a vacation friends jumped into action and before we knew it someone had offered to pay for our hotel in San Antonio.

That trip was a special trip for me. I couldn't help thinking that it might be one of the last trips that we ever took together. I cherished every second I had to spend with Kelly and tried to stay as happy as possible. When we got to New Braunfels we went to our favorite restaurant and spent time walking around the shops. We stayed in a hotel that night and then drove to San Antonio the next day where we ate at a random Mexican restaurant, watched a movie on the IMAX in 3D, and walked around on the river walk. We stayed in a hotel on the river walk that night and then drove back home the next day. It was a pretty uneventful vacation, but every moment of it was so precious to me because of my now very limited time with Kelly.

We got home and before we knew it everybody was there for the holidays and the house was packed. It was a little crazy to have everybody in town, but it was a lot of fun. I don't really remember anything in particular that we did, but I remember the feeling that was there. It was like the news that I wouldn't be around much longer had brought everybody a little closer together. I got lots of hugs, back rubs, and head rubs from everybody and we had lots of tender family moments together. It was a great Christmas!

After everybody left and the excitement was over it seemed like the cancer started to hit me a little more. I was exhausted all of the time, I didn't have an appetite, and I felt like my body was falling apart. Suddenly life became really hard to live through. I cried to Kelly almost every night because I felt so bad for her. My thoughts were constantly on her and what she was going to do after I was gone. I tried to think of everything that I could do to prepare her to take on life on her own. I went over finances with her, I gave her advice on things like where to live and work, and I tried to teach her all of the spiritual lessons that I could think of that would make her life easier.

I was also worried about whether she would get remarried, and if she would still love me after years had gone by. She told me she always would and that she would never find anybody good enough to replace me, and I believed her. I told her all of the time how much I loved her and how amazing I thought she was. It hurt to think that I wouldn't be able to do that much longer. So I decided to start writing the story of our life together so that she could have all of my feelings for her written down for her to read whenever she wanted. I also started writing down things that might help my family if they were to read it too. Then, somehow, I found myself writing this enormous memoir that I felt was full of information that I hoped would help people. I didn't plan on writing a book, but here I am right in the middle of it.

Anyway, Kelly was the original reason for writing. She was my number one concern. I didn't worry about my family as much because they have each other and I just felt like they would be fine. I knew Kelly would be fine also, but I worried a lot about the little things. Things like who is going to cheer her up when she's in a bad mood, or who is going to give her advice when she needs it? I felt so bad that I wouldn't be able to do those things for her anymore.

From then on I decided that I would do everything I could for her while I was still able to, but at that point all I could really do was hang in there and try to live as long as possible. So, if that meant doing chemo treatments until I died just so that she could have more time with me, then that's what I was going to do.

59 NOT THAT STUFF AGAIN!
COCKTAIL #5

I did another set of scans and met with my doctor just before starting up chemo again in January. Of course there was no good news to be told. We found out that the tumors had almost doubled in size in only a month's time. We couldn't believe how fast they were growing. At this rate I felt like I would be a goner in less than a couple of months if the next treatment he gave me didn't work. But my doctor seemed more confident. He said he had a regimen that he felt would work very well at keeping the cancer under control.

Unfortunately, the new chemo regimen that my doctor had in mind was not going to be an easy one like my previous two were. He wanted me to do a mix that was very similar to what I had at the very beginning. It was to include the drugs Adriamycin, Vincristine, Cyclophosphamide, and Etoposide. All were pretty heavy chemo drugs and caused pretty much the same side effects that I experienced during my first round of chemo. However, this time I was going to be able to receive them as an outpatient procedure instead of having to stay in the hospital like before.

I got the treatment at the same facility in Sugar Land, which we loved because by that time we had become such good friends with all of the nurses and staff. This somehow made going in for chemo almost fun. On day one of my treatment I received all four drugs, which usually took about four hours to complete. Then on days two and three I only received Etoposide and on day four I would have to return for a shot to help my white blood cells recover faster. It was a pretty simple treatment, but it beat me up pretty good.

The first night after receiving all of the chemo drugs I would feel pretty awful. I would usually be really wiped out physically, wouldn't have much of an appetite, and would have pretty bad chemo brain. The next day would be even worse because all of the drugs from day one were still in my system and I had to return to get more. I usually spent those first two days lying around on the couch a lot trying to make myself as comfortable as possible. Then on day three I would feel a little better because the drugs from day one would be out of my system. By day four I would start to feel lousy again and I would just go downhill from there.

The whole next week would usually be pretty bad too. My blood counts would drop really low and make me feel sick and completely drained of energy. During that second week I would usually have to go in for several blood and platelet transfusions to keep me alive. The blood transfusions didn't bother me but I couldn't stand the platelet transfusions. Half of the time I would have some degree of allergic reaction to the platelets which would cause me to experience anything from a slight cough, to swelling around my eyes and difficulty breathing. I was always scared to go in for platelet transfusions because I never knew how bad my reaction would be.

Finally by the end of that second week my blood counts would recover and I would start to feel better, leaving me almost a full week of feeling decent before having to go in and repeat the whole process. It was a pretty intense chemo regimen that I was lucky to complete without having any major complications.

60 ROUND 21: JAN 10, 2011

The first round of this regimen was just as bad as I expected it to be. I started on a Monday and by the time I finished all of the chemo infusions on Wednesday I was completely wiped out. A few days later my appetite completely disappeared and I was back to forcing food down just to keep the nausea from getting worse. I was so physically drained that I hardly left the couch for almost a week.

On the second Monday of the three week round I went in to get my blood checked and my platelets and red blood cells were extremely low. I badly needed transfusions, but couldn't get them until the next morning. I went home and tried to pass the time until I could get the transfusion the next morning. My eyes and head ached, my brain felt like it was shutting down, my heart was doing strange things, and I was having a hard time breathing. It was like every part of my body was sounding an alarm to tell me something was wrong. I was scared that I was going to die on the couch at any moment. Luckily I didn't and the blood transfusion the next morning seemed to fix everything, at least for a little while. A few days later my blood counts dropped again and I had to go through the same thing all over again.

I felt a little better after my second set of transfusions and I was looking forward to further recovering so that I could enjoy the good week of the round. But this time when my good week came I didn't really feel that much better. I was still weak and nauseated and it was driving me crazy! Mentally, I needed to feel good during that good week to prepare me to be able to handle the next round of chemo. But the next round was just around the corner and I still felt sick. I started to wonder how many rounds of this stuff I would be able to do before I gave up.

I felt like my body just wasn't as strong as it used to be. Each day I became a little more exhausted and each day it became a little harder to breathe. I just felt like I was slowly wasting away. It scared me that I didn't ever really recover during my "good" week of this round. It made me sad all of the time because I felt like it was just a matter of time until I would waste away to the point that my body couldn't survive anymore. I just wanted so badly to be able to be a normal person again without all of these physical problems with my body. I despised the cancer and the very thought of me being sick.

I had felt this way before, but this time it was with a different intensity. I couldn't stand the thought of being sick and having to do hospital stuff all of the time. I wanted to eliminate everything in my life that reminded me that I was sick. I tried to only be around people and things that helped me feel like a normal person. I found that I couldn't get away from the doctor's visits, treatments, pills, and things like that, but I could get away from people.

Whether it was through conversation or just through my subconscious, people constantly reminded me about my cancer. If I went to church people would come up to me and ask how my treatments were going. If people came to visit me they would talk about my cancer. When friends called to check up, they wanted to know how I was handling everything. It drove me crazy! I told my mom about this and she sent out some emails or something asking everybody not to talk to me about cancer or treatments or anything like that. It worked really well. People stopped talking to me about it.

But from then on, I felt like if somebody random came to talk to me at church they were doing it because they felt bad that I had cancer and they wanted to lift my spirits or something. I felt like when people visited me at home or called, they only did it because I had cancer.

Suddenly everything reminded me of cancer and I turned really anti-social to try to escape it. If I went to church I tried to avoid talking to anybody. I pretty much bored any visitors until they stopped coming, and I almost completely stopped answering my phone. I just tried to surround myself with things that made me feel like I was living a normal life. For the most part, that meant only spending time with Kelly and my parents. Around them life just seemed to go on like normal even though we all dealt with my cancer every day. They made me feel like just a normal person who happened to have cancer, instead of a person with a horrible disease that needed extra attention. I always felt better around them and I am so grateful to them for that.

61 ROUND 22: JAN 31, 2011

Starting a few months back I began to have major problems with my appetite. I didn't feel like eating very often, and when I did, every time I put food into my mouth it made me feel like I wanted to throw up. It had been going on for months now and right before going in for round 22, I met with my doctor to see if there was anything I could do about it. He gave me a couple of medicines to try and said that there was only a small chance that they would work, but at that point I was so sick of not being able to eat that I would try anything. I gladly accepted them and went on my way.

I tried one of the meds and didn't like it. The other was called Megace and I was supposed to take it twice a day. I started taking it and my appetite started coming back right away. It was amazing! All of a sudden I could enjoy eating again. Everything tasted so good and I always wanted to eat so much. The only problem was, after a couple of days of taking the medicine I would eat a big meal and then be hungry an hour later. I couldn't deal with that so I had to cut back on the medicine. I found a good balance of taking it once every few days and was able to feel good and enjoy food from then on.

I think the appetite medicine helped me through that round of chemo because it was a lot easier than the first. I hardly felt nauseated the whole time, and I think having so much food in me gave me more energy and helped me recover a little faster. I was still wiped out during my second week and required two or three platelet transfusions, but overall this round wasn't as miserable, especially compared to the one just before it.

In spite of the easier round, I still felt like my body was getting worse and worse. Mainly by the way that I felt when

I breathed. When I inhaled, it felt like my lungs weren't able to expand enough to get a deep breath in. When I exhaled it felt like I wasn't able to breathe out all of my air. It was the strangest feeling and I thought it might be related to my recent surgeries, but I couldn't help but to think it was being caused by the rapidly growing tumors in my lungs. I worried a lot that the chemo wasn't working, but at that point all I could do was try to relax until we got the results from my next set of scans.

Sometime during my good week we drove out to a little town named Roundtop, Texas and spent the day fishing, shotgun shooting, and just sitting around enjoying the beautiful weather and the Texas hill country scenery. I didn't catch any fish, but somehow was able to hit almost all the clay pigeons that were thrown for me. It was a little difficult too because I was standing on a wobbly rock with my prosthetic and I had to wrap a folded up sweatshirt around my shoulder to keep the gun from kicking my port. It was amazing that I was able to hit anything at all. We all had a great time and it was the perfect get-away from my mundane life at the hospital.

Ever since the doctors told me that they couldn't get rid of the cancer and that I would eventually die from it, I started to think a lot about death and what the next life would be like. I had thought about these things before but the images in my head were always kind of cartoon-like and I never thought about any details.

Now I have realized that my death and the things that I will experience are real. It is going to happen. I think of everything so much more vividly now and I wonder about all of the details. I think of what it will feel like on the other side, what state of mind I will be in, what thoughts I will have, what everything will look like, what I will do there, who I will know, what social interactions will be like, etc. I think about every detail I can. After lots of pondering and some prayer I feel like I have a decent idea of what to expect.

I know everybody has a different belief on what the next life will be like. I personally believe that when we die we don't go straight to heaven or hell but to another place that Christ called paradise. I think of it as almost like a continuation of this life except everything is a little different.

Right before Christ died on the cross he said to the man on the cross next to him "Today shalt thou be with me in paradise (Luke 23:43)." Three days later, after his resurrection he appeared to Mary Magdalene at his tomb and told her "Touch me not; for I am not yet ascended to my father (John 20:17)." I believe that during those three days Christ went to a paradise where God does not reside.

This paradise, in my opinion, is the place where we all go when we die. It is separated into a paradise for those who have lived righteously in their mortal lives, and a type of purgatory for those who did not. I feel like everybody who has died stays there until God's work is completely finished and judgment takes place. People still have responsibilities or jobs, if you want to call them that, they still spend time with friends and family, and they are still able to think and make decisions for themselves.

I don't exactly know what it will be like to get there, like if there is a tunnel of light that I will have to follow, or anything like that, but I feel like once I get there everything will be more beautiful than anything I have experienced before. I'll likely be greeted by family that has passed before me. We will probably have some type of celebration together with lots of good food that I have never tried before. Then they will probably show me around the places where I will be living and spending most of my time.

I feel like our senses will be greatly improved from what they are now, which will make everything feel, sound, smell, taste, and look so much better and more intense. I feel like the plants will grow perfectly, without diseases or deformities and the animals will all be friendly with the people. There will be gardens with more flower varieties than we can even imagine and the colors will cover the entire spectrum and will be so beautiful and vivid. Buildings and roads will be constructed of more precious materials and will not have the typical rust, mildew, and decay that we see in this world. It will truly be a paradise that is beyond our current understanding.

Upon arrival in this spirit world all people will be in the same spiritual state as when they died and they will all continue to work toward perfecting themselves and becoming more like Christ if they choose to do so. The people in the paradise side will all be friendly, respectful, and considerate of everybody, creating a perfect society without any of the crazy problems we have to deal with here. On the purgatory-like side the people will still have the same character problems as they did in life. For the most part, the people there will be unhappy and unpleasant to be around, making it a pretty miserable place to be stuck in. There will also be tons of people there that went through their mortal lives without ever having been given the opportunity to hear the gospel of Jesus Christ. Maybe they lived in a time period where Christianity did not exist. Or maybe they lived and died in a remote part of the world without ever even hearing the name Jesus Christ. In order for judgment to be fair, these people will need to be taught the gospel and given a chance to accept or reject it.

I know that God does all types of things to help us in our lives. He comforts us, teaches us, protects us, and guides us. It seems like most of the time He uses angels on the other side to accomplish these things. I feel like these angels are the righteous people who reside in paradise. Helping those who are still living is a responsibility that one might have after moving to the other side. Another responsibility they might have is to teach the gospel to those who never had a chance to hear it in their mortal life. I'm sure there are all types of jobs on the other side, from leadership positions to construction workers. I feel like the type of responsibility we will be given is determined by the spiritual progress that we made while in our mortal life. Those who were strong, faithful followers of Christ may have very important responsibilities, while those who were not may be given simple tasks.

Apart from the work we will do I'm sure we will have time to spend with family and friends. I'm sure there will be sports, music, hobbies, and crafts of all types to keep us entertained. And of course, some of the most amazing golf courses you can ever imagine. We will all live there in peace and happiness, each day working towards perfecting ourselves and helping others until God's work is complete and judgment takes place. At which point we will move on to wherever we deserve to go.

I feel strongly that after I die one of my main responsibilities will be to watch over Kelly and the rest of my family until they complete their time in life. I will be there to comfort them through hard times, to guide them to make good decisions and to strengthen them in their struggles. It is comforting to me to think that I will still be able to help Kelly from day to day and that I will be involved in her life until she can reunite with me.

62 FINALLY SOME GOOD NEWS!

During my good week of this last round I went in to get some scans done. I was super nervous because I felt like it was another critical moment that would determine how much longer I had to live. If the chemo was working then I could estimate that I would have at least another five months or so. But if the chemo didn't work then I felt like I would only have another month or two left.

We went into the doctor's office and waited forever, like always. When we finally met with the doctor he told us he had good news. He said that the tumors had shrunk. But they didn't just shrink a little. They shrunk by nearly 90% after just two rounds of chemo. He seemed happy, but not overly excited, so I didn't really know what to think. All I knew was that I had just gained a few more months of life and that was all that I cared about.

We went over the scans again a few days later with my other oncologist and he seemed to be a lot more excited about the results. He said that they were almost miraculous and that you couldn't ask for better scans. This made me feel a lot better about my situation. I still knew inside that my prognosis probably hadn't changed so I tried not to get too excited about everything. But when you finally get good news like that, it's hard not to let your mind get carried away and think that this might just be the beginning of a miraculous cure.

63 ROUND 23: FEB 21, 2011

It was a lot easier to start this next round knowing that the chemo was actually helping to extend my life. It somehow made the misery of it all much more worth it. The side effects were a lot more tolerable and I seemed to have a little more energy than the other rounds, although I could have just been making that up in my head.

The week my blood counts dropped was a busy week filled with transfusions. I think I had to get three platelet transfusions and one red blood cell transfusion. By this point I just accepted the fact that I would have to get lots of transfusions with this type of chemo, but unfortunately each round seemed to be a little worse. It was like my counts dropped quicker and were slower to recover with each round. This scared me a little because I knew that if I kept doing chemo my bone marrow would eventually get damaged to the point that my counts wouldn't recover. At that point I wouldn't be able to do any more chemo and I would pretty much be at the end of the line. The scary thing was that we didn't know when this might happen. It could have been this round, or it could be ten rounds down the road. But it was only a matter of time until it happened.

This round was especially interesting for me. A few weeks back I let Kelly get a little puppy. She had been begging me for one for so long and I always said no. But this time I was starting to feel that it might be a good idea to just say yes and let her have one. I knew that it would make her happy and I also felt like if I didn't make it that it would be really good to have a little friend around to cheer her up. So she brought home a little tiny black puppy, half miniature dachshund and half miniature poodle.

It was a lot of fun to have a little dog around but I quickly realized that taking care of a puppy while sick from chemo can be a little annoying. But I had to do it. Most days Kelly would be gone at school and nobody would be home but me. I usually didn't wear my prosthetic when I was sick, so it was really difficult to carry a squirming puppy in one hand while going down the stairs on crutches. A lot of times she would want to play, but I just didn't have the energy to do anything. Taking care of her was definitely a pain in the butt sometimes, but it has been so great to have her around because she makes us laugh when we are sad and is a good distraction from all of the horrible medical stuff we have to deal with.

That round we also moved back into my parent's house. My medical expenses combined with expenses from Kelly's school were just too much for us. We were taking quite a bit of money out of savings each month and we didn't like it. Plus, ever since the surgeries, we had been spending the night at my parent's house almost every night. Our apartment was more of a big storage unit than a place to live. So we gathered some friends together and made the move.

This time, moving back to my parent's house was heartbreaking. The apartment was the only thing that Kelly and I had that reminded me of a normal life with her. All I wanted was a long and normal life with her, but I knew that I wouldn't be able to have it. Moving our stuff out of the apartment that day felt like we were taking the first steps to prepare for my death, but I knew that it was the best thing for us to do. This time when we moved into my parent's house we put a lot of our furniture in our room and set it up just like we had it in our apartment. It helped me to still feel like we had a life together and everything has worked out great since.

We decided to take an extra week off of chemo so that my bone marrow could recover a little. We hoped that taking a break would mean that I wouldn't have to get so many transfusions in the future. We had a lot of fun during our week off. We went to a Broadway show in downtown Houston, and my friend Rob somehow got four court-side tickets to a Rockets game. Rob, Jessica, Kelly and I all went and had an awesome time. We also had some good friends come in from out of town to visit us. That week off was so much fun and gave me some time to recover and feel physically prepared for the next couple of rounds.

Usually when I get bad news I am devastated for a couple of days and then I bounce back and start to look for the positives in my situation. After finding some positives I try to forget about the bad news so that I can stay in a good mood for as long as possible. But then, at some point, the bad news comes back to me and I am devastated all over again. I have gone through this process over and over again ever since I was first diagnosed. It has been a crazy emotional roller coaster ride that I have come to grow so sick of. I felt like everybody else was sick of it too. Dealing with the emotional ups and downs has been the hardest part of this whole cancer mess. Sometimes I looked forward to the day that I die so that the roller coaster can finally come to an end for everybody that I loved. I figured they would all have one big drop and then life would only get better from then on.

After getting the last set of bad news I didn't want to look for the positives anymore. I just wanted to accept the fact that I was going to die and try to prepare myself for it. It was like I was putting up a defensive wall to protect my emotions from being hammered again.

Feeling great during my week off and knowing that my tumors were shrinking at an incredible rate slowly knocked down that wall and gave me hope that maybe I would actually be cured of this horrible cancer, even though deep down I knew that my prognosis hadn't really changed. I was climbing back up that slope and hoping there wasn't another huge drop ahead.

64 ROUND 24: MARCH 21, 2011

Round 24 ended up being about the same as round 23. I felt just as tired and just as nauseated as before. The week off did seem to give me a little extra energy at the beginning, but it didn't seem to help my bone marrow much at all. I still had lots of blood transfusions and my counts seemed to be even slower to recover than before. My white blood cells were practically at zero for an entire week before they started to improve. Luckily I didn't get any infections and never had to go in with fever.

After I recovered a little, a friend of ours offered to prepare for us a will and all of the other documents that come along with it. We gladly accepted. We knew that we needed to do something about those things, but didn't really know how or where to start. He came over and explained everything to us, asked us some questions and went home to prepare the documents. He came back a few days later and we signed everything and got everything set. I am so grateful to him for helping us with that. It was a relatively simple process, but extremely hard for me to go through. It was surreal to be thinking that we were taking another step to prepare for my death. Throughout the whole process I couldn't help but to think about all of the things that Kelly would have to deal with when I was gone. Even though we joked a lot about all of the life insurance money she would be getting and how well off she would be it still hurt inside to think of what she would actually go through.

I had scans again at the end of this round. We went into the doctor's office and the news was still good. The tumors had shrunk even more, although not as much as during the first two rounds. He explained that this was expected and then went on to give us even better news. He told us that with the tumors responding the way they were, he was expecting me to go into some kind of remission after I finished my next two rounds. He didn't give us a lot of details, but he expected the remission to last from anywhere to a few months to almost a year. He also talked a little about doing radiation and possibly a surgery if the tumors shrunk even more. That was like music to my ears because I knew that he wouldn't try to do a surgery or anything aggressive like that unless he thought he could get rid of it for good.

We left the office excited to be able to have some time off of chemo. We started planning all kinds of vacations for the summer and talked about all of the fun things that we would do together. It was going to be like one last big summer vacation. And possibly, the beginning of the rest of our lives if everything worked out perfectly and the cancer was cured.

I was also excited because I felt like I had changed so much through my fight with cancer and that I now had so much potential to do lots of good with the time I had left. I had a huge desire to devote more of my life to serving others and I had gained the confidence to do things that would make that possible. I was eager to start the foundation, and I was constantly trying to think of other ways to help people. Before I felt like these were things that I would never have time to do, but now that I was going to go into remission for a while I felt like I actually would have the time and I couldn't wait to get started.

65 ROUND 25: APRIL 11, 2011

This round I could tell that the chemo was starting to cause more problems with my body. During my first day of infusion the weirdest thing happened. As I was getting the drugs I started to get really weak and light-headed, my skin got all clammy and I felt like I was going to pass out. I called the nurse in and she took my vitals, but they all seemed to be relatively normal. After thinking for a while at what it could be, the nurse finally just suggested that try eating and drinking something. So I had some of the crackers and Gatorade that they give out to the patients. After a few minutes I started to perk up a little and by the time I left I felt pretty normal. The nurses figured it was because I needed to eat and drink, but as far as I can remember, I was plenty hydrated and had eaten not too long ago.

But then I started noticing weird things happening at home. My heart would sometimes palpitate and beat irregularly, I started sweating a lot in my sleep, and I would have these weird dizzy spells. I didn't know if it was something serious that I should worry about or if it was just another "normal" chemo side effect. When I went in the second week to get my blood checked I had another experience like when I was getting the chemo. I had been dropped off, so I was by myself in a wheelchair in the waiting room when all of a sudden I got weak and felt like I was going to pass out again. I didn't really know what to do because I was alone, so I called my mom at work and asked her to come up and help me. By the time she got there a hospital volunteer had already gotten me some Gatorade and I was starting to feel a little better. My mom sat with me until we got the lab results and then dropped me off at the house. I was so grateful that she was willing and able to come up and help me that day because having something happen to you when you are alone is pretty scary.

These kinds of problems kept going on for the rest of the round. My doctor didn't know what the problem was because my symptoms were common and could be related to anything. But he kind of leaned towards the idea that it was related to a cold that I was fighting at the time.

The rest of the round was typical of this regimen of chemo. I laid around a lot feeling sick and weak and I needed several transfusions. Then when my good week rolled around I didn't seem to get my energy back like I normally did. I still felt weak and tired. It made me nervous because I felt like I was just getting closer and closer to the day that the doctors would tell me that I shouldn't do any more chemo. We decided to take an extra week off so that I could be in better shape before starting my final round of this regimen.

Taking a week off ended up being a great decision. The timing worked out perfectly for us to be able to go up to our good friends' lake house with my whole family. We fished, swam, rode around on the boats, and just hung out. It was so nice to be able to get away from the hospitals and into the beautiful scenery at the lake. There is just something about being out in nature that lifts my spirits and brings peace to my heart. Unfortunately, the vacation couldn't last forever. We had to return to finish up this last round of chemo.

At the beginning, when we were in the hospital for my first few rounds of chemo we met a girl that had the same cancer as I did. She finished all of her treatments about six months before me and was in remission for about two years before the doctors called her up and told her that some of her scans looked like there might be some tumors in her lungs, but they needed to do more tests to find out. Considering our experience, Kelly and I were certain that the cancer had come back in her lungs. It made me so mad to think that it was probably going to kill her too, but at the same time, it gave me hope that if her cancer went into remission for such a long time then maybe mine would too.

In that moment I realized how unpredictable cancer really is. The doctors do their best to treat the cancer and give prognoses and time estimates based on other people's experiences, but everybody's outcome with the cancer is different. There are so many cases where a person was supposed to die from some incurable cancer and somehow they miraculously got better. Or where the cancer should be easily curable, but for whatever reason the patient dies quickly. People who are only supposed to last days can last years and people who are supposed to last years may last only weeks. It is a really odd thing, and I can't help to think that it is all because of God's involvement in our individual lives.

I feel that for some people the disease just runs its natural course. But for others, God may be heavily involved in healing, extending, or possibly even shortening a patient's life in order to fulfill the plan that He has for that person and their family. I know that God has a plan for each of us and I feel like sometimes he manipulates the circumstances in order to carry out his work. Especially with cancer because one person's experience with cancer has so much potential to positively impact the lives of so many.

As for my situation, I definitely don't feel like God has been going out of his way to extend my life at all, considering all of the bad news that we get. But it is so comforting to me to know that God is the one in charge of my whole situation, not the doctors. The doctors can tell me whatever they want as far as whether or not they expect me to live or how much time they think I have left. But ultimately it comes down to what God has in store for me. And although now I have a really hard time understanding why He is allowing these things to happen to me, I know that someday it will all make sense and I will be able to see that I and my loved ones are all better off because of what He put us through.

66 ROUND 26: MAY 9, 2011

I couldn't believe that I finally made it to this round of chemo. It was my sixth round of this regimen and my 26th overall. It amazed me to think I had been through so much and I wondered how much I would be able to take if I ever had to do more rounds of chemo. According to my doctor, after my remission I would probably only be able to do a couple more rounds of this regimen before my heart or kidneys give out. After that I didn't know what other treatment options he might have for me. But at this point it didn't matter to me. All I wanted was to be done with chemo for a while and have some time to feel well and have fun with Kelly.

The actual chemo treatment ended up going pretty well. I didn't have any incidents like last round where I felt like I was going to faint or anything like that. Even during my bad week the side effects weren't too horrible. Well, I don't know if they were any easier than normal or if I was just getting more used to feeling so beat up. But this round did hit my blood counts harder than any other I have ever done.

The Monday after my week of receiving the chemo I went in to get my blood checked and my platelets were at three, lower than they have ever been. Usually I can tell when they are low because it's like my entire body is flashing a big warning light. My brain gets all foggy, my eyes start aching, and my heart starts doing all kinds of weird things. This time I didn't have those kinds of symptoms as much, but my gums bled when I brushed my teeth, and my nose constantly oozed blood. Once again I was afraid for my life and wondered if I would make it to the end of the day. I was scared that at any moment my platelets could drop even lower and I could start bleeding uncontrollably. Luckily the doctor scheduled me for a platelet transfusion that night to get them up as soon as possible, but I had to go home and spend the rest of the day waiting and wondering if I would make it to the transfusion.

That night in the hospital I got lucky and didn't have any reaction to the platelets. But it was still a pain in the butt because we didn't get home until after midnight. A couple of days later I returned to the doctor to get my blood checked and my platelets were really low again. I had to get another transfusion downtown at night. This time I wasn't so lucky and had a pretty bad reaction. I coughed uncontrollably and had some swelling in my eyelids. It was another late night in the hospital. We didn't get back home until after midnight. I felt so bad for Kelly because she always wanted to be with me during the transfusions even though we were always there late and she would have to get up early the next morning for school. She was so sweet to go with me all of the time.

My blood counts dropped again later in the week and I had to go back into the hospital for more transfusions. This time I had to get platelets and red blood cells. That night was a really long one. I don't think we got back until about two in the morning. Luckily it was a Friday night and Kelly didn't have school the next day.

After that last transfusion my energy came back pretty quickly and after just a few days I was up and about with all kinds of energy, eager to get going and start enjoying my expected remission. I told myself that I was going to work out every day I was in remission. I felt it might help my body fight any remaining cancer cells and it would make me strong if I ever had to do chemo again. I started to swim laps every day and it felt great. It helped me feel like I was a normal person again and I loved it.

The next week I met with the radiation doctor to talk about radiation treatment options. He explained to me that he felt like he could kill off the remaining tumors using radiation. The radiation would cause further damage to my lungs, which could leave me a little short of breath for the rest of my life, but it was the only chance I had at getting rid of the cancer for good, so I decided to go for it. After agreeing to receive the treatment they took me to a CT scanner where they took images and made marks on my chest to help them shoot the tumors with the radiation. They then scheduled me for my treatments and sent me on my way.

I was really nervous about having to do the radiation treatment. Especially after finding out that it would damage my lungs even more. I didn't want to risk being short of breath all the time, but I didn't want to die either. I was willing to do whatever I could to get rid of the cancer even if that meant ruining my body a little more. I pushed my worries aside and tried to look forward to getting started with the radiation.

67 NOW WHAT? MORE BAD NEWS

A couple of nights after getting my chest all marked up in preparation for my radiation treatments I had this strange itch on my chest. The itch somehow transformed into pain which grew in intensity to the point that I was really uncomfortable. Then the pain started spreading to my back and a little on my arm. It was some kind of strange nerve related pain that wouldn't go away with pain killers. It ended up getting bad enough that it kept me from being able to sleep all night long.

The next day the pain faded and I was able to get some really good sleep that night. But the next morning I woke up and had a different type of pain in my chest. Whenever I breathed in deep it was like a sharp ache in the middle of my chest and it sometimes hurt to swallow. I had experienced similar pain before, but just not as intense, so I didn't worry about it too much. I figured it would just go away after a day or two. But a day or two later it was still there and my resting heart rate had increased to around 110. We decided it was best to get a hold of my doctor so he could tell us what to do. When we called him he told us to just go into the emergency room at the medical center so that they could do whatever tests they needed to do and fix the problem quickly.

We got to the emergency room and had a CT scan of my chest to check for any blood clots or infections that might be there. But when the doctor came in with the results he told us something we weren't expecting. He said that the tumors in my chest had grown and that the symptoms I was experiencing were probably as a result of the tumor growth. The news was heartbreaking! I was supposed to be in remission for at least two months and now the tumors were growing after only two or three weeks. I was scared to death, but tried to calm my fears with the rationale that I would start radiation in a couple of days and the radiation would be able to wipe out the growing tumors. I left the hospital that night wondering what the tumor growth really meant and what the near future might have in store for us.

The next morning the news only got worse. I guess my radiation doctor saw the results of the CT scan and decided to give me a call to talk about them. He kindly explained over the phone that the tumors had grown too much for me to be able to go forward with the radiation treatment. Treating the now larger tumors would damage too much lung and could ruin my ability to breath normally after treatment. He apologized for not having better news and told me to see my oncologist about other treatment options.

When I got off the phone with him I immediately burst into tears. Kelly had overheard the conversation and was right there to hold and comfort me. I apologized to her again for everything I had put her through. We both cried for a while and then sadly accepted the idea that my situation didn't look good and that I might not be around much longer.

We visited with my doctors who informed us that my heart rate had increased because the tumors were restricting blood flow in my lungs. My treatment options weren't very good. I could try to get on a clinical trial, but I probably wouldn't be accepted because of my damaged kidneys. If that option fell through I could try a few different regimens of chemo, each of which would further damage my body. I would only be able to do two or three rounds at most before my heart or kidneys completely shut down. My body and bone marrow were also weak from all of the chemo that I had already been through. Each additional round would have an increased risk of some type of major complication. Plus, the worst part was that he only expected about a 50% chance that the chemo would actually be effective at controlling the tumors. Our other option was to do nothing and to try to enjoy the time that I had left. He estimated that if I didn't do any treatments I would probably have between two to four more months.

I left the doctor's office in a strange mood. I was sad about the options that I was given and about the fact that I would have to leave Kelly, but in a way I was also relieved to know that this whole stressful and emotionally draining cancer ordeal would soon come to an end. At that point we had gone through two and a half years of a continuous emotional roller coaster. It was always so wearing on me and after dealing with it for so long, it was relieving to know that there was an end in sight, even if that meant losing the fight. I was so tired! I had gone through 26 rounds of chemo! Being sick and feeling weak had become a way of life; something that nobody should have to go through. The thought of doing more chemo and going through more torture was too overwhelming for me. That, plus the new potential risks was enough to push me away from that option.

So what we decided is that I would try to get onto a clinical trial if I could and if not, I would try to spend the rest of my days living as normal of a life as I could. It absolutely broke my heart to explain to Kelly that I was tired of doing treatments and that I wanted to stop, but she understood and supported me. Plus it was hard for her to have to see me go through all of the torture and she didn't really want to see me suffer any more either. It has been a hard decision to face and make, but somehow it has felt like the right one.

69 WHY?

By this time in I had been dealing with cancer for over two and a half years, almost one-tenth of my entire life. Throughout this time I, and several family members and close friends struggled with trying to understand why all of this was happening to me. We couldn't figure out why my situation had not improved and why I had gone through so much suffering. I'm sure that lots of other people that were aware of my situation asked themselves that question about me as well. I'm also sure that almost anybody going through a rough patch in life wonders why it is happening to them. At first I was completely stumped and didn't really have any kind of answer. But now, after going through so much, I have been able to put some puzzle pieces together and I can see things a lot more clearly. I'm still not quite sure why I got the cancer to begin with, but I feel like I almost fully understand why God has allowed me to go through so much.

I first have to explain that God created this world that we all live in. For the most part, we all know that. It was a perfect place until Adam and Eve were kicked out of the Garden of Eden, at which point I feel things started to get a little chaotic. The people weren't perfect, crops maybe didn't grow right all of the time, and illness and disease started showing up. From then on, people have been going through all kinds of bad experiences. Some brought on by our own decisions, some brought on by the decisions of others, and some brought on by nature itself. Although God intervenes in this world to carry out his work, I feel that for the most part he just lets things run their course. Unfortunately for me that meant that my body started growing cancer cells. My getting cancer was just a natural consequence of having an imperfect body and living in an imperfect world.

I got cancer because bad things like that just happen to people sometimes. It's a very simple explanation. The questions about God always follow and are a little more difficult to understand. The main one being, "If God is a loving God, then why does he allow such horrible things to happen to his children?" This one is a tough one for lots of people, and it was for me when I was first diagnosed. But after all of the things that I have learned it all makes sense now.

In order for me to understand why God was allowing me to go through so much suffering I had to really understand why I was here in this life to begin with. I knew that we needed to follow Christ's example and that we were given rules and commandments to follow, but what was the underlying purpose of it all? I spent a lot of time thinking about that and there was one scripture in Matthew 5 that kept coming to my mind. It was when Christ was teaching his famous sermon on the mount. He said to everybody "Be ye therefore perfect, even as your father which is in heaven is perfect."

Now, of course, nobody in this life will ever be perfect because we all make mistakes, which is why Christ atoned for our sins. It is true that we are made perfect through Christ and that it is only through him that we are saved. But that is a sin-free type of perfection. I feel like when Christ says to be perfect even as our heavenly father is perfect he is saying that we need to grow spiritually and perfect our character so that it is like God's; perfectly loving, honest, patient, humble, etc.

I feel strongly that during this life we are supposed to try our best to become as perfect and Christ-like as we can be. I also feel strongly that the more we perfect our character and grow spiritually in this life, the greater blessings, privileges, and responsibilities we will enjoy in the life to come. God does love all of his children and he has so many great blessings in store for us, but I feel that there are some of those blessings and privileges that only good, faithful, Christ-like people are able to receive. God wants us to "be perfect" so that we can receive those great blessings.

So what does this have to do with me having cancer? Well, ever since I was diagnosed I started to change. By the end, the way I acted had changed, the way I thought had changed, my attitude changed, I became more humble, I became less selfish, etc. Simply put, my character was improved a little at a time throughout my whole battle with cancer. Now, looking back, I'm a completely different person than I was before, and the same can be said about Kelly as well.

Kelly and I weren't the only people to benefit from me having cancer. All of my family and so many close friends also went through tremendous spiritual growth. On top of that, I always had people tell me that I have been such an inspiration to them. I personally don't really see why, but people would always tell me that I inspired them to be a better person. I started to realize that somehow, my having cancer had triggered spiritual growth and character changes in hundreds of people. After realizing that, and recognizing all of the many blessings that Kelly and I had received, I could clearly see that God was using my experience with cancer to carry out his work.

In the beginning I knew that God could heal me and it shocked me when he didn't. But now I see that if he were to have healed me he would have lost the opportunity to encourage so much spiritual growth in so many people. I know that God could have used other means to impact those people, but there is something about going through really hard times that allows spiritual growth to take place more rapidly and to be longer lasting. My having cancer seemed to be the perfect hard time for providing great spiritual growth and character changing opportunities to all who knew me.

So back to the question, "Why does God allow this to happen to people?" Simply answered, God takes advantage of these types of situations and uses them to carry out his work. He understands that the hardships that we face in this life are like a blink of an eye compared to all of eternity. He also knows that the magnitude of our eternal well-being is determined by the spiritual progress that we make in this short life that we live. Through the suffering of one person God is potentially able to positively impact the eternal lives of many people. From an eternal perspective, the benefits make the suffering well worth it, especially considering the fact that those who suffer most have the greatest potential to gain the most, thus ensuring them greater blessings, privileges, responsibilities and joys in the life to come.

70 IN THE END

So now I find myself near the end of my days in this life. I sometimes wonder in shock and amazement at how my life has come to this. Not too long ago I was strong, healthy, and energetic, with so much potential to have an amazing life. Now my body is weak and damaged and I seem to be wasting away a little more each day. I have all kinds of random pains in my chest, I've developed a horrible cough, my resting heart rate is between 110 and 130 and my doctors say my body could shut down at any moment. At most, I probably only have another month or so to live.

Life has been pretty sad over the past couple of weeks and it feels like I should be really depressed, but somehow I'm not. Right now all of my family is in town to spend time with me and life just seems to go on as usual. We still have fun goofing off and joking around with each other. Although everybody is aware of the sad situation that we face there is a peace and happiness that pushes through the darkness to comforts us.

In spite of the good times that we are having I still break down and cry at least once a day. It just breaks my heart so much to think that Kelly will have to go through life without me. Even though the situation is completely out of my control I can't help but feel partly responsible for the hardships that she faces. I cry for her for what she has to go through and she cries for me because of what I have to go through. Inside I know that God will take care of her and that everything will be alright. He has a way of making things fall into place and work out perfectly. He has done it for us in the past and I feel like he will do that for her in the future. It is kind of strange to think about, but I also feel like I'll be placed as some sort of guardian angel type figure for her. I know that I will still be able to help her from the other side and that she will receive so many blessings to help her through everything.

Even with the understanding that everything will work out for her I am still heartbroken. I try to come up with ways to make me feel better about the situation. Sometimes I try to think logically about the whole thing. I remind myself that anybody who ever gets married will have to be separated from their spouse at some point in their lives. I also tell myself things like, "Death is inevitable and nobody has ever escaped it," but the comfort that those thoughts bring me doesn't last long enough to really help me at all.

There is really only one thing that is able to break away the sadness and bring joy to my heart. And that is the knowledge that God has provided a way for Kelly and I to be together again. After all is said and done, she will still be my wife, my best friend, and my eternal companion and we will be together forever. I can't think of a more joyous time than the moment that we will be reunited. She will be beautiful, as always, and I will be healthy, strong, with a full head of hair and two whole legs. After all of the tragedy that we have been through in this life we will have our happily ever after.

The end.

AFTERWARD

Brent was driven to finish his book. He wanted so much to be able to help other people, and the family members of those who might one day unexpectedly find themselves facing a life changing experience like cancer as he did. He felt strongly that by sharing his story and describing the things that he learned, his words might bring them comfort and help ease their pain. As I watched him fighting fatigue trying to finish the last few chapters, I mentioned to him one time that if he didn't have the energy, it would be alright if he didn't finish it. He immediately replied, "No dad, it wouldn't be alright, it would be a tragedy if I died before I had a chance to finish it."

Well, finish it he did, on July 6th, and you could see the relief in his eyes. After a rapid decline in health, manifested by increased chest pain, and difficulty in breathing, Brent died less than 3 weeks later in the hospital surrounded by his family and his beloved Kelly. He received many visitors from close friends during the last couple of weeks, and in spite of the discomfort he was in, he greeted each of them with warm, kind words, tidbits of wisdom, and that unforgettable, magical smile. We love Brent dearly, and we will miss him. We rejoice in the hope that the gospel of Jesus Christ gives us that someday we will once again be reunited with him.

ABOUT THE AUTHOR

Brent Weaver grew up in Sugar Land, Texas as a healthy, active, energetic young man who loved family, friends, the outdoors, and sports. After graduating with an engineering degree from Brigham Young University, securing a job, and marrying his sweetheart, Kelly, Brent's life took a drastic change. He was diagnosed with a rare bone cancer at the age of 27. While fighting for his life, Brent wrote this book to inform and inspire others affected by this disease. He eventually lost the battle at the age of 29, three weeks after finishing the book.

Made in the USA
Lexington, KY
10 April 2012